Vienna's Golden Years of Music

1850-1900

Vienna's
Golden Years of Music
1850-1900

———•◦•———

EDUARD HANSLICK

———•◦•———

Translated and Edited by

HENRY PLEASANTS III

Essay Index

Essay Index Reprint Series

BOOKS FOR LIBRARIES PRESS
FREEPORT, NEW YORK

STANDARD BOOK NUMBER

8369-0043-X

LIBRARY OF CONGRESS CATALOG CARD NUMBER:

69-18928

PRINTED IN THE UNITED STATES OF AMERICA

CONTENTS

LIST OF ILLUSTRATIONS

vii

Hanslick at the age of forty, already the leading champion of the Leipzig (Schumann-Brahms) school as opposed to the Weimar (Wagner-Liszt) school. He had recently been appointed Extraordinary Professor of the History and Aesthetics of Music at the University of Vienna—probably the first "professor of music appreciation" in the history of education. (See Preface.)

Hanslick at the age of 68. Richard Wagner had died ten years before, but Hanslick was still engaged, through the spoken and written word, in fighting those whom he regarded as his musical heirs—Richard Strauss and Anton Bruckner. (See pages 308 to 314 and 303 to 307.)

The old Kärntnertor Theater, where the court opera performed until 1869, directly behind the site of the present opera house.

The old Carltheater, where Patti sang her first season in Vienna.

The Vienna Court Opera House, which replaced the Kärntnertor Theater.

Contemporary print showing the popularity of a Patti perform- ance at the Vienna Court Opera House.

Ole Bull, one of the great idols of the day, who played only his own compositions. The compositions, Hanslick reports, are inferior, while the playing "excites only surprise." (See pages 65 to 67.)

Of Henri Vieuxtemps, on the other hand, Hanslick wrote: "Listening to him is one of the greatest, most unqualified pleasures music has to offer." He was almost equally enthusiastic about Vieuxtemps's compositions. (See pages 37 to 38.)

The Vienna Music Hall, or Musikvereinsaal. Built in 1870, it comprises three concert halls. (See page 14 for its history.)

Print showing Johannes Brahms accompanying a singer at a recital, made shortly before Brahms's death in 1897.

XIII

Contemporary print of Adelina Patti, the great operatic soprano who enjoyed Hanslick's friendship, piano playing, and dancing. (See pages 187 to 208.)

Amalie Materna as Brünnhilde. Hanslick, despite his opinion of much of the music assigned to Brünnhilde, admired Materna's delivery of it.

Caricature by Heinrich Groeber of Anton Bruckner, regarded by Hanslick as one of those unfortunate composers to come under the influence of Wagnerism. (See pages 303 to 307.)

Giuseppe Verdi from a drawing made in 1879. Hanslick, who was late in appreciating the full stature of this composer, finally rendered him due homage when he heard Otello. *(See pages 287 to 302.)*

Engelbert Humperdinck— whose Hänsel und Gretel *had a success in Vienna that was qualified only by Hanslick's objections to the Wagnerisms in it. (See pages 315 to 321.)*

One of Wagner's champions was Hans von Bülow, for whom Hanslick nevertheless had almost nothing but praise as musician, pianist, and conductor of the Meiningen Court Orchestra. (See pages 209 to 211 and 268 to 274.)

THE EDITOR wishes to express his deep appreciation of the devoted and enthusiastic assistance given him in the preparation of this book by Miss Hella Bronold, of Vienna, in preparing the translation and the annotation; Mrs. Gertrude Meister and Mrs. Anne-Marie Thinnes, also of Vienna, who typed the various drafts; Dean Koch, who assisted in the reading of preliminary drafts; Miss Maria W. Smith, of Gladwyne, Pennsylvania, who read proofs and gave other valuable editorial assistance; and to the National Library of Vienna and the Society of the Friends of Music, who were most co-operative in furnishing photographs, drawings, and source material.

PREFACE

---·◆◆·---

ALTHOUGH this is simply a selection of Eduard Hanslick's reviews and essays, the discerning reader will find, I believe, elements of a drama unique in the history of music. It is no accident that Hanslick alone, of all Wagner's contemporary adversaries, is still remembered. Nietzsche,[1] as a reformed Wagnerite, was an added starter, and his opposition hadn't the dignity of Hanslick's lifelong resistance to "the music of the future." Nor has Nietzsche today the distinction of serving as the historical example of the critical reactionary.

It is characteristic of the tragedy of Hanslick that even contemporary musical historians are inclined to direct their readers' sympathies to Wagner rather than to Hanslick. This can partly be attributed to habit. The critic is seldom the popular favorite in an engagement with an artist of compelling qualities, let alone a genius. But it is more fundamentally attributable to ignorance, particularly with respect to English language historians and critics, few of whom have had the opportunity of knowing Hanslick as well as they know Wagner. During the greater part of his career, Hanslick's battle was defensive. Wagner was a popular idol, and Hanslick knew that his cause was hopeless, that the

---

[1] Friedrich Nietzsche (1844–1900), originally one of Wagner's most enthusiastic disciples [*Die Geburt der Tragödie aus dem Geiste der Musik* (1872), and *Richard Wagner in Bayreuth* (1876)], turned against Wagner with *Der Fall Wagner* (1888) and, a year later, *Nietzsche contra Wagner*.

verdict of his own time was against him, and that immediate posterity was unlikely to reverse it. But he fought to the last, strong in his convictions and his sense of moral obligation to serve what he considered the best interests of the art to which he had dedicated his life.

He seldom referred to this aspect of his career, and when he did so it was usually by way of apology for statements which he later felt might have been biased by personal bitterness and a sense of frustration—an experience common to champions of unpopular causes. It took an unwitting statement of Max Nordau in his book, *Degeneration*,[2] to the effect that "Hanslick . . . finally struck his colors," to provoke him to an uninhibited outburst of personal confession and protest. Referring to the Nordau statement in his autobiography, Hanslick wrote:

"It is only natural that the exalted hero worship of the Wagnerites and their challenging attitude should not have been without effect on the object of their attacks. I and some others who share my views should probably have written more dispassionately about Wagner had not our pulses been agitated by the immoderate, often ludicrous, exaggerations of our opponents. The consciousness of being in the minority embitters the most honest soul and sharpens the vocabulary. I readily confess that in my case this may have happened from time to time. But I must protest Nordau's statement. . . . My most recent discussions of Wagnerian composition and Wagnerian literature are evidence to the contrary. After I had spoken my mind on Wagner for a full two score

---

[2] Max Nordau (1849–1923), studied medicine, wrote several philosophical essays on the general degeneration of mankind, also some novels on the same topic. His book *Degeneration*, published at the turn of the century, disposed not only of Wagner but also of Ibsen, Maeterlinck, the Pre-Raphaelites, etc.

years, my task was finished. There is hardly anything new
to be said on the subject. I would be as wanting in taste as
the Wagnerites themselves, were I to make every single
production of *Tristan* or the *Ring* the occasion for a reopening of the question. . . . I know that I represent a small
minority, and I know that I shall not live to see a reversal of
taste in this regard. Younger critics may. I shall not dare to
predict how long Wagner's music will command public
enthusiasm, but I do not doubt that in fifty years the writings
of the Wagnerites will be looked upon in amazement as the
relics of an intellectual epidemic."

Hanslick's collected writings run to twelve volumes,
including two volumes of autobiography. None of his reviews and essays, with the exception of the early *Beauty in
Music* (*Vom Musikalisch-Schönen*) has, to the best of my
knowledge, been published in English. Some fairly extensive
excerpts are quoted by way of example in Stewart Deas'
In Defense of Hanslick (Williams & Norgate, Ltd., London,
1940). It would have been possible to compile a book from
the essays on Wagner alone, but after careful examination
of all the material it seemed that this would be fair neither
to Hanslick nor the reader. It is impossible to appraise his
attitude toward Wagner without having some idea of his
approach toward music in general. A book devoted exclusively to Wagner would, moreover, give the impression
that his quarrel was with Wagner alone, and that it was
motivated by personal antipathy. Such was not the case.

Hanslick and Wagner were personally acquainted.
They were, for a time, even on good terms. They met in
Marienbad in 1845, when Hanslick was twenty years old
and still a student at the Prague University. Wagner noted
his interest and invited him to Dresden to hear *Tannhäuser*,

an invitation which Hanslick accepted, along with an invitation from Schumann, in the summer of 1846. Following his move to Vienna in the autumn of the same year and his introduction to music criticism as an avocation while still studying law, he became Wagner's first articulate prophet in the Austrian capital. His enthusiasm cooled, however, with *Lohengrin* (about which he wrote unfavorably after its Vienna *première*), and when Wagner came to Vienna in 1862, with the manuscript poem of *Die Meistersinger*, Hanslick found himself caricatured in the person of Veit Hanslich, later renamed Beckmesser. They never spoke to each other again. Hanslick made no effort to heal the breach. He was far too independent to practice the fawning idolatry which seems to have been a prerequisite for Wagner's friendship. He maintained, nevertheless, a considerable degree of objectivity in his reviews of the later operas.

"I have often been asked," he wrote in his autobiography, "by those disposed to think of all criticism as personal, what it is that I have 'against Wagner.' Nothing at all! That he should have been so cool as a result of my review of *Lohengrin* was to be expected. In such matters I had already had a good deal of that experience in which I am now over-rich. I was even less offended later, in 1869, when Wagner smuggled me into his *The Jew in Music*.[3] Wagner couldn't stand a Jew, and consequently he developed the habit of regarding as a Jew anyone he didn't like. I should be most

---

[3] *The Jew in Music* (*Das Judentum in der Musik*) appeared anonymously in 1850, referring in general terms to Jewish musicians. In 1869, Wagner reissued the essay under his own name, with a lengthy postscript in which he referred to Hanslick's "gracefully hidden Jewish origin" (*"Hanslicks zierlich verdeckte jüdische Abkunft"*) and offered him as the embodiment of Semitic, anti-German art criticism.

flattered to be burned by Father Arbuez Wagner [4] at the same stake with Mendelssohn and Meyerbeer; unfortunately I must decline the distinction, for my father and all his ancestors were of Catholic peasant stock and, moreover, from a region where Jews were known only as wandering peddlers.[5] Wagner's inspiration of describing *Beauty in Music* as a libel evolved with extraordinary cleverness for the purpose of 'musical Jewry' is, to put it mildly, so incredibly childish that, while it might annoy my enemies, it could certainly not annoy me. . . . I cannot, however, deny that his entire personality was thoroughly uncongenial. A stranger would have seen in his face not so much an artistic genius as a dry Leipzig professor or lawyer. He spoke incredibly much—and fast—in a monotonous singsong Saxon dialect and always of himself, his works, his reforms, his plans. If he mentioned the name of another composer it was always in a tone of disparagement. It is the same in his books. . . . The more I knew and learned of him in the course of the years, the more my respect for his character diminished. That all this had nothing to do with the impression his operas made upon me and upon my estimate of them, requires no further assurance."

---

[4] The reference is to Peter de Arbuez (1441–1485), who, as the first Inquisitor of Aragon, so distinguished himself in the destruction of heretics that he was assassinated in front of his altar by a conspiracy of the families of his victims. He was beatified in 1661, and canonized in 1867.

[5] Hanslick's books were banned by the Nazis because, according to their racial researchers, his mother was a Jewess. It will be noted in Hanslick's statement that he refers only to his father's side. Whether Goebbels' henchmen actually established the facts in the case or simply took Wagner at his word is a mystery hardly worth solving. It should be noted, however, in judging the possible hypocrisy of Hanslick's disavowal, that the concept of half-Jew, or *Mischling*, had not the significance then that it gained subsequently under the Nuremberg Laws.

Hanslick never denied Wagner's genius or the measure of his accomplishments. "I know very well," he once wrote, "that he is the greatest living opera composer and in a historical sense the only one worth talking about. . . . But when an art enters a period of utmost luxury, it is already on the decline. Wagner's operatic style recognizes only superlatives, and a superlative has no future. It is an end, not a beginning. Starting with *Lohengrin*, he broke a new path, dangerous to life and limb. This path is for him alone. Whoever follows will break his neck, and the public will contemplate the disaster with indifference. . . . The most recent example of his reforms does not represent an enrichment, an extension, a renewal of music as did the art of Mozart, Beethoven, Weber, and Schumann. It is, on the contrary, a distortion, a perversion of basic musical laws, a style contrary to the nature of human hearing and feeling. One could say of this tone poetry: there is music in it, but it isn't music."

Hanslick's quarrel was not with Wagner alone. He rejected Berlioz and Liszt just as consistently, and later Richard Strauss and Anton Bruckner. Wagner was simply the most gifted, and the most influential, of the prophets of the "music of the future" and, therefore, the most dangerous. If one were required to define the basis of Hanslick's objections to this school, one might cite: (1) the introduction of foreign elements (prose, poetry, color for graphic purpose), and (2) transcendentalism. He was against program music because he felt that music lost rather than gained by being pegged to a specific plot or idea, and his fundamental objection to Wagner was directed against the subordination of melodic development to the elucidation of the text. Had he been in the habit of rereading his own essays he would

certainly have been struck in 1881 or 1891 by what he wrote
of Beethoven's Ninth Symphony and the Mass in D, in 1861
"In artistic richness, in intrepid greatness, in the free unleashing of an immeasurable fantasy, these two compositions
stand unique and alone, like colossal Pillars of Hercules at
the gates of modern music, saying, 'No farther!' " To
Hanslick, twenty or thirty years later, it would have seemed
that these Pillars of Hercules had known whereof they spoke
and that no good had come of ignoring their fair warning.

A number of reviews in this selection are not necessarily
concerned with the musico-ideological conflicts which
dominated Hanslick's career as professional critic. They
have been included for various reasons. It seemed advisable,
for one thing, to show Hanslick in the act of giving praise.
In evaluating a critic, it is important to know his likes as
well as his dislikes; it is, moreover, an axiom of criticism
that it is more difficult to praise than to condemn. It also
seemed appropriate to seize this opportunity to pass on to
the English-speaking reader Hanslick's thorough, first-hand
estimates of such world-famous artists as Joseph Joachim,
Johannes Brahms, Clara Schumann, Adelina Patti, Anton
Rubinstein, Franz Liszt, Lilli Lehmann, and Richard Wagner (as conductor).

A more fundamental consideration prompted the
selection of such works as Bach's *St. Matthew Passion*,
Handel's *The Messiah*, Beethoven's Mass in D, Schubert's
"Unfinished" Symphony, the Brahms symphonies, Tchaikovsky's "*Pathétique*" Symphony, and Verdi's Requiem and
Otello. They are of interest not only because of the light
they shed on Hanslick as a critic, but also because of the
light Hanslick sheds on them. It should be remembered that
in most cases he was reviewing first performances, or at

least performances which occurred before the pieces in question were invested with the sanctity they enjoy today. These reviews will have justified their selection if they do no more than re-stimulate a critical approach to composition in an age when the verdict of a generation or two is accepted as final and when criticism, for want of new, original material, tends to concentrate on performance.

To conclude on a personal note, I confess that I was compelled to do this work of selection and translation by a strong feeling of sympathy with Hanslick and his views, and by a feeling of obligation to give him the opportunity of being read and judged by what he himself wrote and not by what others have written about him. In this sense, it may be considered a former critic's tribute to a distinguished and noble colleague who fared badly, in his own time, at the hands of "the Wagnerites," and worse, in later years, at the hands of those from whom he might have expected more appreciative treatment.

Henry Pleasants III

VIENNA, 1949

VIENNA'S GOLDEN YEARS OF MUSIC

1850–1900

EDUARD HANSLICK

———— • ● • ————

[1825–1904]

EDUARD HANSLICK was born in Prague on September 11, 1825. His father was an enthusiastic philosopher and musician, of Bohemian peasant stock. His mother, the daughter of a well-to-do merchant, had been one of his father's piano pupils. The marriage was extremely happy, and life in the Hanslick family appears to have run an untroubled course. In later years Hanslick wrote: "I have the inestimable good fortune to be able to look back upon a pleasant and undisturbed youth and to remember my parents with nothing but the deepest love and gratitude."

His own marriage was similarly happy. There was in his life little of the emotional *Sturm und Drang* which characterized the adolescence, and even the maturity, of so many of his generation, particularly those with whom he took such critical issue—Berlioz, Liszt, Wagner, Bruckner, Strauss. The harmonious circumstances of his emotional and intellectual growth may well have contributed to the development of a rationalistic point of view at odds with the romantic spirit of his time. Generally speaking, however, he considered himself utterly identified with his own generation, as witnessed by his devotion to Schumann and Brahms and by the part he played in bringing them to public attention in Vienna. And he was not particularly drawn toward older

1

music. He once confessed that he would rather see the complete works of Heinrich Schütz [1] destroyed than Brahms' *Ein Deutsches Requiem*, the complete works of Palestrina than Mendelssohn's, all the concertos and sonatas of Bach than the quartets of Schumann and Brahms, and all of Gluck than *Don Giovanni, Fidelio,* or *Der Freischütz.* "A shocking confession," he added, "but at least an honest one!"

From his father Hanslick had his love and talent for music; from his mother, his leaning toward the theater and French literature. As soon as the children were old enough, his mother subscribed to two seats in the Prague theater, and took the children in turns. Hanslick's first opera was *The Magic Flute;* his first play, *William Tell.* He displayed a lively interest in music at the age of four or five. His first impressions were of his father playing the overtures to *Don Giovanni* and *The Marriage of Figaro,* and Beethoven's "Prometheus" Overture. He received his first instruction from his father, who, in time, entrusted his talent to a local pedagogue and later, in view of rapid and impressive progress, to Wenzel Johann Tomaschek, the foremost Czech composer and teacher of his time,[2] with whom young Hanslick studied for four years. The curriculum included piano, theory, harmony, counterpoint, fugue, instrumentation, and experimental composition. In his autobiography Hanslick relates that Tomaschek required that a Bach prelude and fugue be prepared from memory for each lesson. He also assigned the Beethoven sonatas (excluding the very

---

[1] Heinrich Schütz (1585–1672), the foremost German composer of church music of his time.

[2] (1774–1850). When Berlioz paid a courtesy call upon him during his visit to Prague in January of 1846, Hanslick acted as interpreter and recorded Berlioz's comment: *"Il a l'air bien enchanté de lui-même!"*

late ones) and works of Chopin, Thalberg,[3] Henselt,[4] and Liszt. Hanslick learned to play them all well and acquired a respectable "capital" of technique upon which he was able to draw in later years when his legal studies at the University of Vienna, and subsequently his official duties as a public servant, put an end to practicing the piano.

He emerged from these four years with Tomaschek not only with the inevitable certificate and a good technical and theoretical schooling, but also with the problem of whether or not to adopt music as a career. Tomaschek was all for it, and his father was not opposed; but Hanslick was not drawn to the career of virtuoso and felt himself insufficiently gifted to attempt a career as composer. For a bourgeois intellectual the most attractive, as well as the most conventional, calling was law. Not that it promised rapid or brilliant advancement. On the contrary, there were talented and industrious young men in Prague who "practiced" ten or twelve years in the public service without pay until a salaried position became open. But a bureaucrat in the imperial service of absolutist Austria had a highly respected and, as a rule, secure position. One was promoted according to seniority and thus had, as Hanslick later pointed out, no stimulus to overexertion or spectacular accomplishment. The career of a bureaucrat promised, moreover, sufficient leisure for musical and literary pursuits, where Hanslick's inclinations really lay.

While studying law at the University of Prague, he

---

[3] Sigismond Thalberg (1812–1871), the foremost piano virtuoso and composer for the piano of the pre-Liszt generation.

[4] Adolf von Henselt (1814–1889), eminent Bavarian pianist, pupil of Hummel at Weimar and Sechter in Vienna. He developed a pianistic style which laid great emphasis on *legato* and on the stretch capacities of the hand.

3

found time to devote himself to a side of music neglected in Tomaschek's severe but unimaginative curriculum: history and aesthetics. Stimulus in this direction came from his father, who, as a professional bibliographer, recommended Kiesewetter's ⁵ *History of Music* and Hand's ⁶ *Aesthetics of the Art of Music.* "These two works," wrote Hanslick, "long since rendered obsolete both as to conclusions and method, struck me as heaven-sent gifts. They provided the initial basis upon which I was subsequently able to build without much difficulty and entirely on my own." At the same time, he and his circle of young intellectuals at the university became acquainted with Schumann's *Neue Zeitschrift für Musik*, published in Leipzig, and through it they were introduced to the contemporary world of Mendelssohn, Chopin, and Berlioz. They even formed their own Prague chapter of the *Davidsbündler*,⁷ among whose activities that of four-hand sight-reading of new and unfamiliar music, as well as symphony and opera arrangements, was one of the most engrossing.

There was published in Prague at that time an intellectual periodical called *Ost und West*, whose editor, Rudolf Glaser, was married to the sister-in-law of Tomaschek. At the suggestion of mutual friends, Glaser sought out Hanslick and offered him the post of music critic. Hanslick wrote his

---

⁵ Raphael Georg Kiesewetter (1773–1850), musicologist and writer on musical subjects. He spent most of his life in Vienna.

⁶ Ferdinand Gotthelf Hand (1786–1851), professor of Greek Literature at the University of Jena.

⁷ David Guild, founded by Schumann and his friends in 1834. Its official organ was the *Neue Zeitschrift für Musik*, which he edited for ten years. The name David derived from the biblical story of David and Goliath, Schumann and his friends thinking of themselves in their adventurous reformatory zeal as leaders of a fight against the Philistines.

first review in December, 1844.[8] "My modest first attempts at music criticism," he later wrote, "benefited me greatly in that I took them entirely seriously. I never criticized a composition that I had not read or played through, both before and after the performance—a custom which I have conscientiously followed for almost half a century. My activities as a critic further stimulated in me a livelier interest than I had previously felt for symphonic and chamber music. As a youth my deepest musical impressions had come from opera."

The dominant figure in the concert life of Prague in the forties was an ambitious young conductor named Friedrich Kittl,[9] Director of the Conservatory of Music and conductor of the Conservatory's orchestra. Among the novelties he introduced was Schumann's *Das Paradies und die Peri*.[10] This performance inspired a long article by Hanslick, which came to the attention of Schumann and prompted the latter to invite the young critic to visit him in Dresden. Hanslick accepted eagerly, the more so since the visit offered not only the opportunity of meeting Schumann but also the prospect of renewing a fleeting acquaintance he had made with Wagner in Marienbad in the summer of 1845. It was during this visit in Dresden that he heard the performance of *Tannhäuser*,

---

[8] And had his first encounter with the censor. The concert included a performance of the first finale from Gluck's *Armide*. In commenting on the absence of Gluck from the repertoire of the Prague Opera at that time, and upon the fact that Gluck's spirit had thus to be content with such fragmentary productions, Hanslick compared the admirers of Gluck with the early Christians who had been compelled to hold the Communion Service secretly in the catacombs. All this was cut, since references to religion were forbidden!

[9] Johann Friedrich Kittl (1806–1868). He wrote an opera, *Bianca und Giuseppe*, to a text by R. Wagner.

[10] *Das Paradies und die Peri*, opus 50, a work for solo voices, chorus, and orchestra, composed in 1843, based on Thomas Moore's *Lalla Rookh*.

under Wagner's direction, which prompted him to come out as Wagner's champion when he moved to Vienna in the following autumn for the fourth and last year of his legal studies.

He arrived in Vienna just in time, at just the right age (twenty-one), and with just the right background. The Revolution of March, 1848, was less than two years off, and although its political consequences were destined to be other than its agitators had dreamed, it was symptomatic of social development of bourgeois cultural life in the second half of the nineteenth century. Toward the end of his life Hanslick was to write:

"It has always been a valuable memory to me to have experienced the last years of pre-March (1848) Vienna. How trivial was public musical life at the end of the thirties and in the early forties! Sumptuous and trivial alike, it vacillated between dull sentimentality and scintillant wit. Cut off from all great intellectual interests, the Vienna public abandoned itself to diversion and entertainment. Not only did the theaters flourish; they were the chief subject of conversation and occupied the leading columns of the daily newspapers. Musical life was dominated by Italian opera, virtuosity, and the waltz. Strauss [11] and Lanner [11a] were idolized. I would be the last to underestimate the talent of these two men . . . but it can readily be understood that this sweetly intoxicating three-quarter time, to which heads as well as feet were abandoned, combined with Italian opera and the cult of virtuosity, rendered listeners steadily less capable of intellectual effort.

---

[11] Johann Strauss, Senior.

[11a] Joseph Franz Karl Lanner (1801–1843), credited with being founder of Viennese dance music. A rival to Johann Strauss, who alternated with him as conductor in the large and small Redoutensaal of Vienna.

"The year 1848 marked the borderline between the old and the new Austria—not only in political and social matters but also in the literary and artistic life of the nation. The way had, of course, been prepared, partly in the nature of growing dissatisfaction with musical life as it was, partly in a growing sense of need for something more elevated and substantial. That the dominance of virtuosity would lead to satiation was inevitable. The public had not only grown tired of astonishing accomplishments of superficial bravura; it had also grown tired of its own enthusiasm. The intoxication it had indulged in for the better part of a decade under the stimulus of Liszt, Thalberg, and others could not continue indefinitely. And the serious music lover who had had his fill of virtuosity could find little respite in other sectors of musical life. The inadequacy and the dilettantism of the 'Society Concerts' [12] and the 'Spirituals' [13] had long been obvious. The brilliant but fleeting phenomenon of the Philharmonic Concerts under Nicolai [14] had made the dark-

[12] The Society of Friends of Music (Gesellschaft der Musikfreunde). It was founded in 1813 and has functioned ever since as one of the principal institutions of Vienna, along with its executive adjuncts, the Singverein (choral society, a mixed chorus of 300–350 members), founded in 1858, and the Orchesterverein (orchestra society), founded in 1869. Among its musical directors in Hanslick's time were Hellmesberger (1851–1859), Herbeck (1859–1870 and 1875–1877), Rubinstein (1871–1872), Brahms (1872–1875), Kremser (1878–1880), Gericke (1880–1884 and 1890–1895), Richter (1885–1890), Perger (1895–1900), and Loewe (1900–1904).
[13] Concerts Spirituels, so called because of their origin in the Church of St. Augustine, when their founder, Franz Gebauer (1784–1822), was choir director (he was otherwise celebrated in his time as a mouth organ virtuoso). The Concerts Spirituels began in 1819, with the choir and congregation of the church as a nucleus, and rendered great service in promoting interest in serious music at a time when such interest was not general. Unlike the Society of Friends of Music, this institution has not survived. The last Concert Spirituel was given on April 23, 1848.
[14] Otto Nicolai (1809–1849), best known to contemporary music lovers as composer of The Merry Wives of Windsor, of which the overture, at least, is familiar in the United States. The opera still survives in the repertoire of

7

ness more perceptible by contrast. The 'Tonkünstler-Gesellschaft'[15] was wholly petrified in the annual performances of *The Seasons* and *The Creation*. No notice was taken of the new creative talents in Germany. Schumann, Gade,[16] Heller,[17] Sterndale Bennett,[18] Karl Loewe,[19] Robert Franz,[20] and Wagner were almost entirely unknown. Mendelssohn had found only a belated hearing in Vienna; his *St. Paul* was performed in the smallest provincial cities of Germany, and even in America, before it was finally given in Vienna.[21] And there wasn't much enthusiasm for it even then.

"The mighty storm of the March Revolution almost

German and Austrian opera houses. Nicolai was conductor of the Court Opera in Vienna in 1842, when it occurred to him that there would be merit in employing the opera orchestra for concert performances. The result was the first Philharmonic Concert, given on November 27, 1842, in the large ballroom of the Palace (Grosser Redoutensaal). The Philharmonic Concerts continued under Nicolai's direction until 1847, when the conductor left Vienna to assume the directorship of the Berlin Opera. They were continued only spasmodically until 1854, when Karl Eckert gave them a new impulse. Nicolai's service is commemorated in contemporary Vienna by an annual Nicolai Concert, traditionally devoted to Beethoven's Ninth Symphony, performed by the Vienna Philharmonic.

[15] The first oratorio society in Vienna. Its founding in 1771 marked the beginning of concert life in Vienna in the modern sense of public productions. It was a beneficial society, created to provide pensions for destitute musicians. The musical nucleus was made up of members of the Court Orchestra. The Tonkünstler Society traditionally presented two oratorios a year, one at Christmas and one at Easter, usually Haydn's *The Seasons* or *The Creation*. It was reorganized in 1862 as the Haydn Society and continued its activities well into the second half of the century, considerably overshadowed, however, by the Society of Friends of Music and its associated bodies.

[16] Niels Wilhelm Gade (1817–1890), Danish composer, a protégé of Mendelssohn.

[17] Stephen Heller (1815–1888), Hungarian pianist and composer.

[18] Sir William Sterndale Bennett (1816–1875), English composer and teacher, protégé of Mendelssohn and Schumann.

[19] Johann Karl Gottfried Loewe (1796–1869), German composer, remembered chiefly for his ballads.

[20] (1815–1892), German composer, remembered chiefly for his *Lieder*.

[21] In 1839.

immediately found a trembling echo in Vienna's artistic life, first in the expulsion of Italian opera. The Italian season was to have begun on April 1, 1848, with Verdi's *Ernani*, but no sooner had the placards been posted than they were defaced or torn down. These demonstrations prompted the Court authorities to postpone, and finally to cancel, the season. Behind this demonstration lay two powerful emotional currents. The first was one of which everyone was conscious and which found open, unashamed expression. This was a general trend toward all that was German— manners, politics, art. Away with the mortal enemies of Germanism! Down with the Italians! The second motive was less conspicuous, but it played an undeniable part. It was of a democratic nature. Italian opera was regarded as an exclusive artistic luxury, as the music of the Court, of the aristocrats, and of the rich. Thus it was the artistic expression of anti-German, and specifically aristocratic, entertainment."

But to return to 1846: Hanslick had been in Vienna only once before—in the Easter holidays of the same year, when he had indulged in a kind of reconnaissance of the terrain. He had been unimpressed by the physical aspects of the city itself. There was no Ringstrasse in those days. Vienna was still a walled city, and Hanslick found that the narrow streets and the constricted, crowded urban centers, such as Graben and Kohlmarkt, compared unfavorably with Rossmarkt and Graben in Prague. But life in Vienna, its artistic and personal stimuli—that was something else again. He had called on Liszt, bearing a letter of introduction from Berlioz, and had heard him play. He had also heard a Philharmonic Concert under Nicolai (Beethoven's Ninth Symphony) and a performance of Verdi's *Ernani* which opened the three-month Italian *stagione* of 1846, traditionally on Easter Monday. He did not like it. Only much later did he learn to appreciate Italian opera.

When he returned to settle permanently in Vienna in the fall, Hanslick took modest lodgings in the suburb of Landstrasse and learned to enjoy a bachelor's leisurely breakfast at a coffee house on Wollzeile, near the old university, seated on a red velvet sofa and reading the newspapers, in true Viennese fashion. His university studies did not so occupy his time as to restrict his opera and theatergoing—nor his critical enthusiasm. Finding that Wagner was virtually unknown in Vienna, and anxious to refresh his own stimulating experience with *Tannhäuser* in Dresden, he borrowed a score from Liszt and began a lengthy analysis of the opera, which the *Wiener Musikzeitung* published in eleven installments. It did little to stimulate Viennese interest in Wagner, but it brought Hanslick to Dr. August Schmidt, publisher of the *Musikzeitung*, and fairly launched him on his career as a music critic.

He did not immediately become the first critic of the *Musikzeitung*. Schmidt assigned him to small concerts in the suburbs, much as contemporary editors of metropolitan dailies are accustomed to do with our budding music critics. Nor was he paid. More important to him at the time were occasional opportunities to contribute essays—also gratis— to the *Sonntagsblätter*, the foremost literary periodical of pre-1848 Vienna. It was in the columns of the *Sonntagsblätter* that Hanslick struck the first critical blows for Schumann when the latter, hitherto known to the Viennese only as "Clara Wieck's husband," came to Vienna as a composer, shortly after Hanslick's arrival. In this manner Hanslick gradually established a modest reputation for himself as a music critic, and when the official court newspaper, *Wiener Zeitung*, was reorganized in January of 1848, he was offered the post of music editor.

In the wake of the social and political changes attendant upon the explosive events of 1848 came administrative changes which were to affect Hanslick's career directly. In 1849 he received his Doctorate of Law and was ready to enter public service. Many of the best public servants in the field of finance had been transferred to the newly created district attorneys' offices, leaving a number of vacancies in the provincial fiscal offices, and there were sudden calls from the provinces to Vienna for replacements. Hanslick was assigned to Klagenfurt. It seemed to him at the time not only an unpleasant but even a disastrous circumstance. It meant separation from the urban cultural life to which he was so strongly drawn and also relinquishment of his position on the *Wiener Zeitung*, at a time when his name was just beginning to become well and favorably known in a field far closer to his heart than that in which he had chosen to make his profession.

In Klagenfurt he made the best of an unrewarding situation by cultivating such social opportunities as were afforded by a provincial city as yet not even connected with the national capital by railroad, and dependent for musical pleasure on what he and a few other accomplished amateurs themselves contributed. He was recalled to Vienna in 1852, to a position in the Ministry of Finance, and eventually restored to the musical editorship of the *Wiener Zeitung*. Shortly afterwards he was transferred in the public service to the Ministry of Education and assigned to the University Department.

Now he was able to settle down to the dual routine of

official duties and music criticism, combining both with an active and rewarding social life which brought him into personal contact with most of the musical and literary figures of the Vienna of the fifties, and with many of its distinguished visitors. His own standing was bettered in 1855 by a move from the *Wiener Zeitung* to *Die Presse*, then the most widely read and influential newspaper in Austria. He remained with *Die Presse* until 1864, when the publisher refused to raise the salaries of several key employees who then walked out and founded *Die Neue Freie Presse*. Hanslick went with them, and thus began a long and celebrated association which lasted until his retirement from active life in 1895.

During the fifties, Hanslick devoted a great deal of his spare time to the study of the aesthetics and history of music. This was to bear fruit in 1854 in the form of the brochure *Beauty in Music* (*Vom Musikalisch-Schönen*), his first important publication and the first to carry his reputation appreciably beyond the confines of Vienna. It had its origin in the musical-aesthetic theories which were subsequently to characterize his opposition to the major trends of popular musical taste of his times. Of the impulses which prompted this book, he wrote in his autobiography: "Reading so many books on musical aesthetics, all of which defined the nature of music in terms of the 'feelings' it arouses, and which ascribed to music a definite expressive capability, had long excited in me both doubt and opposition. The nature of music is even harder to fix within philosophical categories than painting, since in music the decisive concepts of 'form' and 'content' are impossible of independence and separation. If one wishes to attribute a definite content to purely instrumental music—in vocal music content derives from the poem, not from the music—then one must discard the precious pearls of the musical art, in which no one can demonstrate a 'content' distinct from the 'form,' nor even deduce it. On the other hand, I readily agree that it is idle to speak of absolute lack of content in instrumental music, which my opponents accuse me of having done in my treatise. How is one to distinguish scientifically in music between inspired form and empty form? I had the former in mind; my opponents accused me of the latter."

It was about this time that Hanslick set to work on a new project, destined to play an important part in the shaping of his future career. This was to qualify and be recognized as a lay lecturer (in the sense that no salary was involved) on the history and aesthetics of music at the university. Despite the fact that nothing of the kind had ever been done before at the University of Vienna (nor probably at any other university) the authorities were most co-operative. They accepted *Beauty in Music* as a qualifying treatise and waived the normally requisite dissertation. They even accepted his doctorate, despite the fact that it was for law rather than music. He began his lectures in October, 1856, at the Old University building, and continued them for nearly forty years, always in the afternoon five o'clock period. He created a minor sensation when he had a piano placed beside his reading desk to give actual examples and, on occasion, perform entire compositions. His lectures were well attended right from the beginning, and by a widely varied and often distinguished audience, including students from all departments, public servants, lawyers, physicians, and artists. Hanslick was probably justified in considering himself the originator of musical appreciation courses.

He continued, nevertheless, with his bureaucratic duties at the Ministry. These became increasingly irksome, particularly since the preparation of his lectures and his work as a music critic made demands on his time which were difficult to accommodate with mornings spent at an office. But he could only give up the latter if he could get a paid professorship, and this seemed unlikely, since there had never been a chair of music at the university and since the Ministry of Finance could not be expected to look with favor upon the establishment of such a "luxury." Hanslick was now so anxious, however, to devote all his time and energy to music that he interested influential friends in the proposition, and in 1861 the improbable occurred. In October of that year he was named Extraordinary Professor of the History and Aesthetics of Music and relieved of his office duties at the Ministry.

He was now able to settle into the routine which was to be his for the next forty years, subject only to interruption by an occasional service on musical juries at world fairs or occasional out-of-town assignments, such as the *première* of *Die Meistersinger* in Munich in 1868, the opening of Bayreuth in 1876, the first *Parsifal* in Bayreuth in 1882, an early *Otello* in Milan in 1887, and the first Rome performance of *Falstaff* in 1893. His season was from October to July, and his beat a comparatively small area of Vienna embracing the Musikvereinssaal,[22] the Redoutensaal,[23] the

---

[22] There have been three Musikvereinssaale (literally, Music Society Halls) in Vienna. The reference here is to the second, opened in 1831, which was built on the site of the first, more familiarly known as "Zum rothen Igel" (Red Hedgehog), on Tuchlauben, in the Inner City. It served as the home of the Society of Friends of Music and Vienna's principal concert hall until the opening of the third Musikvereinssaal in the Musikvereinsgebäude (literally, Music Society Building), just off the Ringstrasse, on January 6, 1870. The Musikvereinssaal is the largest of three concert halls contained

Kärntnertor theater,[24] the Carltheater,[25] the Theater in der
Josefstadt,[26] the Theater an der Wien,[27] and, after 1869, the
"new" opera house on Ringstrasse, and the "new" Musikvereinsgebäude.[28] He wrote one or two pieces (*feuil-
letons*) a week, covering several events at a time or devoting a whole piece to one event, according to the news
interest or controversial value of the productions in question. Unlike American critics, he was not plagued by the
necessity of making the next morning's late city edition. His
reviews appeared anywhere from two days to a week after
the event. This was the custom in Vienna in those days and
remains the rule today. Only once did he permit himself to be
hurried. This was in connection with the Munich *première* of
Die Meistersinger in 1868, when he agreed to forward his review to Vienna the day after the performance. He felt ever
afterwards that this haste had contributed to making it one
of the few reviews of his career about which he had subsequent reservations. Haste, combined with resentment at the

within the building (the others are the Brahmssaal and the Kammersaal, used
for recitals and lectures respectively) and has been, for the past eighty years,
one of Vienna's two principal concert halls.

[23] The large ballroom of the palace. It is still used occasionally for operas
and plays by the State Opera and the Burgtheater (State Theater). *Cosi fan
tutte*, for instance, is almost always given there.

[24] Home of the Court Opera, until the opening of the new Opera House
on the Ringstrasse, on May 25, 1869. It was situated approximately on the
site now occupied by the Sacher Hotel, directly behind the present Opera.

[25] In the Leopoldstadt. It was an all-service theater, frequently used for
independent opera enterprises. (Patti sang her first Vienna season there.)
Only the façade still stands.

[26] The oldest and most beautiful theater in Vienna. It was the scene of
Max Reinhardt's triumphs in the 1920's and is presently the home of an
excellent repertory theater.

[27] After the Josefstadt, the oldest theater in Vienna. It was the scene of
the première of *Fidelio* in 1805 and of many other epoch-making *premières* in
both grand and light opera. It is now the temporary home of the Vienna State
Opera, pending completion of the restoration of the house on the Ringstrasse
which was destroyed by bombs in March, 1945.

[28] See page 14, note 22.

idolatry of the audience, prompted him, he later admitted, to write in greater heat than an objective approach warranted and to render too harsh a judgment. He came to prefer *Die Meistersinger* to all other Wagner operas with the possible exception of *Tannhäuser*. Six years later, when he was assigned to cover the first Bayreuth Festival, he accepted only on condition that overnight coverage would not be required.

The Vienna concert season of Hanslick's time was about as variable as a New York, Philadelphia, or Boston season today—that is, virtuosos came and went, while certain staple institutions went on forever—or seemed to. Indeed, some of Vienna's institutions have achieved a certain relative immortality. The Society of Friends of Music (*Gesellschaft der Musikfreunde*) was thirty-three years old when Hanslick came to Vienna, and it is still the foundation stone of Vienna's concert life, having survived both world wars and the normal sequence of economic and political crises. It is similar to what was, in Hanslick's days, the Court Opera (Hofoper), which became the State Opera (Staatsoper) after the fall of the Hapsburgs in 1918. Last but not least of the permanent institutions which contributed to Hanslick's season was the Philharmonic Orchestra, then as now one of the world's finest.

Just as his arrival in Vienna, in 1846, had coincided with the impending changes in Vienna's musical life attendant upon the Revolution of 1848, so his appointment as Extraordinary Professor in 1861, and his release from the constraining duties of a public servant, roughly coincided with the beginning of the period of full bloom of the renascent musical forces liberated in 1848. This period is difficult to bracket by dates, but since it was a reflection of Vienna's

16

sudden expansion to the status of cosmopolitan, political, and economic capital of southeastern Europe, it can—if only for convenience's sake—be said to have begun with the Christmas edict of 1857, directing that the city walls be torn down. This Imperial directive signaled the beginning of an ambitious building program which led to the opening of the Ringstrasse in 1865, the laying of the cornerstone of the imposing new Rathaus (City Hall) in 1866—and the completion of the new Court Opera and the Music Society Building in 1869.

It also coincided with Hanslick's own coming of age as a critic. The twenty-two-year-old enthusiast who had volunteered as Wagner's champion in 1846 had grown into a thirty-seven-year-old professional critic, still Wagner's admirer, but no longer his champion. The 1846 essay on *Tannhäuser* had revealed a great critical talent, if hardly a great critic. It showed knowledge, discernment, the selective urge which is essential to real criticism, and, above all, the capacity for enthusiasm without which all criticism sours. It had also disclosed great self-confidence, which is hardly less important in a critic's natural endowment than enthusiasm. Without it, a critic becomes at best a dispassionate, more or less literate reporter, possibly instructive but incapable of making either himself or his art an object of controversy. If it were the custom to evaluate the debuts of critics as one evaluates the debuts of artists, Hanslick's debut with his *Tannhäuser* essay could have been greeted as a work of great promise, and his subsequent book, *Beauty in Music*, as a fulfillment of that promise. But in 1846, his critical talent was more striking than the critic himself, whose personality had thus far been revealed only by its positive side. In this respect, Hanslick's career can be regarded as paralleling Wagner's; *Tannhäuser* is to the *Ring* more or less what Hanslick's essay on *Tannhäuser* is to his *Letters from Bayreuth*. Between 1846 and 1861, Liszt had written most of his symphonic poems; Weimar, as represented by Liszt and Wagner, had broken with Leipzig, as represented by Mendelssohn, Schumann, and Brahms; and Hanslick, in his *Beauty in Music*, had aligned himself with Leipzig as the defender of the musical art against the transcendentalists in Weimar, who had decided that the "music of the future" had to consist of elements other than music alone. Hanslick's rejection of Liszt was a lively skirmish, but no more than that, since Liszt was not the real enemy. He joined the battle proper in 1858, with his review of the Vienna production of *Lohengrin*. How bitter it would become was indicated by Wagner's caricature of Hanslick in the character of Beckmesser. The personal element reached a climax one night in the fall of 1862, at the home of Dr. Standhartner, personal physician to Emperor Franz Josef, where Wagner, with Hanslick present, read the *Die Meistersinger* text in a draft in which Beckmesser was still called Veit Hanslich.

The further course of the struggle on Hanslick's side is mirrored in the following pages, in the critic's own words. It is apparent that, while he may have had some misgivings now and then, wondering if he had not gone too far, he had none about the correctness of his aesthetic principles. It has become the fashion among twentieth-century commentators and historians to write of Hanslick as a fine critic who, in indulging the human being's proneness to err, erred monstrously (in his opposition to Wagner). Those who write of him in this manner can hardly have read him, since, if he erred on Wagner, he also erred on Berlioz, Liszt, Bruckner,

18

Wolf, and Strauss, which is a high error count even for a Beckmesser. And their charity is misdirected. There can be no doubt that Hanslick, were he alive today, with all the musical developments of the last half century to go on, would stoutly deny that his judgments on the great composers of his time had been mistaken. He might readily admit to a horde of minor errors, but not to mistakes based on aesthetic principle.

He enjoyed the fight. Every good critic lusts for controversy, just as he lusts for good music; and Hanslick, in his time, had plenty of both—but not too much. In the closing days of September, 1894, toward the end of his career, he was asked by his friend, Billroth,[29] with whom he was staying near Salzburg, whether he did not dread the imminent exposure to another round of concerts, recitals, and operas.

"No," Hanslick replied, "I must say that at the close of every summer vacation I find myself happily anticipating the winter program of Philharmonic Concerts, the concerts of the Society of Friends of Music, and the quartet programs, menus which I sample with a gourmand's happy anticipation. I have been writing music criticism for half a century, and, while it does not come to me as easily now as it once did, my receptivity is still fresh. From early youth I have always regarded the job of the music critic for an eminent newspaper—next to a professorship—as the most enviable of occupations. The poet is left to his own creative resources. The critic has the advantage of constant exposure to new materials. Not a year passes but that the sources of artistic creation bring us a golden nugget, or two, or three.

---

[29] Theodor Billroth (1829–1894), famous German surgeon and musical amateur, an intimate of Brahms and Hanslick and author of a book, *Who Is Musical?* edited by Hanslick. Almost all of Brahms' chamber music was played privately in Billroth's apartment prior to the first public performances.

Along with the worthless, there are certain to be some works of originality and excellence. Nor is it the excellent works alone that stimulate and occupy the critic; the pretentiously ugly, the consciously perverted, also belong to his province. They are the 'interesting cases,' such as you have at your [Billroth's] clinics.

"But," he concluded, "we critics, unfortunately, cannot heal or cure."

H. P.

" TANNHAUSER "[1]

[1846]

I

THERE is no denying that the present condition of German opera is sad. It almost seems as if we had entered upon a period of poverty and impotence, a state of barrenness after an ample harvest. Many splendid operas can be credited to the post-Mozartean epoch, but the masters who wrote them are dead.

"Dead?" the reader asks reproachfully. "Are not many still alive whose works are recorded in golden letters in the history books of German opera?" True, to be sure; but the artists in them are dead. There is, first and foremost, Heinrich Marschner,[2] the robust, profound singer of Hans Heiling and Ivanhoe, so serious and yet so ardent, so learned and yet so romantic! And Spohr,[3] the noble dreamer and bard, with the sweet voice and the deep blue eyes! Both have achieved fame, but their creative span is finished. The fresh

---

[1] This was the essay with which Hanslick, then a student of law, just twenty-two years old and fresh from Prague, introduced himself as a music critic to the city which was to be his home and his battlefield for the next fifty years. It ran in eleven consecutive issues of the *Wiener Musikzeitung* in November and December of 1846. In its preparation, Hanslick used Franz Liszt's personal copy of the orchestral score. He was rewarded with a lengthy letter of thanks from Wagner, dated January 1, 1847. The version of Hanslick's dissertation given here in translation is necessarily severely abridged.

[2] Heinrich Marschner (1795–1861).

[3] Louis (Ludwig) Spohr (1784–1859). Although now remembered primarily as a composer for the violin, he was one of the foremost opera composers of his generation. His stage masterpiece was *Faust* (1816).

bloom of song has withered, the youthful fantasy grown old. Their most recent works, for all their truly admirable details and masterly workmanship, must be classed among the weaker products of German opera.

What of Lortzing? [4] We gratefully acknowledge the charming products of his comic muse—accompanying the acknowledgment with the modest request that he give us a second *Czar und Zimmermann*. And, in any case, the cheerful Lortzing is not for serious grand opera. Flotow? [5] He is at the threshold of his creative work and may yet accomplish something superior to his overrated *Stradella*.[6] Thus far I consider him a composer with a flair for instrumentation and personal advantage, who, with a couple of pretty tunes, leads art and the public around by the nose. I guess that's about all—save Meyerbeer! [7] Gifted genius, composer of *The Huguenots!* For years he has been carrying *Le Prophète* back and forth between Berlin and Paris in his suitcase, possibly in an effort to determine whether prophets may travel customs-free.[8] It is possible that the master has kept the greatest of beauties hidden away, but a hidden beauty is, in effect, no beauty at all, and an opera in a suitcase is as little help to art as a change of clothes. Thus, is German opera entirely widowed? Is there no one else? No one?

---

[4] Gustav Albert Lortzing (1801–1851). He was, at the time of Hanslick's writing, conductor at the Theater an der Wien where, on May 30 of the same year, he had presided at the *première* of his opera, *Der Waffenschmied*, which is still a staple item in the repertoire of German opera houses.

[5] Friedrich Flotow (1812–1883).

[6] He did, with *Martha*, introduced at the Court Opera on November 25, 1847. The opera was commissioned as a result of the previous success of *Stradella* in the Theater an der Wien, and subsequently at the Court Opera under Nicolai.

[7] Giacomo Meyerbeer (1791–1864).

[8] Meyerbeer had more serious intentions. *Le Prophète* got out of the suitcase and onto the stage of the Grand Opéra in Paris, in 1849, whether customs-free or not history doesn't tell.

We shall see. Nothing is to be gained from complaining and fault-finding. In continual mourning for what we do not have, we are likely to end by ignoring what we do have. Let us look around and see if there may not be a glimmer of hope. We must look for a man who has already accomplished enough to justify founding one's hopes upon him but not so much that we can expect nothing further. I think we have such a man. He is Richard Wagner. If there is anyone among contemporary German composers from whom we can expect something distinguished in the field of serious grand opera, it is he. Richard Wagner is, I am convinced, the greatest dramatic talent among all contemporary composers.

The first work with which he presented himself to the world was the big, five-act opera, *Rienzi*. It was first given in Dresden,[9] with the utmost brilliance, and was received with noisy jubilation. Listeners were so enraptured by the freshness of this new music, and so dazzled by its impact, that there was a general tendency to regard the young composer as a suddenly revealed regenerator of dramatic music, the Messiah of German opera. Richard Wagner was the man of the hour, and his fame was established overnight. A superficial examination of the score sufficed to convince the critic that here was, indeed, a great musical talent, an uncommon gift for dramatic expression. The work was animated by a youthful vigor and enthusiasm which carried the listener away. But with regard to strictly artistic requirements it was inadequate, and I was thus unable to join in the enthusiastic praise which even Liszt, himself a genius, uttered in my presence.

---

[9] October 20, 1842.

Wagner's second opera, *The Flying Dutchman*,[10] aroused sympathy right at the outset, if only because of its uncommonly poetic, exotic substance. It represents unqualified progress beyond *Rienzi*. The characters are drawn more simply and with greater repose; the situations are more tightly compressed and more confidently represented. The musical forms still lack the ultimate finish, and the instrumentation lacks moderation here and there. But in both respects a significant improvement is undeniable. *The Flying Dutchman* alone would have sufficed to assure Richard Wagner a seat and a voice among contemporary dramatic masters.

Then came his third and newest opera, *Tannhäuser*,[11] which I heard this summer in Dresden. It is not a composition in which I could find pleasure merely by understanding how nicely this or that had been accomplished. It was, rather, a musical experience, carrying the listener irresistibly with it, in such a way that what occurred in the orchestra and on the stage became part of his own life. I am of the firm opinion that it is the finest thing achieved in grand opera in at least twelve years, that it is the most significant dramatic creation since *The Huguenots*,[12] and that it is just as epoch-making in its time as were *The Huguenots*, *Der Freischütz*,[13] and *Don Giovanni*,[14] each for its respective period of musical history.

In order to substantiate my judgment, I must undertake a critical analysis of the opera; and, difficult and unsatisfactory as it may be to try to "tell" music, the reader may, nevertheless, permit the attempt more willingly, since this interesting and significant work (just like Wagner's

---

[10] Dresden, January 2, 1843.   [11] Dresden, October 19, 1845.
[12] 1836.   [13] 1821.   [14] 1787.

earlier operas) is *terra incognita* in the Austrian monarchy. I intentionally refrained from going into detail about the two earlier operas, partly because my topic was *Tannhäuser*, partly because I have never heard an actual performance of either of them. For I feel that with a dramatic composition the over-all impression in actual performance is at least as necessary as, even if less decisive than, the mere study of the cold notes; the most exact preconception which the skilled musician may evoke from a study of the score can receive its ultimate completion and confirmation only through the actual sensual conception. Will not the most accomplished score reader here and there overlook the effect and importance of some little touch later discovered, and will he not, on other occasions, in actual performance, often recognize as mere paper effect something that had struck him as particularly promising in his study?

II

The *Tannhäuser* libretto has a rich dramatic plan and the virtue, significant for a grand opera, of taking place within the framework of a familiar folk legend and a no less familiar national-poetic institution, the Wartburg Song Contest. The element of the supernatural, without which no grand opera is quite complete, appears in fortunate concord with the content of the whole. Pictorial fantasy, sentiment, medieval atmosphere, German character and customs—all are included and, even more important, all are capable of musical expression and development.

I regard it almost as a matter of regret that, in accordance with traditional requirements, in Wagner's operas, too, the overture comes first and is therefore the first object of critical judgment. For purely instrumental composition is not his forte. He needs the live word, the developing situation, as a firm basis for his melodies. As programmatic musical summations of the respective operas, his overtures offer much of interest and even of genius, but they are not satisfactory as independent musical compositions. The overture to *Tannhäuser* brings us—fairly well put together, but often too monotonously repeated—the following themes: the Pilgrims' Chorus from the third act, the Venusberg music from the first act, Tannhäuser's Hymn to Venus, and, as finale, the Pilgrims' Chorus again, with violin figuration. We shall encounter all these pieces in the course of the opera itself and we shall have later occasion to speak of Wagner's art of instrumentation, demonstrated particularly well in the overture.

At the rise of the curtain, we see a spacious grotto, illuminated by a roseate light, representing the inside of the Hörselberg, where the enchantress Venus holds her court of love. The background is a blue lake, in which bathing naiads are visible; in the middle ground are dancing nymphs and bacchantes. Tannhäuser sleeps quietly in the foreground, his head in Venus' lap. In the orchestra there begins a slow tremolo in the much divided violins, which sustain, with and without mutes, a truly charming, continuous whispering, whirring, and buzzing. The viola sets off quietly on the characteristic demoniacal ascending passage whose significance has already been impressed upon us in the overture. The nymphs and bacchantes begin a suggestive dance which grows steadily more abandoned, accompanied by a kindred crescendo in the orchestra, interrupted from time to time by a single stroke on the triangle or tambourine. The dancers pause for a moment in the middle of their dance to listen to the charming, insinuating song of the sirens, heard from afar and without accompaniment.

It is always difficult to describe music in words, and in this instance sheerly impossible. The magical trembling and fluttering of the music, the diabolically alluring upward and downward rhythmic curves, the fairy-tale weaving and dancing and singing, which strike us so magically and attractively, and, at the same time, so strangely and uncannily— it is all absolutely unique. Even in Wagner's earlier operas, the instrumentation excited the greatest attention and established beyond doubt his great talent for descriptive and characteristic treatment of the orchestra. He has now outgrown the excessive noise and outlay of brass which was often so disturbing in *Rienzi*. In resourceful, descriptive, and original use of the orchestra, *Tannhäuser* ranks among the finest accomplishments of musical history.

The music to the ensuing scene between Tannhäuser and Venus is extremely passionate and dramatic, the accents of pleading and rejection being alternated with great cumulative effect. And here we encounter a fault—or a habit, if you will—into which Wagner almost always falls in the description of violent emotional tension. I refer to the frequent and compounded use of the chord of the diminished seventh. It is, of course, only natural to have recourse to these sharp, penetrating, and, at the same time, easily assimilable chords to describe strong, restless effects. But, quite aside from the fact that the creative artist must never be more vigilant than against stereotyped means of expression and mannerisms, the use and abuse of the diminished seventh chord has already been rendered *mauvais genre* by mediocre composers.

With the last word of Tannhäuser's ultimate convulsive outcry, the scene changes with a thunderclap into a delightful, verdant valley, smiling upon us in cheerful stage illumination. On a hill to the left sits a young shepherd blowing on a reed pipe. Tannhäuser stands to one side, stiff and motionless, as if in a trance. This sudden transformation is indescribably effective and excellently reflected in the music. On the last note of the shepherd's pipe, one hears from afar the simple, devout chorale of pilgrims on their way to Rome.

Now, in the distance, echo the sounds of woodland horns heralding the approach of the Landgrave and his hunting party. In many operas we are confronted with the situation of an approaching hunting party, but in musical representation they are as alike as peas in a pod. One hears, as a rule, two horns stationed behind the scenes, occupying themselves with sixths, fifths, and thirds in such a manner as to prompt the assumption that hunting music, as handed down from the time of King Nimrod to Prince Albert, has always consisted of these same meager progressions. Now let us see how Wagner, who composes the smallest scene with the greatest care, describes the approach of a hunting party. As the last note of the distant Pilgrims' Chorus dies away, we hear a single horn call from the background of the theater; during the ritornello after the chorale, we hear two horns enunciating the melody of the fanfare. Only then comes a bit of a hunting song, in three-part harmony, from one side of the stage. This principal theme is answered from a different direction in a different tonality. We hear it now from one direction, now from another, from far and near, interrupted now and then by single horn calls. The hunt converges upon us from all directions. The fanfare grows stronger and more distinct until taken up in full harmony by the entire horn choir.

Wagner's description is as new and original as it is true to nature. Look into the score and see how he achieves and orders this effect. He uses twelve horns, disposed on the stage in the following manner: two horns in C, nearest; three horns in F, farther away; three horns in F, still more distant; four horns in E flat, most distant. These instruments, so disposed, throw the melody back and forth, answer or interrupt one another, draw nearer, until they are finally united and playing in concert. This passage is one of countless examples of the exactitude and care with which Wagner not only arranges every effect but also determines the practical aspects of execution and thus protects his intentions against unforeseen circumstances.

The Landgrave comes striding down the hill, accompanied by six knights and singers, among them Wolfram von Eschenbach, Walther von der Vogelweide, Biterolf, Reimar von Zweter, etc. They recognize in the praying figure of Tannhäuser a long missing companion and greet him with unanimous pleasure. There follows a very successful, melodious, and well-rounded male septet, interwoven with violin figurations. The friends plead with Tannhäuser to return with them. Tannhäuser, in great confusion, refuses. Wolfram intercedes. "Here dwells Elisabeth!" he cries. At the urging of the Landgrave, Wolfram recounts how, during Tannhäuser's absence, the affectionate sentiments entertained for him by the saintly Elisabeth (the Landgrave's niece) had so far matured as to promise the happiest fulfillment upon his return. The others now join in Wolfram's song. Tannhäuser is persuaded and won over. The hunting party assembles from all sides. The horns blast away with full force and bring the act to a jubilant close.

The second act begins with an aria by Elisabeth, preceded by a rather long orchestral introduction. The aria is affectionate, candid, chaste, and exuberant. This is possibly by way of establishing Elisabeth's German character, preserved most consistently throughout the entire development of the role. Wolfram is a similarly genuine old-German character, and likable, despite his utter passivity. The characters of Wolfram and Elisabeth indicate without doubt that Wagner is splendidly qualified for the composition of German subjects and that it is in the national field that he will grow the most beautiful flowers.

The next number is a duet between Tannhäuser and Elisabeth, an excellent piece of work, with the possible exception of the over-rich accompaniment. After Tannhäuser has hurried away, the Landgrave appears and announces the song contest, for which the nobility of the land has gathered from far and wide, in great numbers, and with splendid ceremony. The justly celebrated song contest is the climax of the whole plot, the point toward which all that has gone before has been directed. It is the keystone of the piece, although not in respect to music. It is known that the improvisations of the minnesingers consisted, after the fashion of the Greek rhapsodies, not in rhythmically rounded melodies, but in free, unconfined song, somewhat like our large-scale recitative, and supported by the accompanying instruments in a declamatory rather than musical manner. Wagner has successfully captured the character of free, inspired improvisation, but he damages the musical effectiveness of the scene by sticking to it too consistently and for too long a time.

Tannhäuser brings the contest to a close by boldly opposing Wolfram's reverent hymn of love with his own hymn of praise for Madame Venus. With a general exclamation of horror the entire assemblage comes to its feet. The ladies take to their heels. The knights, with drawn swords, close in upon the blasphemer. Elisabeth, with much dignity, steps between them and pleads for him. The music to this stormy scene is effective and dramatic, although one would have preferred a more moderate employment of the tremolo and the diminished seventh. The vengeful knights finally defer to Elisabeth's gentle majesty. The Landgrave severely reprimands Tannhäuser and banishes him forever from his presence. He allows him, however, for the good of his soul, to join the pilgrims, now gathering in his district to undertake the journey to Rome.

This whole finale is imaginatively conceived and artfully contrived, although it seems to be rather the product of artistic cerebration than of spontaneous inspiration. Nor can it escape the charge of excessive length. This may, indeed, be the proper place to mention in general Wagner's characteristic fault of overextending his individual numbers, particularly the finales. It is neither impiety nor presumption but, on the contrary, true love for Wagner's creations which prompts me to express the conviction that they could only benefit by appropriate cuts designed to heighten the effect of the whole opera by easing the task of musical perception and leaving the audience fresher and more receptive.

Between the second and third acts lies Tannhäuser's pilgrimage to Rome, and the introductory entr'acte bears the title in the score, "Tannhäuser's Pilgrimage." The title and, even more so, the content of this entr'acte suggest that we have here not so much an independent piece of music as a purely dramatic introduction extending back to the second act, gathering together in epic reminiscence the threads of the story and then leading in preparatory manner to the occurrences of the act to come. It is elaborated with the utmost mastery and with a provocative choice of instrumental color.

Twilight is well advanced. We see a wooded valley in the shadow of the Wartburg, which looms up gray and forbidding out of the green of the fir trees. To the right, the slope below the Wartburg, Elisabeth kneels in prayer. Opposite her, at some distance, is the faithful Wolfram, in sorrowful contemplation. Now we perceive the pilgrims, returning to their German homeland, their sins redeemed. Elisabeth, who has arisen with their approach and now anxiously and expectantly searches for the loved one for whose salvation she has been praying, notes with dumb anguish that he is not among them. Her fading strength is sufficient only for a prayer. It is of solemn, religious character, somewhat in the manner of many church chorales. The mood of renunciation is beautifully and effectively captured, but the piece as a whole is rather too long.

Wolfram steps toward Elisabeth and offers to accompany her, but she indicates by a gesture that he is not to follow, that she has a high holy office to perform and wishes to make this last journey toward her life's goal alone. Slowly she advances toward the mountain. Wolfram remains alone with his sorrow. He begins a moody, melancholy song, accompanying himself on the harp, a wonderfully lovely, deeply felt episode in six-eight time, "O thou sublime, sweet ev'ning star." At its conclusion, Wolfram remains, supporting himself on his harp, lost in meditation. The cello repeats the entire melody, accompanied by harp and pizzicato chords in the violins—a genuinely poetic moment. Wolfram, overcome with deep melancholy, sings no second verse, but the song lives on and sings further in his heart.

Four shattering horn calls, with an abrupt movement of

the basses, interrupt the ritornello. Tannhäuser comes down
the woodland path, pale and distraught, bareheaded, his
clothes in tatters. With an errant stare he asks the way to
the Venusberg. Wolfram, horrified, exclaims: "Hast thou
not been in Rome?" "Speak not of Rome," replies Tannhäuser indignantly. Finally, affected by Wolfram's touching
sympathy, he tells him how the Holy Father declined to proclaim his forgiveness, pronouncing, instead, a papal edict:
"And as this barren staff I hold ne'er will put forth a flow'r
or leaf, thus shalt thou never more behold salvation or thy
sin's relief!"

The entire narrative is of great dramatic and declamatory truthfulness, particularly successful at the beginning.
A discreet cut, however, would undoubtedly increase its
effectiveness.

Scourged by this annihilating pronouncement, Tannhäuser had fled Rome and wandered, confused and mis-
anthropic, with only one wish, one desire in his heart. The
tremolo in the violins and the diabolically alluring viola
motive tell us what it is he is seeking. Suddenly, we see the
distant Horselberg, aglow in rosy light through which
dancing figures are visible. Music now resounds with
exultant sensuality from within the mountain. This ensemble is set up in the deepest background of the stage and plays
strongly and loudly, but thanks to the distance and the
appropriate acoustical dampening the audience hears it
faintly. The effect is as new as it is surprisingly convincing.
We hear soft music, but even as we hear it, we are certain
that it must be the devil of a racket at the point of origin.
The alluring call of the sirens drives the ecstatic Tannhäuser completely out of his mind. "Venus!" he cries.
Wolfram attempts in vain to restrain him, invokes his

spiritual salvation to resist the diabolical temptation. "An angel prayed for you on earth!" he cries. "Soon shall it send you His blessing from Heaven: Elisabeth!"

During this last exchange between Tannhäuser and Wolfram, the violins alone sustain a tremolo. With the convulsive cry "Elisabeth!" the whole orchestra breaks forth, including trombones. Transfixed by the thunder of this name, Tannhäuser stands motionless. In a devout, expiring voice he repeats, "Elisabeth!" His exclamation is accompanied merely by flutes, clarinets, and oboes, double piano, on a sustained chord. It was a good idea on the part of the composer to have Wolfram exclaim the name Elisabeth, as in the first act, with the sudden entrance of the whole orchestra on the sustained six-four chord. With the same name, the same tones, with which Wolfram had recalled his errant friend from dark enchantment to radiant life, he now recalls him from eternal damnation to eternal salvation.

The reddish glow of torches is visible on the Wartburg, and one hears the muffled mourning music of a chorale for the deceased Elisabeth. The funeral bell of the chapel mixes its bright peal with the melancholy song of the men's voices. "Heinrich, thou art absolv'd!" cries Wolfram in a rush of emotion. Tannhäuser sinks to the ground and expires in his friend's arms. And now, in a joyous movement, the younger pilgrims arrive, swinging green branches in their hands and accompanied by numerous country folk. In a devoutly jubilant chorus they proclaim a miracle which has just occurred in Rome. The barren staff in the hand of the Holy Father has suddenly sprouted leaves.

The narrative of the miracle leads directly into a maestoso in three-two time which, on the exclamation

"Hallelujah," breaks into the Pilgrims' Chorus. During this exalting final song the sun rises. The whole valley brightens in the red of dawn. The pilgrims assemble on the knoll by the image of the Virgin and move on. The faithful Wolfram remains kneeling beside Tannhäuser's body.

III

It is natural that the more deeply a musical creation is derived from the soul, and the more finely and tenderly the motivation of the spiritual aspects constitutes the basic texture of a work, the more difficult is the task of the listener. It is also natural that the more individual and artful the composition, the more often it must be heard in order to be fully understood. Wagner has had the monstrous notion of writing for something higher and bigger and more enduring than the pleasure of the youngsters in the parterre, the homage of the theater journals, and the sweat of the potpourri writers. This is one of the two reasons why his works are not more often performed. It is the more important of the two, and the more general, in that it applies to other works of serious aspiration. The other consideration is a special one: they are extremely difficult to perform properly.

And yet here, too, there has been a tendency to exaggerate, to assume, in view of the excessive demands imposed upon singers, orchestra, stage director, and audience in *Rienzi*, that the same is true of Wagner's later operas. It is not. In *The Flying Dutchman*, excessive vocal difficulty is avoided and the technical stage requirements are within the means of any good provincial theater. Only in the orchestra are things still a bit rebellious, but there are no impossibilities. In *Tannhäuser* the grand scope of the subject and the intensity of the passions represented require the employment of more forceful means, but even here we find no excess. The tasks given the orchestra are in accordance with the high prevailing standards, but they do not transcend what can reasonably be expected nowadays of a good orchestra. As for the voices, only the role of Tannhäuser demands exceptional strength and endurance. What makes it so strenuous is the continuous psychic agitation, against which the protagonist can hardly protect himself. But once the problem of casting the title role is solved, the difficulties of staging, assuming the availability of a good orchestra, are limited to precise and careful preparation under an imaginative conductor, to providing for the numerical requirements of chorus and instruments, and finally to establishing the necessary scenic splendor.

All this suggests, quite properly, that it would be best to reserve the performance of *Tannhäuser* for court theaters. And, indeed, I regard it as one of the noblest missions of such a court opera to break down the Chinese Wall of the standard repertoire and to prepare a proper entrance for the German *Tannhäuser* and its proud banners of progress! [15]

---

[15] The Vienna Court Opera took its time about accepting this excellent advice. *Tannhäuser* was first performed at the Kärntnertortheater on November 19, 1859. It had had an earlier Vienna production at the suburban Thalia Theater in 1857. The "immorality" of the libretto was the reason given for the Court Opera's long resistance to *Tannhäuser*, and even when this resistance, as a result of the great success of *Lohengrin* in 1858, was finally broken down, the word "Rome" had to be expurgated from the text. Hanslick, in his autobiography, recalls the comical effect of the third-act dialogue in which Wolfram asked Tannhäuser, "Were you not there?" and Tannhäuser replied, "Don't speak to me of 'there'!"

VIEUXTEMPS

[1854]

JUST as in the life of an individual a single enlightening experience may have the effect of bringing brightness and
warmth to whole periods of daily humdrum, so in artistic
life do we regard a period as rich when a single imposing
personality relieves the monotony of mediocrity. He stands
out like a flag of victory planted on a pile of stones. We
could look back upon the musical events of the past few
weeks with pleasant satisfaction had they offered nothing
else than the playing of Vieuxtemps.

Listening to him is one of the greatest, most unqualified
pleasures music has to offer. His playing is as technically
infallible and masterly as it is musically noble, inspired, and
compelling. I consider him the first among contemporary
violinists. Some may counter with Joachim, who is now in
his prime and said to be unsurpassed in the interpretation
of the classics of the violin literature. But for one who has
not heard Joachim, the existence of a greater player than
Vieuxtemps is hard to imagine.

He is also one of the best of the modern composers for
his instrument. His concertos are imaginative, gracious,
well made, and contrived with great technical knowledge,
particularly with respect to instrumentation. They do not,
for all that, rank with the truly great examples of instrumental composition, and a local critic who rated Vieux-

temps' Concerto in D minor with the violin concertos of Beethoven and Mendelssohn was overdoing it. His compositions are, however, quite interesting. That which is most striking in music always involves a certain departure from the purely beautiful, and such departures—carried sometimes to extremes—are encountered throughout his works. His compositions give a marked impression of contrivance. The musical invention is genuine but not especially rich; the craftsmanship is incomparably more notable. Thus, in the remarkable exposition and development of the Concerto in D minor, we come upon many imaginative passages; the main themes, on the other hand, suggest no extraordinary native invention.

Vieuxtemps' great talent has had too much intimate traffic with Beethoven not to have assimilated a considerable degree of German solidity, but at the same time it is too deeply rooted in French romanticism to deny the dubious charms of that school. What Vieuxtemps has over his composing colleagues are his well-developed capacity to think in terms of the orchestra and his artistic consistency, which, in his larger works, he allows to prevail, even at the expense of the virtuoso. Excluding Spohr,[1] he may be considered the finest composer among contemporary violinists, and the finest violinist among contemporary composers.

[1] See page 21, note 3.

CLARA SCHUMANN

———— • • • ————

[1856]

IN HER second concert,[1] Clara Schumann confirmed and heightened the impression she had so definitely created in her first. This is the impression of pure satisfaction, experienced when an ideal project is realized harmoniously and within the appropriate frame. She gives a perfect reproduction of each composition, having first understood it in its entirety and then studied it in the utmost detail. The artistic subordination of her own personality to the intentions of the composer is, with her, a principle. And she is, indeed, rarely qualified to grasp and to identify herself with those lofty intentions. Brought up on Bach and Beethoven, she has become so much at home in the thoughts of august composers that she finds profound beauties where others find only riddles. As a young girl she already stood above the insipid trifles of virtuosity and was one of the first to preach the gospel of the austere German masters. And yet she did not grow stale in the one-sidedness of a single

---

[1] In January and February, 1856, Clara Schumann gave five scheduled concerts in Vienna. The tremendous success of these concerts prompted her to give a sixth on March 6. Apart from smaller pieces by Mendelssohn, Chopin, and Weber, the programs included the following: Brahms, Sarabande and Gavotte, C major Sonata; Henselt, *Wenn ich ein Vöglein wär'*; Schumann, Quintet, Trio No. 1, *Carnaval, Symphonic Études*, Two Ballads, Canon in B major (From *Studien für Pedalharfe*), *Des Abends, Traumeswirren, Jagdlied aus Waldszenen, Schlummerlied*; Beethoven, Sonata, opus 106, Sonata, opus 101, Sonata, opus 31, Variations in C minor, Concerto in E flat, Sonata, opus 81a.

school. She made Schubert, Chopin, Schumann, and, above all, Henselt [2] available to the public at a time when the dawn of their fame had hardly risen above the musical horizon.

Her penetrating understanding of every kind of music —as long, of course, as it is still true music—is such that she can treat the whole range of technique as a matter completely dominated and utterly at her disposition. In one or another aspect of virtuosity she may be surpassed by other players, but no other pianist stands quite as she does at the radial point of these different technical directions, focusing their respective virtues on the pure harmony of beauty. Although mere correctness is hardly her objective, it forms the essential basis on which she builds. To give a clear expression to each work in its characteristic musical style and, within this style, to its purely musical proportions and distinctions, is ever her main task. She seems to play rather to satisfy a single connoisseur than to excite a multitude of average listeners. If one of the latter, however, may have wished for just one small audacious deviation from the pure linearity of the Greek profiles, I cannot blame him. The effect of her playing is never to overpower or to transport. It is a most truthful representation of magnificent compositions, but not an outpouring of a magnificent personality. This is not only more appropriate to the true task of virtuosity; it is also its fulfillment, and we should be compelled to declare her playing ideal, if everything human were not imperfect, and if every virtue did not have its deficiencies.

She could be called the greatest living pianist rather than merely the greatest female pianist, were the range of

---

her physical strength not limited by her sex. The compelling power of a pianist resides principally in his touch. Only he who can draw the full tone from an instrument can project the full impression, be it in the tempest of an allegro or in the long-drawn cantilena of an adagio. Every personal artistic performance, as a twin product of body and mind, must obey the terms of both, and one need not be a musical Karl Vogt [3] to find the effective power of a pianist more in the muscles of his hand than in the greatness of his soul. I

[3] Karl Vogt (1817–1895), famous scientist and researcher, one of the first propagators of Darwinism in Germany.

41

remember, for instance, Rubinstein or Dreyschock,[4] whose more powerful touch, compared with Clara Schumann's, got them more compelling effects. The softest little hand can caress, but only the fist can grip. Thus, the second variation and the finale of Schumann's *Symphonic Études*, opus 13, did not make the same impression when Clara Schumann played them as they made when played by others more appropriately equipped.

She is not given to the choice of extremely forceful pieces; but in what she does play she rather shames the brilliant virtuosos of our time, by the masculinity of her playing. There is nothing effeminate and retiring, nor any overabundance of emotion. Everything is distinct, clear, sharp as a pencil sketch. The frequent small accents which she affects differ remarkably from the stresses which the majority of female pianists use to place a personal emotional imprint upon every single note. What in their case is an affectation of subjective emotion is with her only a careful elucidation of rhythmical or harmonic contrasts. If one were to express a preference for one aspect of her so excellently developed technique, it would be for the dazzling facility with which she plays delicate fast movements. She succeeds best with tender, light, graciously moving pieces.

But also in this typically feminine realm of emotion, I observed more profound understanding than profound feeling. As compared with the common misuse of rubato, she maintains, almost without exception, a strict conformity of measure. Some may have been surprised by her metronomi-

---

4 Alexander Dreyschock (1818–1869), eminent Bohemian pianist and, like Hanslick, a pupil of Tomaschek. According to Hanslick (*Geschichte des Konzertwesens in Wien*), he "completed the succession of those virtuosos whose bravura was capable of attracting and fascinating a numerous public which admired technical magic and was happiest in—astonishment."

cal playing of the middle movement of Chopin's D-flat Impromptu, sharply marked even in the bass. Nobody can object to it, but whether Chopin's music gains by the dispersal of its misty nostalgia is open to question. I fancy that the softly affectionate, thoughtful expression with which the less robust Wilhelmine Clauss [5] plays such pieces is more to the point.

Clara Schumann's noble selectivity in the composition of her programs has been generally recognized. It is, indeed, an essential expression of a truly artistic nature not to abase itself in the service of the profane. As unusual as is the inclusion of Beethoven's Sonata in A minor, opus 101,[6] in a modern recital, Clara Schumann's program was just as exceptional in its unblemished purity as a whole. Recitals starting with Beethoven and ending with Kullak [7] threaten to become the order of the day. But in this mania to satisfy all and sundry lies the root of decay.

Clara Schumann not only plays well; she also chooses well. We are particularly indebted to her for several performances of piano works by her excellent husband, Robert Schumann. This profound and inspired composer has produced a great number of works for the piano, not only of extraordinary beauty but also, in many cases, of such extraordinary difficulty that only a virtuoso of the first order can master them. Franz Liszt, unfortunately, has

---

[5] Wilhelmine Clauss-Szarvady (1834–1907). She gave six concerts in Vienna in 1855. Hanslick wrote: "The characteristic reflective quality of her playing, the tenderness and gentility of her interpretive style, more than made up for what she lacked in strength."

[6] The acceptance of Beethoven's late sonatas into the piano repertoire was the joint accomplishment of Clara Schumann and Brahms.

[7] Theodor Kullak (1818–1882), German pianist and teacher, pupil of Czerny, Sechter, and Nicolai. Among his own pupils were Moszkowski and the Scharwenka brothers, Xaver and Philipp.

never honored this artistic debt. The more courageous and successful, then, the achievement of a woman in fulfilling the double mission of artist and wife.

Two items, as notable as they were valuable, were Schumann's settings, for declamation with piano accompaniment, of two ballads by Friedrich Hebbel.[8] Although we own to a bias against this melodramatic genre, where music shyly separates itself from the spoken word like oil from water and one art injures the other instead of supporting it, I found pleasure in this instance in what struck me as a generally pure impression. Hebbel's masterly ballads—the first (*Schön' Hedwig*) a charming picture of maidenly trust and knightly love, the other (*Der Heideknabe*) a gruesome nocturne of overpowering force—are interpreted in Schumann's music with sensitive and appreciative restraint. The music renounces its own material substance and follows the visions of the poet like a shadow, now light, now dark. Since an equal mistress of declamation (Marie Seebach) [9] joined forces with the mistress at the piano, and since, in her performance, the supreme art of declamation joined forces with a fine musical sensibility, the whole melodrama passed before the double facets of our fantasy as if created and sustained by a single force.

---

[8] Schumann wrote three such ballads for declamation with piano accompaniment. *Schön' Hedwig*, composed in 1849, was his opus 106. The *Ballade vom Heideknaben* and *Die Flüchtlinge*, composed in 1852, comprise Nos. 1 and 2, respectively, of opus 122.

[9] Marie Seebach (1834–1897), actress, member of the Burgtheater, married to Albert Niemann, played in the U. S. in 1871, and later.

LISZT'S SYMPHONIC POEMS

———•••———

[1857]

WHEN Franz Liszt, the most gifted virtuoso of our time, grew tired of triumphs won with other people's compositions,[1] he set about to surprise the world with large creations of his own. One who is accustomed not only to intellectual activity but also to having his activity crowned with laurels cannot leave the public arena; he can only change it. In Liszt's case it was his intention that the composer should overshadow the virtuoso. Enthusiastic friends and obliging writers heralded this transfiguration as a phenomenon of immeasurable advantage to the development of music. It seems more likely that the musical world has suffered, in the virtuoso's abdication, a loss which the composer's succession can hardly compensate.

He who attentively observed Liszt's artistic individuality during his long career as a virtuoso might pretty well guess the character of his new works. His piano compositions were consistently of such mediocre invention and execution that barely one of them could have claimed lasting existence in musical literature. A profound knowledge of pianistic effect and several interesting ideas are all that can be mentioned with praise. With a virtuoso of genius such

---

[1] In 1847. His last public concert as virtuoso was in Elisabetgrad, now Stalingrad, in October of that year.

45

attributes may be taken for granted. Well aware of his insufficient power of invention, Liszt habitually elaborated the melodies of others in transcriptions, fantasies, etc. Every one of his popular works belongs in this category. His purely original works represented a mixture of trivialities and oddities, tolerable only when he played them himself.

Now, suddenly, he has resolved to come out with great and profound compositions. He has tackled the job with his usual intellectual agility and with enviable energy. Too intelligent not to recognize his most obvious shortcomings, he has chosen to approach music from an angle where, inspired by external ideas, it occupies the comparative intellect and stimulates poetic or picturesque fantasy. He has, as if with one stroke of the pen, brought forth nine symphonies, or, as he calls them, "symphonic poems," issuing them with special explanatory programs. The titles of these poems are: *Ce qu'on entend sur la Montagne*; *Tasso*; *Les Préludes*; *Orpheus*; *Mazeppa*; *Prometheus*; *Festklänge*; *Heroïde Funèbre*, and *Hungaria*. If one adds that he is presently working on a musical transcription of Schiller's *Ideale*, of Dante's *Divine Comedy*, of Goethe's *Faust*, and other similar trifles, one must concede that he has high aspirations. He fancies his music capable of fiddling and blowing the most magnificent phenomena of myth and history, the most profound thoughts of the human mind. A musician cannot but find this method hazardous from the very start, since it demonstrates that music is only the afterthought. First place is taken by the poetical material; the music is a kind of brilliantly illustrated marginal notation. Assuming descriptive music to be justifiable at all, there is still a great difference between the subjects chosen for it. In *Meeresstille und Glückliche Fahrt,*[2] in the *Midsummer Night's Dream,* in the program of the "Pastoral" Symphony and similar pieces, no one will misunderstand the spontaneity of the musical allusion. But a *Mazeppa* is absolutely anti-musical; a *Prometheus* is so far removed from every musical reference that just to associate such titles with symphonies can only create the impression of braggadocio.[3]

It is hardly necessary here to raise the issue of whether program music can be justified or not. Nobody is now so narrow-minded as to deny the composer the poetical stimulation offered by reference to an external theme. Music certainly will never be able to express a definite object, or to represent its essential characteristics in a manner recognizable without the title; but it may take the basic mood from it and, with the title given, present an allusion, if not a graphic representation. The main prerequisite is that music be based on its own laws and remain specifically musical, thus making, even without program, a clear, independent impression. The main objection to be raised against Liszt is that he imposes a much bigger—and abusive—mission on the subjects of his symphonies: namely, either to fill the gap left by the absence of musical content or to justify the atrociousness of such content as there is.

The "symphonic poems" are published with explanatory prefaces by Liszt, drawn up in that horrible sentimental bombast associated with Richard Wagner. Just as with these prefaces, which provide an explanation as a ballet program explains a deaf-and-dumb dance, the pronunciamento printed on top of all Liszt scores throws a revealing light upon the

---

[2] By Mendelssohn, an overture in D major, opus 1, No. 27, based on a poem by Goethe.

[3] Beethoven's *The Creatures of Prometheus* was a ballet.

falsity of his method. "Although I have endeavored," it runs, "to elucidate my intentions by definite instructions, I cannot deny that many, even the most essential ideas, cannot be put down on paper." I leave it to the musically educated reader to decide how one can still speak of musical compositions when the "most essential ideas" cannot be conveyed by notes. Conductors and players, therefore, have to be gifted with a special divine insight—and audiences, too.

It was to be expected that Liszt's compositions would be superficially novel. Thus, his symphonic poems stand somewhere between the extended overtures of Mendelssohn and the conventional four-movement symphony. He makes the three or four distinct parts which constitute his symphonic poems pass easily one into another, as in free fantasy, so that the whole is performed as an ostensibly uninterrupted entity. This does not prevent the constituent parts from being assembled, mosaic-like, or jumbled chaotically. The one-movement symphony might have a future if it were cultivated by truly musical men. Orchestra pieces of an intermediate size are needed for concert performances, and all of Liszt's "Poems" are advisedly short.

From a purely musical standpoint the most lucid and agreeable of Liszt's musical dissertations is *Les Préludes*. And even *Les Préludes* is essentially a matter of music added to a finished program by mere cerebration. One finds no theme that could be called original or profound; quite the contrary, there are signs of banality in both its pathos and its sentiment. Still less does one find in these poetical vagrancies the thematic development desirable in every larger composition. The ambitious endeavor to achieve surprise at every moment with a new, ingenious idea introduces a restlessness redolent of dilettantism.

48

Despite all this, the listener may find *Les Préludes* stimulating. It shows a lively sense for the grouping of tone colors, as, for instance, in the instrumentation of the rather ordinary theme [4] in E major, broadly played by four horns and divided violas, and lightly accompanied by violin and harp chords. Similarly, the rising chromatic sixths of the string quartet, at first supported only by bassoon and clarinets in the bass, and then by oboes and flutes, stir up a real tempest. The last movement is not much more than a march, dressed up with all the brass of a regimental band. Liszt never misses such an opportunity. He knows too well that such a purely sensual effect never fails of popular response, and his "good friends" take proper care that the brassy noise is interpreted as profundity.

But it remains the critic's main concern that the qualities which attract the public and interest the musician in Liszt's symphonic poems do not flow from the pure fountain of music; they are artificially distilled. Musical creation does not come freely and originally with Liszt; it is contrived. Everyone who has thought about music knows that an intelligent man endowed with fantasy, who has completely mastered the outward forms of musical technique, is not necessarily a creative composer. If a poet such as Victor Hugo were to possess full musical knowledge and be tortured by a desire to compose—the result would be similar to the "symphonic poems." There would be intelligence, poetry, and imagery in abundance, but no musical essence.

Liszt belongs to those ingenious but barren tempera-

---

[4] This is essentially the theme known since the eighteenth century as *Marlborough se va t'en guerre* and, more recently, in the U. S. as *We Won't Be Home Until Morning*.

ments who mistake desire for calling. If a whim should prompt him to write tragedies he would probably do it intelligently, but nobody would think of comparing him with Shakespeare, save possibly one of those literary lackeys whom Macaulay calls "an intermediate phase between man and baboon" and who, unfortunately, are always among us. Only those who do not know the works of Berlioz or Richard Wagner could mistake Liszt for a musical discoverer or reformer. They were models, and one could scarcely find an effect in his works which has not been anticipated by something similar in theirs. Where the good and the bad are as obvious as in Liszt's symphonic poems, it is not difficult to draw the artistic balance. The interest commonly excited by intelligent detail, technical brilliance, and the energetic prosecution of one special principle wins them a higher position than is the lot of numerous student works which elaborate a similar insufficiency correctly but without intelligence; i.e., his works are preferable to those of his numerous pianist colleagues.

But to assume this relative position to be absolute, and to offer Liszt's symphonies as musical artistic creations, as masterpieces, or as the starting point of a rejuvenation of music, is only possible if we first abandon once and for all every previous conception of purely instrumental music and every remembrance of Haydn, Mozart, Beethoven, and Mendelssohn.

" L O H E N G R I N "

[1858]

THE success which Richard Wagner's *Lohengrin* enjoyed here three months ago was so brilliant that certain observations pertinent to the work may not be amiss, even at this late date.[1] We cannot be certain whether, as we are assured, the popular enthusiasm for *Lohengrin* is subsiding; it suffices that attendance is still excellent. The splendid production,[2] unsurpassed on any German stage, would alone account for the continuing good houses. The general enthusiasm would, in any case, be more readily understood by a deaf person, subject only to the impression of the stage sets, the processions, the groupings, the miming of the

---

[1] On August 20, 1858, two days after the first performance of *Lohengrin* at the Court Opera, there appeared a short report of the performance in *Die Presse* with the remark that, in view of the importance of the event, a detailed review would be reserved to Hanslick, who had been prevented by sickness from attending the *première*. Hanslick's review appeared on November 9 and 10.

[2] With Alois Ander in the title role, Luise Dustmann as Elsa, and Johann Nepomuk Beck as Telramund, Heinrich Esser conducting. Liszt's pupil Alexander Winterberger, who had heard *Lohengrin* under Liszt at Weimar (where it was first performed on August 28, 1850), wrote to Wagner that the Vienna production was so far superior that "he simply could not have recognized the opera given at Weimar." Everyone was quite overcome with delight, said Winterberger; the audience applauded like mad, and every performance was a veritable festival. Wagner had occasion to check on these reports in May of 1861, and found them not exaggerated. He wrote to Minna: "[It] surpassed all my expectations, and, for the first time in an artistic career full of trouble and struggle, I experienced such complete pleasure as to make up for everything . . . orchestra, singers, chorus, all splendid, incredibly beautiful."

51

principals, than by someone who knew nothing of *Lohengrin* but the music.

Although the verdict of the public as a whole has been impressively unanimous, the judgment of individual listeners has been just as impressively varied. We must, of course, leave to *Figaro* or *Kladderadatsch* [3] the most amusing aspect of the matter, namely the perspiration-drenched enthusiasm of those who dare not at any price be considered "unprogressive" or "dated." But even sincerity has gone to remarkable extremes. It is a fact that persons of the most diverse sorts and conditions, and even those who make no secret of their indifference to music of any kind, who are ordinarily never to be seen at an opera or concert, have seen *Lohengrin* half a dozen times and enjoyed it. And it is also a fact that some of our most cultivated and dispassionate musicians were so dispassionately bored at the first performance that they sought diversion elsewhere after the second act.

A very numerous, moderate center describes the novelty, quite correctly, as "interesting." When it comes, however, to going further into the matter and determining just what it is that is so interesting, one encounters a conspicuous uncertainty of opinion. Many admirers of *Lohengrin* who haven't much to say for the music find ample compensation in the "incomparable text." I must confess that I find as little to admire in the text as in the music.

To begin with the libretto, we find, unfortunately, that it, too, has been published as a self-sufficient work of art, an ultimately poetic accomplishment, a complete drama capable of immediate presentation in the legitimate theater. For those who can take such a claim seriously, I am merciless

---

[3] Political-satirical weekly published (after 1848) in Berlin, with famous cartoons of Napoleon III and Bismarck.

enough to hope that they may someday be required to experience a practical test. If we examine the *Lohengrin* text
we find the sum of its virtues in a few poetically or, rather,
graphically conceived situations. It is undramatic in the
telling and in the characterizations, and the diction is hard
and bombastic. On every page there are such tasteless
verses as *"Lass mich ihn seh'n wie ich ihn sah, wie ich ihn sah,
sei er mir nah!"* (*"Let me see him, as I saw him; as I saw
him, let him be near me!"*) Such verses are not necessarily
disturbing in an opera, but they shouldn't be offered as the
work of a great poet. I regard *Lohengrin* as a skillfully contrived opera libretto, not only musically more effective but
also more compact and carefully executed than most of its
brothers; whoever considers these qualities to be sufficient
for an independent drama is welcome to regard *Lohengrin* as
such.

First of all, the choice of the Grail legend is unfortunate; doubly so in view of Wagner's own dictum that an
opera text must be, above all, popular, easily comprehended,
appealing to national characteristics, and so on. Now, an
operatic hero can hardly be more exclusive than this knight
of the Holy Grail. Who is Lohengrin? What is the Holy
Grail? With what audience can one presuppose any knowledge of this medieval legend, about which everything in
Lohengrin revolves? We are a world removed from the
moral views of that time and its poesy, motivated by what
could be called armed ecstasy. Even the literary enthusiast
given to immersion in these Christian epics of the Middle
Ages would decline to find them dramatic. Our first re-
quirement of a drama is that it present us with real characters, persons of flesh and blood, whose fate is determined
by their own passions and decisions. We wish to witness

the reaction of free will to great conflicts and to volunteer our own emotional and intellectual participation. What does Lohengrin know of such things? He is a knight of the Holy Grail on Monsalvat, the precious vessel containing the blood of Christ, celebrated in the medieval sagas as the miraculous and dominant center of the earthly Kingdom of God. The Holy Grail sends its knighthood forth on adventures in its service; it alone commands and occupies their thoughts, their feelings, their deeds. By the grace of the Holy Grail they are of divine nature and faultless, although required to preserve the secret of their miraculous sponsorship. Can we really be impressed by Lohengrin's virtue and righteousness, knowing that they are not the product of his own free will but the mere reflected splendor of the Holy Grail? Can we be moved to joy and sorrow by his love for Elsa, knowing that his only real emotional problem is the safeguarding of his secret? Can his insistence that Elsa, his "beloved wife," may never ask his name or his origin strike us as other than inhuman? The bond of love is fashioned by confidence, not by secrecy. We find ourselves on Elsa's side as she succumbs to "culpable curiosity" and loses her husband. In vain she pleads at Lohengrin's feet that he remain as "witness of her penance." He has no other answer than: "I must go, I must; the Grail will be angry with me if I remain." A person who "must" is no hero of a drama, for he is not of our kind. He is a "seraphic soldier," whose will and consciousness repose not in his own bosom but in the furrows of his divine field commander's brow.

That Wagner himself has characterized *Lohengrin* as the "type of the only real tragic subject" need not be taken too seriously, especially in view of the familiar vainglory of Wagner's salutatory pronouncements on his own works. It remains an incongruity to seek the regeneration of opera in a return to this kind of mythological-symbolical subject matter, in itself barren of any dramatic movement and no longer even remotely a part of the national consciousness. The true opera of the future is the historical.

The advantage of Wagner's Christian-mythological opera texts over the once fashionable classical-mythological subjects is their national character. They are German, and those scenes in *Lohengrin* which picture German customs will always have the most enduring effect, however much Wagner may insist upon the mythical-symbolical element as the real heart of the opera. I have been unable to find a specifically dramatic force in the *Lohengrin* poem; rather mere lyric endowment combined with an uncommon feeling for the theater. How meager are the individual characters in *Lohengrin* compared with the life of the masses in it—a collection of stereotypes without development and without climax!

This knack of Wagner's for building groups and introducing situations which cannot fail of pictorial effect is perhaps the most characteristic facet of his talent and the aspect most deserving of closer analytical examination. He is neither a great musician nor a great poet. He can be called, at best, and in the higher sense of the term, a decorative genius. The ultimate that such decorative genius can achieve, supported by imagination and cultivation is— Wagnerian opera. One can admire in its creator the energy and the insight with which he has identified himself with an art form utterly adequate to his talent, the only artistic specialty within his reach, and at the same time the only one which could be reached by him alone. The ultimate artistic profit accountable to Wagner's investment is not, however, the ultimate profit for art. What counts decisively against the presumed absolute greatness of Wagner's operas is their musical barrenness. They lack what they cannot obtain and what they cannot do without—the divine dowry, the generative force, the inborn wealth, in short, the whole beautiful injustice of nature.

When the celebrated Jonmelli [4] had to decide in a dispute about the talent of Piccini,[5] he did so with the solemn exclamation: "He's an inventor!" With these three words he felt that he had given his admiration for Piccini the most forceful expression; actually, he aptly characterized the essential element of artistic production in general and musical production in particular: continuous invention and creation. The composer who is not an "inventor," who lacks the mysterious power to create in tone and from tone something independently beautiful, may become the most imaginative experimenter in the history of music—but never a master in his art, never a musical genius!

No one can persuade me to desert the musical standpoint with respect to Wagner as long as his operas are sung and played from beginning to end, and as long as reasonable people continue to go to the opera to hear music. It is only a sad indication of extensive derangement that even persons who admit Wagner's musical impotence claim for him a different set of criteria and celebrate the interdependent and harmonious relationship of his music to his poetry as the great new achievement, next to which the question of the

[4] Niccolò Jonmelli (1714–1774), composer of operas and church music, one of the leaders of the Neapolitan School, one of the first composers to appreciate the dramatic possibilities of the accompanied recitative. He is sometimes referred to as "the Italian Gluck."

[5] Niccolò Piccini (1728–1800), Italian opera composer and party of the second part—and loser—in the famous feud with Gluck in Paris in 1778, in which Gluck's enemies made Piccini their champion.

beauty of the music as such is of no concern. It would be a pity if the memory of the German musical public were so short. Have we never had, heretofore, operas which combined the freshest of melodies with the earnestness of dramatic truth? Have the greatest masters of three nations striven in vain to be dramatic composers? Has the whole history of opera been—as Wagner would attempt to persuade us—only a kind of sin in perpetuity, awaiting redemption through *Lohengrin?*

I do not find that Wagner, in respect to pregnant and gripping representation of dramatic situations, has progressed beyond—for example—Beethoven in *Fidelio*, which is music through and through and in the most exclusive sense, quite aside from the dramatic character of the opera. Is there in the whole of *Lohengrin* a single number which quickens the listener's heartbeat as does the trio or the quartet in the prison? Has Wagner, with his declamatory apparatus, ever awakened the pulse of life as Beethoven did with his purely musical materials? Or has *Lohengrin* a single character who could step from the painting as plastically and naturally as any of the characters of *Don Giovanni?* What lifeless stage props are Telramund and Ortrud, compared to similar characters in the operas of Weber and Spontini!

Let us put the purely musical element aside for the moment and ask merely if Wagner has really achieved anything new and unprecedented in the way of dramatic truthfulness—as is claimed for him by his vindicators—or if he has even equaled what the aforementioned masters have already achieved. The latter knew and respected the demands of the poet, but at the same time they were musicians —and inventors. They had the gift which Wagner disdains —because he doesn't have it: the gift of melody, of independent, self-sufficient, beautiful musical thought. It is a great error to represent melody as the enemy of all dramatic characterization. It can be committed only by one who is, by nature, without melody and who must be content with the lesser profits yielded by clever effects. The truth is rather that in the formal musical thought, in the melody itself, there resides a dramatic force which emotional declamation and all the instrumental wizardry in the world can never equal. In repeated and attentive examinations of the score of *Lohengrin* I have found imaginative intentions and effective passages but not a single eight-measure theme which could compel the exclamation: "These eight measures could have been written only by a musical genius of the first order, by a creator in his art!"

As paradoxical as it may sound, it is fundamentally true that Wagner's opera music derives essentially from declamation and instrumentation. These two factors, which have figured heretofore as ornament and support of the basic musical thought, have been "emancipated" by Wagner and pushed to the foreground as dominant musical elements. That Wagner understands declamation is one of his most decisive attributes. That he presumes to replace melody with rising and falling recitation is at once the root and flower of his error. In place of true song he introduces a melodically sustained recitation. It is a matter of indifference whether Wagner was really led to this theory by free conviction or by the limits of his musical-creative endowment; I believe the latter, for as long as there has been a history of music, contempt for melody has been identical with melodic impotence. Be that as it may, with Wagner the text is dominant and the music tags along, sacrificing its own dignity and significance. True musical

58

characterization, as we find it with all great composers, does not destroy the musical form simply in order to qualify the text word for word. It abides by the mood of the whole.

The despotic degradation of music to a mere means of expression accounts, in *Lohengrin*, for those extended scenes in which one takes in little more than a continuous fluctuation of featureless, fluid tonal matter. Melody, self-sufficient song, from which alone the intrinsic musical body can be constructed, is lacking. Take, for example, Telramund's scenes with Ortrud and the finales of the second and third acts. What there is of real melody in *Lohengrin* is either utterly commonplace or conspicuously reminiscent of Carl Maria von Weber. If one looks closely at certain of Elsa's phrases, at the trio in the Wedding March, at the church procession in the second act, or at the first finale (worthy of Weber or Marschner at their worst), and other similar examples, one is inclined to see in Wagner not so much a pioneer of the music of the future as the last of the romanticists. Yet these few tunes enjoy the most grateful reception. And why not? What real song could be so insignificant as not to seem like manna in the wilderness after the declamatory exercises of the King and his Herald?

Let us see how Wagner exploits the individual musical factors to serve his dramatic ends. In order to match every turn of dialogue with a surprising musical coloration, he has recourse to perpetual modulation. I know of nothing so fatiguing as these half-recited songs in *Lohengrin* which never stay four measures in the same key but, with infinite evasiveness, continue from one deceptive cadence to the next until the ear, exhausted and resigned to its fate, lets them go where they will. Wagner likes best to modulate on the basis of abrupt pure triads. The exotic, fablelike impression which this device achieves initially is quickly dissipated by abuse. In this cold plunge of harmonic surprises the listener soon reaches the point where he is incapable of further astonishment. There is something so intense about this trait that it actually sustains the declamatory emotionalism of *Lohengrin* at a certain level. But on this level it moves with the empty uniformity of some preachers. Hand in hand with the monotony of this irritating modulation hunt goes the monotony of meager rhythm. Music is hopelessly constrained in these dragging periods of two- and four-measure rhythms. And since, as far as Wagner is concerned, contrapuntal devices and everything that one understands as "thematic development" are as good as nonexistent, what counterbalance has he for the depressing weight of this melodic monotony?

It is to be found in his treatment of the orchestra. Here Wagner has not only distinguished accomplishments to his credit but also real originality. Mendelssohn and Berlioz did not write for the stage (not counting some quickly forgotten youthful experiments); Wagner, who has modeled his instrumentation mostly upon theirs, is therefore the first to exploit fully the magic of new and daring orchestral effect for dramatic purposes. His instrumentation, with its clever use of tone colors and its elastic application to the text, is interesting to the musician and irresistible to the layman. It is what makes Wagner's music seem dazzlingly new, exotic and fabulous, and completely acceptable to many listeners as a substitute for real music.

Wagner has achieved for the theater that dramatic vitalization of the orchestra which Berlioz had in mind for the symphony. There can be no essential objection except for the deafening use of the brass and the recourse to such quickly stereotyped devices as the tremolo of the violins *divisi* in the highest position, and so forth. The manner, however, in which, in *Lohengrin*, orchestral brilliance alone is relied upon to salvage many a scene from the poverty of musical ideas can be demonstrated with well-nigh mathematical certainty by reference to the so-called "complete piano score with text." It is astonishing how tiny the hero of the nursery rhyme looks.

Despite its dazzling exterior, the music of *Lohengrin* leaves behind it the over-all impression of unpleasant desolation. Excited initially by the charm of the instrumentation and the strangeness of the modulations, one quickly tires of a composition in which the musical essence is wanting. One is never at ease, never secure in one's sensations; it is rather like being exposed to the deluge of an ever-turning mill wheel. Attracted by many a lively detail, I cannot recall a single larger musical episode of which I could say that it gripped the listener with an immediate force or struck him in his emotional vitals. Wagner's music affects the soul less than the nerves; it is not moving so much as eternally exciting, painfully concentrated, sensually and poetically exquisite. This latter characteristic can certainly escape only the most credulous enthusiast. In *Tannhäuser*, it often gave way to genuine emotional rejoicing; in *Lohengrin* it is dominant throughout. Wagner makes the impression less of a volcanic nature bursting its bonds than of a shrewd contriver who, secretly aware of his essential sobriety, continually forces himself into a state of exaltation.

The most valuable and the most beautiful aspect of Wagner's activity is the sincerity and the strength of his effort. He is not vulnerable with respect to his artistic morality. With a rare fund of uncurbed energy he pursues the path which he is convinced is the only right one. This ethical enthusiasm permeates *Lohengrin*, too. Everyone feels instinctively that here is a work of the greatest and sincerest exertion. Nor is there any want of pleasant details amidst the stupefying uniformity of the whole. These are almost always episodes which move in that realm so natural to Wagner—the supernatural. Such, for instance, are Lohengrin's initial entrance, with the lovely choral episode in A major, and certain other simple episodes which hold together, such as the Bridal Song, etc. The love duet in the third act I found not so much gripping or deeply affecting as interesting by virtue of the mysterious expression of a certain lurking suspense.

In conclusion, a word on the much discussed relationship of *Lohengrin* to *Tannhäuser*. The latter strikes me as decidedly superior with respect both to text and music. The *Tannhäuser* saga and the cleverly interwoven legend of the song contest on the Wartburg are closer to us both historically and traditionally than the myth of the Holy Grail. Not only is the demoniac element more moderately treated in *Tannhäuser;* it is also introduced as an effective contrast. We have Elisabeth as opposed to Venus, the Wartburg as opposed to the Hörselberg—extreme contrasts against which each element stands out the more clearly and forcefully. In *Lohengrin* the supernatural element is not opposed to the human by way of contrast but is inseparably contained within it in the person of Lohengrin. It happens regularly that our hero, whenever we expect human feelings and behavior from him, takes refuge within his seraphic dignity and frustrates our sympathetic participation. The *Tannhäuser* libretto is also superior technically. The motives are more intelligible, the structure is more compact, and the catastrophe more gripping.

Although Wagner himself and his whole knighthood have characterized *Lohengrin* as representing a decisive advance beyond *Tannhäuser*—so much so, indeed, that the whole divine realm of the music of the future is to be regarded as beginning with *Lohengrin*—I have no scruples about rating *Tannhäuser* musically superior, too. I find in *Tannhäuser* incomparably more freshness and vitality—often suppressed by boring declamation, to be sure, but still putting in a friendly reappearance after each such assault. There is, in *Lohengrin*, as little of such melodies as the Chorus of the Sirens and the Song to the Evening Star as there is of such musically effective ensembles as the male septet. This misfortune, about which Wagner's disciples complain so bitterly—namely, that in *Tannhäuser* a few real melodies actually escaped him—was not, as it now develops, irreparable. In *Lohengrin* Wagner is more single-minded and consistent, but he has become fanatic in his tunelessness. *Tannhäuser* enjoyed, along with certain "futuristic" tendencies, so much of the musical present that one had every reason to expect that the composer, steadily advancing in beauty and significance, would soon dominate the German stage. In view of the poetic and musical direction of *Lohengrin*, however, and in view of all that we hear of Wagner's *Der Ring des Nibelungen*, I have had to modify this expectancy. Wagner's star will continue to shine in the German operatic firmament—as long as all around is darkness. As for the public, what pure gold of genuine enthusiasm will be left when the sediment of curiosity has been washed away will be revealed in the next few years. It will depend upon whether a general fundamental familiarity with Wagner's music will work in the latter's favor or not. If I might be allowed to express an assumption, it would be that the public will have had enough of these rare delicacies as soon as it occurs to three or four other composers to write in Wagner's "one and only true style."

OLE BULL

———•◦•———

[1858]

EIGHTEEN years have passed since Ole Bull gave his first recitals in Vienna and Prague. I remember well the pale Nordic youth who had only to take the violin in his hands to excite the most vivid popular sympathy. All hearts went out to him. He was celebrated as a Nordic Paganini, and what the tones of his violin could not express distinctly a sympathetic public read in his visionary shining eyes.

The life story of the young artist was, with more or less elaborate details, common knowledge. His father wished him to become a theologian and, for safety's sake, even deprived him of his violin. He studied in Göttingen, but music was an irresistible attraction. Spohr, in whom he confided, was so uncomfortably affected by his eccentric manners that he let him go without encouragement. He went to Paris, the high school of fame. But there, too, his start was unfortunate; everything, even his violin, was stolen. Without lodging, contemplating suicide, he roamed the streets until a genteel elderly lady, the widow of Count Faye, whose grandchild he later married, saved him. A recital played on a borrowed violin was such a success that his career as a virtuoso was secured; he was able to go abroad for further schooling and further fame. The subsequent story has been no less romantic: having lived for many years as a farmer in the United States, he now suddenly reappears in Europe.

But whether we have become more rational in our conception of life or more idealistic in our conception of art, he exercises little of his old magic.

Ole Bull was always given to a one-sided virtuosity, to a combination of sovereign bravura and bizarre manners which might best be called "Paganinic." Enthusiasm for this kind of thing, which leaves heart and mind untouched and excites only surprise, has decreased astoundingly during the last twenty years. We look for deeper satisfaction even from a virtuoso. The heaping-up of technical difficulties and their ever so brilliant mastery can only give pleasure as a medium for more spiritual purpose, a transitory device for a nobler effect. We demand of a virtuoso, himself insignificant as a composer, that he place his technical abilities at the service of superior music. Now, as he did twenty years ago, Ole Bull plays only his own compositions. They are, if we are not greatly mistaken, the same pieces. No one can be expected to be edified by these formless and thoughtless fantasies. It used to be fashionable to interpret a certain artistic obscurity as sublimity and profundity, to admire as "truly Nordic" what could not be admired as truly musical. I, for my part, was never able to see in it more than the immature product of a fantasy in hopeless ferment. Barely a few measures showed traces of originality. Dependence on reminiscence remained the basic characteristic.

Ole Bull's muse is consistent only in two things: inconsistency of musical construction and preponderance of bravura. As an example of the first we need only to cite the *Polacca Guerrière*. Form and title lead us to expect a homogeneous piece of vigorous vitality. And, indeed, the orchestra does start off with a polonaise which, for lack of any inner animation, at least marks the rhythm with drums,

66

triangles, and cymbals. This martial introduction leads directly to a pitiful recitative, followed by a long adagio and a sentimental andantino in four-four time. The andantino concludes the piece without subsequent reference to the introduction, which should dominate the whole composition or develop into a brilliant climax. With all his bizarre recitatives and elaborately ornamented andantes, the composer has completely forgotten that he set out to write a "martial polonaise." Such want of the most elementary artistic discipline can probably not be found elsewhere in the literature of music.

Ole Bull's "concertos" are similarly formless fantasies, indulging partly in broadly expansive adagios, partly in antiquated bravura. The superabundance of the latter constitutes Ole Bull's second consistency. One can find the same tricks in every work. There are two which he prefers: flageolet and double stops. Both are executed with brilliant security and purity; but by setting lengthy episodes of no intrinsic importance exclusively in flageolet or double stops, he dulls the listener's interest. Still more brilliant are his staccati, which he renders unsurpassably, both up bow and down-bow. Other aspects of his technique, formerly admired, have become common property. His tone has a beautiful softness, but it is sometimes whining in the adagios. By way of summation we can say that his virtues are purely technical. The whole orientation of his playing has become obsolete, and it needs all his personal charm to recall it even partially to a fictitious life.

BEETHOVEN'S
"MISSA SOLEMNIS"

———◆•◆———

[1861]

Many of my works were immediately effective; others, not equally fathomable and compelling, required many years to achieve recognition. In the meantime, these years, too, have passed, and second and third generations have doubly and triply made good to me what I had to endure from my earlier contemporaries.

THESE words of Goethe, from the introduction to *West-Oestlicher Divan*, were found underlined in Beethoven's copy and written out in his own hand in his diary. Beethoven was convinced that he would not live to see his later, more difficult works understood by his contemporaries, and he was resigned to his fate. The hope for which he sought sustenance in Goethe's words did not deceive him. Of this we had an opportunity to convince ourselves recently when a performance of his *Missa Solemnis* in the Redoutensaal was so mobbed that the adjoining Small Redoutensaal had to be opened to accommodate the overflow.[1]

The impression was powerful. Of that there can be no doubt, however difficult and oppressive much of it may have

---

[1] By the Society of Friends of Music on March 17, Herbeck conducting. This performance represented the climax of a musical renaissance which began in the forties with Nicolai's performance of the Ninth Symphony with the newly founded Philharmonic Orchestra and in which Beethoven's late works were finally accorded general popular recognition.

seemed to the audience. There is no other work of Beethoven's which crushes the unprepared listener with such gigantic strength, at the same time raising him up again, deafened, delighted, confused. The Mass in D, and its companion piece, the Ninth Symphony, are creations which recall Zelter's dictum: "I admire Beethoven with awe." [2] Only devoted and extensive study can dispel this awe. A work by Beethoven, conceived in the full power of his imagination and fully characteristic of his utter lack of compromise, is not to be enjoyed as easily, as freely, as a symphony by Haydn. In the Mass in D, Beethoven set down everything he possessed in the way of sublime ideas and religious feelings; he gave to this music three years of his life then in its sunset and brilliantly aglow with its double majesty of genius and adversity.

The more closely and confidently one approaches the Mass, the more pure its outlines appear, the more solid its structure, the more profound its meaning. In the course of a few rehearsals—the dry study of the score is not sufficient—the Mass in D struck me as clearer and more sympathetic than the Finale of the Ninth Symphony ever did. Certainly it is more distinct, more harmonious, and, for all its forcefulness, more sparing of the singing voice. In artistic richness, in intrepid greatness, in the free unleashing of an immeasurable fantasy, the Mass in D and the Ninth Symphony stand unique and alone, like colossal Pillars of Hercules, at the gates of modern music, saying, "No farther!"—the one to sacred music, the other to the symphony. It is no more possible to build upon them than to find Beethoven's genius, with all its personal convictions, conflicts, and destinies, all

---

[2] Karl Friedrich Zelter (1758–1832). German composer and long-time friend of Goethe. Mendelssohn was one of his pupils.

its psychological and pathological prerequisites, repeated in another human being.

There is no doubt that the Mass, in its whole and in its parts, stands at the outermost boundary of sacred music. And yet one must be careful about accepting the often repeated objection that it is "unchurchly." Whether a church composition is appropriate to the requirements of a particular service, or whether it is imbued with a religious spirit, are two entirely different questions. Although both are perfectly justified, they are not of equal validity when reviewed from a more elevated standpoint. Beethoven's relationship to the Catholic Church was casual, probably limited largely to the friendly echo of childhood impressions. After the oratorio, *The Mount of Olives*, which he himself later disparaged, and his first Mass, which already overstepped the boundaries of the churchly in many aspects, he let years pass without further thought of sacred music. Then the installation of his noble pupil and friend, Archduke Rudolph, as Archbishop of Olmütz [3] provided an occasion for the composition of a great religious office. He obviously began the work, intending, for all its immensity of concept, that it should meet the requirements of the church.

The "Kyrie," with its calmly ordered, harmonious masses of sound, its devout mood, gives no hint of anything contrary to churchly convention. But in the "Gloria," overpowering grandeur of conception tears the composer from convention and carries him along with it. It was simply contrary to Beethoven's nature to constrain within the framework of a church service a work begun so greatly and impelled by such an inspirational force. With unexampled

---

[3] In 1820, but the Mass was not finished until three years later.

self-assurance, he builds up every particle of the text with the profoundest mysticism, pursuing the individual word to the very kernel of its meaning and making of the "Gloria" such a perfect whole that, in grandeur of conception and wealth of contrasts, it can be called a kind of holy office in itself. And the penetrating insight, the illustrative power of his music, so mounts in the "Credo" that the individual articles of faith are spoken with the subjectivity of a genius bowed by the exaltation of faith.

The further he goes, the more the walls of the cathedral seem to fall back before him. Everything becomes higher and broader. The waves of tone are directed no longer at the church and its community; they seem, rather, to flow back to the origin of being. The mood calms gradually after the "Credo." The transubstantiation is represented by a wonderfully beatific praeludium in organlike progressions for flutes and violins. It leads to the "Benedictus," in which a single violin accompanies the prayer of the singers with phrases now intimate, now mysterious and mystical. The "Agnus Dei" rises solemnly, deeply founded, goes into a pastoral-like, evenly moving six-eight rhythm, and seems about to burst into a bright A major when the scene suddenly changes. There is a succession of soft, pulsating beats on the kettle drum. Muffled sixths scurry by like clouds before a storm, and the sound of distant trumpets brightens the scene like pale, lingering flashes of lightning. "Agnus Dei" the alto sings in recitative, as if in unspeakable anxiety; then it is repeated more importunately by the tenor, until the chorus breaks in with the shattering outcry, "Miserere nobis."

This passage, the most disparaged in the whole Mass, is, in my opinion, its most moving. He who has experienced its power will never understand how even so submissive a

Beethoven admirer as Schindler [4] could have proposed the expurgation of this "offensive dramatic episode." No more churchly, at any rate, is the orchestral presto which later bursts in so passionately, and which could well have been taken from the finale of a symphony—a Beethoven symphony, to be sure. All this does not prevent me from regarding the spirit which breathes in this Mass as magnificently religious, although certainly transcending churchly conventions.

I have remarked before that Beethoven was never especially attached to the articles of the Catholic faith, that his belief had rather the character of a liberal theosophy, responsive only to ethical dictates. His faith—tested in adversity—in an unalterable moral order, in a just and supreme being, never left him. Bettina,[5] in the enthusiastic letter she wrote about Beethoven to Goethe, had the former say: "I have no friends, but I know that God is closer to me in my art than the others. I go with Him without fear—I have always recognized and understood Him—nor am I worried about my music; it can suffer no unhappy fate. He to whom it is readily understandable must be free of all the misery that others bear with them." Although it is hardly likely that Beethoven actually expressed himself in this fashion, Bettina's quotation certainly has a truly Beethovenesque ring, as is plain from other things he said to her. The consecration of a lofty and liberal religiousness and the earnestness of an unbending morality are discernible as a

---

[4] Anton Schindler (1795–1864), Beethoven's closest personal friend and his first biographer.

[5] Bettina von Arnim (1788–1859), a writer of the romantic school; her famous book *Goethes Briefwechsel mit einem Kinde* contains a fictitious correspondence between herself and Goethe, written in a rather extravagant style.

principle in all of his life and works. Would he have deserted these principles in the very work in which he devoted his best efforts to a religious subject? On the contrary, he offers us in the Mass the ultimate intensification of that devotion which we find in all his greater works.

All his music was to him religious; in art he always felt himself to be in a church, and that is why, in this particular case, it did not occur to him to don specifically churchly raiment. "With devotion," he wrote at the beginning of the "Kyrie" and the "Sanctus"; and, indeed, what music has the character of devotion if not this? The imposing and austere spirituality of this holy office strikes me as significantly more religious than the brighter spirit of the Haydn Masses, although the latter may be incomparably more valuable and useful to the church. Comparison of the respective treatment of the text of the Mass by Beethoven and Haydn reminds us of an analogous contrast in the respective interpretation of the Bible by Klopstock [6] and Goethe. While the devout bard of *The Messiah* simply opened the Bible in unquestioning faith, we see the young Goethe, surrounded by a maze of learned commentaries, examining the Book of Books with respectful skepticism. The unthinking, childish credulity of Klopstock was lost upon Goethe and his time. We see the same contrast repeated in the field of sacred music in Beethoven and his predecessors.

Heinse [7] once said of an effective piece of sacred music, and with reason, that "it filled the spirit of the listener without making itself felt." In this sense we have the ideal of

---

[6] Friedrich Gottlieb Klopstock (1724–1803), German poet, whose epic *Messias* was the outstanding artistic expression of the pietist religious feeling of the time in Germany.

[7] Johann Jakob Wilhelm Heinse (1749–1803), German novelist and critic who was influential in the romantic movement.

true church music in the Masses of Palestrina; they are the community sublimated in music. The harmonious stream, crystal clear, moves with calm repose; there is no melodic excitement, no rhythmic stimulation, no disconcerting instrumental color. Palestrina represents that point in the history of music where music had advanced sufficiently far to command respect as an art, but not so far that its resources had outgrown the purposes of the church. Palestrina's music is what the church likes music to be, namely, a means of intensifying religious devotion. It belongs completely to the church, just as do the sacred pictures, the painted windows, the costly vestments, and other art products which the church employs, not to awaken the artistic senses but to stimulate devotion. The ultimate advancement of art is not profitable to the church. People think that they, too, are devout when they listen to a Mozart or Beethoven Mass in church, but therein they confuse aesthetic devotion and religious dedication.

Beethoven himself, after completing his Mass in D, wrote to Zelter that he "regarded the *a cappella* style as the one true church style." Thus, despite the forceful, symphonic treatment of his Mass, he had at heart the correct feeling that the interests of the church require simpler music. In the conflict as to whether the church or music itself should dominate in his own sacred music (in the concept of any sacred music there is an inner conflict), he decided in favor of art, courageously, and fully conscious of the import of his decision. And it is on this basis that one must follow the grandeur of his genius, whole-heartedly, without concern as to whether this passage or that seems too dramatic or too symphonic. Even as the composer of a Mass, Beethoven neither could nor would deny his own great artistic person-

74

ality; he was inspired by the idea of faith, and in his music he gives us religion as he saw it. After the impression which I experienced myself and which I observed in others, I cannot doubt that for the Mass in D, as for the Ninth Symphony, the time is approaching when shock and surprise will give way to understanding, admiration, and love.

JOSEPH JOACHIM

————•••————

[1861]

THE most important event of recent weeks was the appearance of Joseph Joachim.[1] He had played in Vienna many years ago as a child prodigy, but the man prodigy has remained a stranger. As the site of Joachim's schooling, if not his birthplace, Vienna has cause for complaint at its neglect by this much-traveled artist. Young as he still is, Joachim has been regarded for some ten years as the greatest living violinist; if Vieuxtemps[2] is sometimes ranked with him, that in itself is proof of his greatness. It was no easy task for the artist to meet the intense, long-nourished expectation of so experienced a public as ours. Joachim did it, however, and most brilliantly.

He began with the Beethoven Concerto. After the first movement, it must have been clear to everyone that here was no mere stunning virtuoso but rather a significant and individual personality. For all his technique, Joachim is so identified with the musical ideal that he may be said to have penetrated beyond the utmost in virtuosity—to the utmost

---

[1] During this visit to Vienna, Joachim (1831–1907) gave five concerts in the Musikvereinssaal and a sixth in the large Redoutensaal. Born in Kittsee, near Bratislava, he entered the Vienna Conservatory in 1838 as a student of Joseph Boehm. He moved on to Leipzig in 1843 and did not return to Vienna until 1861, when he gave the concerts here discussed.

[2] Henri Vieuxtemps (1820–1881), pupil of de Bériot and, after Joachim, the greatest violinist of his time.

in musicianship. His playing is large, noble, and free. Not even the slightest mordent has the flavor of virtuosity; anything suggestive of vanity or applause-seeking has been eliminated. This noble dedication is so striking in Joachim that only afterwards does it occur to one to consider his great technical equipment.

What a flood of strength there is in the tone which his large, sure bow draws from the instrument! For the first time we heard none of that sawing and scratching, even in the most emphatic treatment of the lower strings, which occur here and there in the playing of even the most famous violinists. His trill is incomparable in its purity and evenness. In his playing of multiple-voiced passages, the individual voices are at once so co-ordinated and so sharply differentiated that one often has the impression that there are two players.

On the basis of this first concert, one would assume the great, the noble, and the tragic to be the qualities most congenial to his nature. The Beethoven Concerto, particularly the almost improvisatory, profoundly motivated presentation of the Adagio, was proof of a distinctive individuality. This concerto sounded more brilliant, more lively, when Vieuxtemps played it; Joachim searched it more deeply and surpassed, through a truly ethical force, that which Vieuxtemps had achieved through an irresistible temperament.

Next came an Adagio by Spohr, whose one-sidedness lost all trace of heaviness in the rhythmic force and variety of Joachim's playing. Most surprising, however, was his interpretation of Tartini's "Devil's Trill" Sonata. Violinists will agree that this represented a colossal and, at the same time, classically articulate technique hitherto unexampled.

Not only did he set forth the most difficult bravura with secure facility; he even managed to distribute innumerable significant touches throughout this roaring tumult of sound, to throw light here and there which gave the whole composition a new, expressive character. There is hardly another violinist whose achievements seem to come so completely from a single mold, at once so clear and harmonious in their effect.

From Joachim's Concerto in Hungarian Style one can draw conclusions as to the extent and nature of his creative gift only with due caution. It is too expansive and complicated, and, through the role played by the element of virtuosity, too striking to be fully evaluated at a single hearing. At any rate, it commanded and occupied the interests of the listeners to the utmost. Its significance appears to lie more in the energy with which the mood is controlled, and the imaginative manner in which this energy is varied, than in a real wealth of melodic invention.

Joachim's further offerings, truly enormous accomplishments of a brilliant but always subordinate technique, were selected movements from J. S. Bach's violin sonatas and a Fantasy with Orchestra by Schumann (opus 131).[3] Since there is none of the vanity common to the virtuoso about him, it must have been largely piety which prompted him to play a piece at once so unpleasant and so difficult. Schumann wrote it toward the end of his lucid days and dedicated it to Joachim. It is a dark abyss across which two great artists clasp hands. Martyrlike, gloomy, and obstinate, this Fantasy struggles along, depending upon continuous figuration to make up for its melodic poverty. Only seldom is the

---

[3] The same "Concerto" which Yehudi Menuhin "discovered" and played with much attendant publicity throughout the season of 1938–39.

tiresomeness of this device interrupted by something harmonically or orchestrally imaginative.

We cannot remember ever having heard Beethoven's Romance in F, opus 50, played in public. Beethoven wrote

BETTMANN ARCHIVE

Joachim crossing bows before a caricatured duel with his great Spanish rival Sarasate.

two Romances for violin (with octet accompaniment). Both bear the unmistakable stamp of his genius, but they are obviously not the product of creative impulses alone. They have the character of "occasion" pieces. Although they belong to his strongest and most characteristic period, many a conventional, obsolete device suggests his "first period." Joachim projected it with wonderful breadth and repose, playing the melody simply on the bright E-string, when hardly any other violinist would have failed to darken it artificially.

This modest, unadorned greatness appears to be the most outstanding characteristic of Joachim's playing. Many fine, immediately touching effects are thereby lost. The large, dramatic style will always excite admiration before love: it occupies the mind and cannot, therefore, progress so swiftly to the heart. As in the personal character of human beings generally, so also in artistic individualities we find that certain attributes are bound to be mutually exclusive. In many a Beethoven passage Hellmesberger's [4] fine, stimulating naturalness would have played more directly to our hearts than Joachim's unbending, Roman earnestness.

[4] Joseph Hellmesberger (1828–1893), member of a distinguished Viennese musical family and, like Joachim, a pupil of Boehm. He was Director and Professor of Violin at the Vienna Conservatory, concertmaster of the Court Opera and Philharmonic orchestras, and founder and leader of the famous Hellmesberger Quartet. He was also for a time (1851–1859) Director of the Society of Friends of Music.

B R A H M S

[1862]

JOHANNES BRAHMS has now presented himself as composer and virtuoso in a concert of his own.[1] His compositions are hardly to be counted among those immediately enlightening and gripping works which carry the listener along with them in their flight. Their esoteric character, disdainful of popular effect, combined with their great technical difficulties, makes their popularization a much slower process than one had been led to expect from the delightful prophecy Schumann gave his favorite as a parting blessing.[2] Of his larger compositions, not a single one had been heard previously in Vienna, and of the smaller pieces only a series (unpublished) of Hungarian Dances, introduced by Clara Schumann. Thus, to the Viennese, he was actually a stranger.

An appraisal of his talent and effectiveness at this time is an undertaking of considerable delicacy. Even for those who have grasped his works more fully than I, it is by no means easy to achieve an absolutely certain orientation. It is

[1] This was Brahms' first visit to Vienna, which was to become his second home. After serving a year as director of the Singakademie (1863–1864), he left Vienna to live off and on in Hamburg, Zurich, and Baden-Baden, returning in 1869. He was director of the concerts of the Society of Friends of Music from 1871 to 1874. In 1875, he moved to Heidelberg, but he returned to Vienna again in 1878, this time to stay.

[2] Presumably a reference to Schumann's entry in his diary in September, 1853, "Brahms to see me (a genius)."

not as though he were still in the tumult of the first fermentation. More mature creations have long since followed upon those bitter youthful works whose untamed genius was so irresistibly and, at the same time, so forbiddingly attractive. From the two exuberant piano sonatas to the F-sharp minor Variations,[3] and then on to the two piano quartets, the Handel Variations, etc., what progress there has been in the free, secure command of technique, and what a gain in moderation and formal clarity!

One cannot speak here of a beginner. But it is precisely in Brahms' latest works that one encounters question marks and picture puzzles which will be solved only in his next creative period. The solution will be decisive. Will his originality of invention and melodic richness hold pace with the ultimate development of his harmonic and contrapuntal art? Will the natural freshness and youthfulness continue to bloom untroubled in the costly vase that he has now created for them? Will they grow even more beautiful and free? Does that veil of brooding reflection which so frequently clouds his newest works presage a sudden burst of sunlight, or a thicker, less hospitable twilight? The very near future will tell.

Brahms is already a significant personality, possibly the most interesting among our contemporary composers. In the form and character of his music he suggests Schumann, although rather in the sense of an inner kinship than of actual imitation or modeling. Only with the utmost difficulty could such an individual entirely escape the spirit of Schumann, which so undeniably permeates and determines the musical atmosphere of the present. His music and Schu-

---

[3] Variations on a Theme by Schumann, opus 1, No. 9.

mann's have in common, above all else, continence and inner nobility. There is no seeking after applause in Brahms' music, no narcissistic affectation. Everything is sincere and truthful. But with Schumann's music it shares, to the point of stubbornness, a sovereign subjectivity, the tendency to brood, the rejection of the outside world, the introspection.

Far surpassed by Schumann in richness and beauty of melodic invention, Brahms often matches him in wealth of purely formal structure. This is his greatest strength. The imaginative and intelligent modernization of the canon and the fugue he has from Schumann. The common well from which they both draw is Johann Sebastian Bach. Even in Brahms' first variations (on a theme of Schumann) one feels an uncommon structural force at work. Those that followed—one on an original theme, the other on a Hungarian melody—are of a generally similar standard. He has now surpassed them all with the *Twenty-five Variations on a Theme of Handel*. His talent has thus far found the variation form the most congenial. It requires, above all, richness of formal outline and consistency of mood, which are just his most decisive virtues. The Handel Variations (I cannot help recalling the second and the twentieth, two models of inspired harmonization) won the most applause at his concert.

Less favorable was the effect of the Piano Quartet in G major. The shadowy aspects of his creative spirit are here more decisively in evidence. For one thing, the themes are insignificant. Brahms has a tendency to favor themes whose contrapuntal viability is far greater than their essential inner content. The themes of this quartet sound dry and prosaic. In the course of events they are given a wealth of imaginative derivatives; but the effectiveness of a whole is impossible without significant themes. Then, too, one misses the continuous stream of development. There is a continual pulling together and taking apart, preparation without objective, promise without fulfillment. In each movement there are excellent motives, but none of the type which could carry the whole piece. Knowing the quartet from a single hearing one can, of course, describe only the first impression, not the work itself. A closer study, as is always the case with Brahms, would doubtless bring many virtues to light. But study is not much help to the actual effect of the work in performance. This demands the plastic presentation of the melodies, a broad intensification building to a single objective, and, finally, development.

The Piano Quartet and others of Brahms' more recent works, unhappily, suggest Schumann's last period, just as his earliest works are reminiscent of Schumann's first period. Only for Schumann's crystal-clear mature middle period has his favorite pupil thus far offered us no companion piece.

Brahms' piano playing is all of a piece with his artistic individuality in general. He is motivated solely by the desire to serve the composition, and he avoids, almost to the point of shyness, any semblance or suggestion of independent importance. He has a highly developed technique which lacks only the ultimate brilliant polish, the final muscular self-confidence required of the virtuoso. He treats the purely technical aspect of playing with a kind of negligence. He has a way, for instance, of shaking octave passages from a relaxed wrist in such a way that the keys are brushed sideways rather than struck squarely from above.

It may appear praiseworthy to Brahms that he plays more like a composer than a virtuoso, but such praise is not altogether unqualified. Prompted by the desire to let the composer speak for himself, he neglects—especially in the playing of his own pieces—much that the player should rightly do for the composer. His playing resembles the austere Cordelia, who concealed her finest feelings rather than betray them to the people. The forceful and the distorted are thus simply impossible in Brahms' playing. Its judicious softness is, indeed, such that he seems reluctant to draw a full tone from the piano. As little as I wish to gloss over the minor shortcomings, just as little do I wish to deny how insignificant they are compared with the irresistible spiritual charm of his playing. This was most deeply effective in Schumann's Fantasy in C major, opus 17.

The fanciful magic of this tone picture, one of the most remarkable works of Schumann's *Sturm und Drang* period, had not been previously played in Vienna by anyone. Liszt, to whom it is dedicated, never played it in public, a portion of the great debt to Schumann of which Liszt can never be absolved and which, with admirable frankness, he subsequently recognized and regretted. In this Fantasy, Schumann originally had in mind a supplement to the Beethoven Monument in Bonn, and he intended its three movements to represent the "Ruins," "Arch of Triumph," and "Wreath of Stars" of the monument. In subsequently abandoning this idea he robbed his disciples of an "interpretive" field day. How unfailingly would the "thought analysts" have heard Beethoven's whole biography in this piece, which now, without title, enjoys a certain immunity from such experiments!

I cannot imagine a more profoundly, more genuinely effective performance of this remarkable piece than that which Brahms gave it. What pleasure it is to hear him play! The instant he touches the keys one experiences the feeling: here is a true, honest artist, a man of intelligence and spirit, of unassuming self-reliance! Brahms appeared to be in especially good form. By that I do not mean to say that every passage was ultimately immaculate or that in every leap he hit the mark unerringly. His technique is like a big, strong man, negligent in attire and given to loitering. He has too many more important things in his head and heart to be constantly concerned with his external personal appearance. But his playing is always compelling and convincing.

" T H E M E S S I A H "

————•◦•◦•————

[1862]

IN *The Messiah* Handel erected a monument to himself, not only as a composer but also as a devout Christian well versed in the Bible. He compiled the text himself from the Holy Scripture. "Does Your Lordship believe," he said in his blunt, hearty manner to a high-ranking individual who offered to write a text for *The Messiah*, "that I do not know God's Word, or that Your Lordship would write something better than the Apostles and Prophets?"

It was not his intention to write a Passion; he conceived his task in a free, grand manner, casting an eye over all of history, from the promises of the prophets to the appearance and sufferings of the Saviour and the enduring effects of His expiatory death. In the first part, he sings of the promise of the Messiah, the longing for Him, His appearance as a teacher and comforter; in the second part, he sings of the work of redemption, of suffering and death, of the dissemination of the new teaching, of the defiant revolt against it, and of the ultimate triumph "of Him who shall reign for ever and ever"; in the third part, he sings in devout confidence and expectation of the blessings Christianity promises for the future.

The musical manner of expression is mainly lyrical. The epic, narrative element is relegated to the background; the dramatic, with the single exception of the chorus, "He

Trusted in God," is completely excluded. The whole work thereby achieves a grandeur and unity, a kind of deeply founded repose and intensity, present in no other work treating the same subject. All trifling, genre-like traits have been avoided: even the person of Christ is not introduced as singing, a dangerous rock where even Beethoven was ship-wrecked.[1] The prevailing lyrical, meditative atmosphere of *The Messiah* could not, however, be maintained with such uniformity without disadvantages. Dramatic shadows are lacking, and with them the strength of characteristic con-trasts which delight us in *Judas Maccabaeus*, *Samson*, and *Belshazzar*. The listener's fantasy finds little stimulus in *The Messiah*, where it is not intended that the subjective devotion, the continuity of feeling, be interrupted by de-scription of external action.

The majority of Handel's oratorios are actually Biblical dramas without scenic setting. They achieve effectiveness through the full perception of dramatic life. *The Messiah*, by renouncing this effect, suffers from a certain monotony of expression not easily tolerable. Apart from this monotony, which cannot fail to appear in so narrowly limited a range of emotion, the impression is forceful and profound. Devo-tion is present with such strength and spiritual health, everything is so genuine, grand, and whole, that one has a sense of being in the presence of an imperishable work of art and dedication.

The main burden is borne, of course, by the chorus, in the grandiose treatment of which Handel is unique in the history of music. Who does not know the most rousing of all choruses, the "Hallelujah," with its compelling rhythm,

---

[1] In the oratorio *The Mount of Olives*.

its polyphony, lucid despite its complexities, its imposingly cumulative climax! This "Hallelujah" is unique in its humanity and resplendent magnificence; there is, however, no lack of grand counterpieces in *The Messiah*. How deeply affecting is the austerely mournful "Surely He hath borne our grief" after the melancholy alto aria! [2] What solemnity in the "Wonderful" of the first part! In this respect we could find no end of examples of the grand and powerful.

In the arias, Handel often surpasses himself. In warmth and intensity of feeling, in freedom from conventional limitations, the majority are far above even his average. But he who does not wish to admire indiscriminately (by which the truly admirable always loses) must discriminate among them. Some belong to those purely formalistic, contrived pieces where the text serves as only the pretext for a musical composition. Usually beginning with a powerful motto (as in "Every valley"), they continue with a characteristic stiffness, adorned with coloratura, which does not bother much with the single words. I would place nearly all the arias of the first part in this category, with the exception of "He shall feed His flock." Through Handel's great successors we have become so accustomed to a more individualistic treatment of the solo voice, to a freer and warmer melody, that it is difficult to be sincerely enthusiastic about this manner of expression. There are, however, a number of solo pieces in *The Messiah* where word and music have been integrated, where every note has its own importance and every phrase is deeply felt. Coloratura is either completely absent or is of the descriptive sort, as in the rugged figurations for the basso in the aria, "Why do the

---

[2] "He was despised" (?)

nations?" The arias "I know that my Redeemer liveth," "The people who wander in darkness," and "He was despised" (particularly after the interlude in C minor) belong to this category—admirable vocal pieces, unequaled in any other oratorio of this master.

Herbeck,[3] in the best interests of the work (which is not presented in full even in England), omitted several pieces, among them, unfortunately, the chorus "He trusted in God," whose incomparable dramatic energy I would not wish to miss at any price. There is no need to labor the right of the conductor (who wants to draw the public to Handel, not to frighten it away) to make cuts. Against Professor Gervinus,[4] who considers the cutting of an aria a sacrilege, it may be pertinent to quote old Thibaut of Heidelberg.[5] One of the greatest admirers of Handel and a strict purist (Haydn and Mozart made him uncomfortable), Thibaut, in his *Über Reinheit der Tonkunst*, pleads for cuts, comparing Handel's oratorios to "a box where jewels lie wrapped in cotton," and pitying "those who consider it their unconditional duty to perform a Handel oratorio in full, believing they have thus brought about something truly miraculous."

---

[3] Johann Franz von Herbeck (1831–1877), the foremost Viennese conductor of his generation and Nicolai's most illustrious successor as leader of the musical renaissance begun in Vienna by the latter with the founding of the Philharmonic Orchestra in 1842. He was conductor of the Society of Friends of Music concerts from 1859–1869 and again from 1875. He was first conductor of the Court Opera from 1871–1875.

[4] Georg Gottfried Gervinus (1805–1871), German literary historian, a great admirer of Handel. He participated in the preparation of Chrysander's Handel Edition and wrote a book, *Handel and Shakespeare*.

[5] Anton Friedrich Justus Thibaut (1774–1840), Professor of Jurisprudence at the University of Heidelberg. *Über Reinheit der Tonkunst* (1825) did much to stimulate interest in old music.

TAUSIG

———•••———

[1862]

TAUSIG'S recital in the Musikvereinssaal failed to dissuade me from my previous unfavorable opinion. I regret it the more because it showed him to be uncommonly gifted and extraordinarily enterprising. His bravura, power, and endurance are astonishing in so frail a youth. Similarly astonishing is his memory, which permits him to present a long succession of the most varied compositions with consummate security. Neither can one deny that his playing has spirit, although it asserts itself coquettishly and without motivation in the one-sided kind of brightness which Heine called "a mere sneezing of the intellect."

Not one single piece left a pure, satisfactory, or even profound impression. I was painfully struck by his deliberate cultivation of the most ugly of all possible mannerisms of touch: that of jabbing the keys. Not only in actual bravura passages, but also in cantilenas, which should be played softly and metrically, he has a habit of striking single notes with a force which simply makes the piano groan. At other times he labors as if he had to chop frozen notes out of ice. What must one think of the ear of an artist who does not hear the howling metallic rattling of the abused chords or is not disturbed by it? And what a choking, squeezing, and strangling of tones you get when he finally sets loose his whole technical pack of hounds!

91

If this love of tonal strife could be considered the over-flowing of boundless youthful strength, it might be possible to accept its extravagance. But it is not abundance of strength but rather sophistication which is the basic characteristic of Tausig's playing. Excited massacres are succeeded in turn by long periods of indifference; the keys, having been jabbed and beaten, are now merely brushed, swept, slightly touched, in a nearly inaudible pianissimo. Wanting is the healthy middle way, the quietly resounding touch. Many a passage enjoys temporarily a certain tonal beauty, even feeling, but it never lasts long: a single stabbed note, and the harmonious continuity is spoiled.

He began most beautifully with the *Andante spinato* of Chopin. We recognized the gentle voice of the composer, this Ariel of the modern piano; but the anxiety, the fearful certainty of having one's mood wrecked in the next measure, left us under a strain which excluded secure enjoyment. It is the curse of sophistication that one distinguishes it even when it is actually silent, that one no longer has confidence in virtuous impulses.

Tausig had assembled an interesting program. Beethoven's Sonata in E major, opus 109, is among the most rarely played sonatas, and was welcome if only for this reason. Every work of the master, even if not one of his important ones, exercises a magic fascination. At worst, we accept it as a memorable page from Beethoven's autobiography. This sonata—it was composed in 1821—tells of unhappy days. Melodies full of proud rapture and noble grace are impulsively interrupted by bad humor and a weary lowering of the wings. Lenz, the foremost of Beethoven's admirers, calls the first movement of the E major sonata "*faible, diffus, et maigre dans sa diffusion.*" It is certain that this

92

Allegro, interrupted twice by an Adagio, has no proper center and resembles rather a free improvisation than a sonata. The first movement is followed by a short, brilliantly surging Prestissimo and an Andante with variations. The Andante is a simple and thoughtful theme, and there is a magnificent first variation; but the following ones are somewhat snowed under in a blizzard of notes.

A nocturne by Field, after this stormy Beethoven landscape, had the effect of a graceful, dainty pastoral by Watteau, a truly musical pastel. A Suite by Handel (G minor) and a polonaise by Chopin were followed by the varicolored and charming *Carnaval,* one of the most delightful of Schumann's piano compositions. Let me confess frankly that it was painful to hear this delicate piece so butchered. To support the confession I need only remind him who knows this music and was present at the recital of the breathless harassing of the first and last movements, of the rude assault on the graces of "Chiarina" and "Estrella," and of the unlovely rumbling in the "Deutscher" and "Vornehme" waltzes.

Incomparably better was his playing of Liszt's transcription of the Spinning Song from *The Flying Dutchman,* a bravura piece full of the most charming pianistic effects.

Tausig again stuck to his trying practice of presenting himself alone the whole evening, admitting neither singing nor accompanying instruments. The concert was well attended, and there was no lack of applause.

THE "ST. MATTHEW PASSION"

[1862]

THE Singakademie [1] offered Bach's *Passion Music After the Gospel According to St. Matthew.*[2] For Vienna this was the first performance of a work hardly equaled in religious sublimity and artistic perfection in the whole literature of music. Marx [3] went so far as to call it the "Fifth Gospel." The impression we experience through the elemental form of this music is fully explained and justified when we consider its ancient and venerable roots.

Bach's music is the final rich flowering of a centuries-old religious art form. The Passion in music, now regarded as the undisputed property of the Protestant faith, owes its

---

[1] Founded 1858, the year of the founding of the Singverein of the Society of Friends of Music. The objectives and composition of the two organizations were similar, but the Singverein had the advantage of an orchestra of its own (the Orchesterverein) and sound financial backing, not to mention the excellent conductors who, at one time or another, served as musical directors of the Society of Friends of Music (Herbeck, Rubinstein, Brahms, Richter, etc.). Both choruses used the Musikvereinssaal for their weekly rehearsals and the large Redoutensaal for their public performances. Brahms was conductor of the Singakademie in the season of 1863–64.

[2] April 15, 1862, Ferdinand Stegmayer (1803–1863) conducting. It was the first complete performance in Vienna. It had been given in a private performance with piano accompaniment by the Bach Verein, forerunner of the Singakademie, in 1854. The *St. Matthew Passion* was reintroduced to the world, so to speak, by Mendelssohn, in a performance by the Berlin Singakademie, in Berlin, on March 11, 1829.

[3] Adolf Bernhard Marx (1795–1866), German author and musician, co-founder (with Adolf Martin Schlesinger) of the *Berliner allgemeine musikalische Zeitung* in 1824 and (with Kullak and Julius Stern) of the Berlin Conservatory.

origin and early development to the Catholic Church. Until the twelfth century, it was the custom of the Catholic Church to represent the suffering of Christ musically in epic-dramatic form during Holy Week. Long before Palestrina's time the story of the Passion was so represented in the Sistine Chapel, one singer giving the words of the Evangelist, a second the utterances of Christ, and a third all the other speaking parts. The multiple-voiced chorus would enter at intervals, representing the people. The Latin words of the Bible were given psalmodically, in a manner regulated by the Church and called "accents."

The Evangelical Church adopted this tradition in its liturgy. At the direction of Luther, the story of the Passion of Our Lord was sung every Good Friday, in German, by the priest at the altar, in monotoned psalmody uninterrupted by any chorus. Toward the end of the sixteenth century, the musical part of the church service began to expand and develop. This is not the occasion to describe in detail how, through enlargement of the chorus, the introduction of arias and duets, and the more precise characterization of Biblical personalities, the form reached its first peak in the four Passions of Heinrich Schütz,[4] and how it achieved a still more artistic development through Sebastiani of Königsberg[5] (continuous instrumental accompaniment, for example).

The form and character of the Passion music took a new course at the beginning of the eighteenth century in Ham-

---

[4] Schütz's *Story of the Suffering and Death of Our Saviour Jesus Christ* comprised the Passions According to St. Matthew, St. Mark, St. Luke, and St. John, written in 1665–1666.

[5] Johann Sebastiani (1622–1683). His *Suffering and Death of Our Lord and Saviour Jesus Christ* was written in 1672. He also introduced chorales, "to stimulate more devotion."

burg. Freely composed pious observations and applications were juxtaposed to the words of the Evangelist (no longer in strict adherence to the Bible) alongside the chorales of the congregation. The most celebrated attempt in a whole array of poetically deplorable, but devoutly intended, Passion texts was the *Jesus Who Was Martyred and Died for the Sins of the World*, by the Hamburg City Councilor Brockes.[6] It was set to music by R. Keiser,[7] Mattheson,[8] Telemann,[9] and others. The poetic and religious concepts of this work are the soil from which Johann Sebastian Bach's wonderful Passion grew and flowered.

Bach's Passions are intended for the church in that their form is a constituent part of the Protestant service. And yet they are not so deeply rooted in churchly soil as the Catholic Masses. Having more the character of the oratorio, they are much easier to detach from the liturgical ritual. In Bach's Passion, the Evangelist tells the story of Christ's suffering in the words of the Bible. Christ (bass), Peter, Judas, Pilate, the Jewish people, etc., appear in speaking parts in the course of the narrative and lend it dramatic life. The specially dramatic moments are punctuated by arias, choruses, and chorales, sometimes assigned to the actual congregation, sometimes to an idealized congregation. Great choruses, in which the congregation dedicates itself to devout meditation, open and close the work. One perceives that the epic and the dramatic are essential in this oratorio, as well as the lyric, which provides, however, the

---

[6] Barthold Heinrich Brockes (1680–1747), German poet. He combined religious feeling with a deep feeling for nature.

[7] Reinhard Keiser (1674–1739).

[8] Johann Mattheson (1681–1764), from 1715–1728 cantor and musical director of the Cathedral at Hamburg.

[9] Georg Philipp Telemann (1681–1767), contemporary and friend of J. S. Bach, and one of the most gifted and prolific composers of his day.

fundamental character and also dominates it externally. The *St. Matthew Passion* offers incomparable examples of each of the three types of expression. When the narrative broadens to a deeply felt aria, or breaks out like lightning in a violent dramatic chorus—to subside soon again in a long echoing chorale—it is difficult to prefer one to another. And yet the most significant element is the lyrical, which was closest to Bach's own spiritual life.

In the first chorus, possibly the most perfect of the whole work, we have a polyphonic wonder whose enormous craftsmanship one admires without being oppressed or overwhelmed by it. It is a double chorus of the Daughters of Zion and the faithful, upon which float silvery tones of a third chorus (boys' voices) more highly placed. One can imagine no more majestic portal to the Gothic cathedral, with which the *St. Matthew Passion* is so often—and correctly—compared. Among the arias, the most significant are those in which the solo voice is projected upon the mighty, firmly secured masses of the chorus, such as the tenor aria in C minor (No. 27), the alto aria, *"Ach, nun ist mein Jesus hin,"* etc.

The smaller arias are less imposing and artful, but no less profound and thoughtful. Their enjoyment is rendered difficult for the general public, however, by antiquated form and uncommonly paltry instrumentation. The solo voice is frequently accompanied only by oboe and cello, or by flute and doublebass, each going its own independent way and usually in a strict counterpoint to the voice. The thin accompaniment (especially, as in the Vienna performance, where the complementary organ was missing) and the absence of any brass instrument lend these arias an unusually chaste, earnest, and, at the same time, exotic expression.

97

After the extended dominance of the flutes and oboes, it is actually refreshing when a violin takes up the accompaniment of the second part of the beautiful alto aria. Of smaller aria episodes of delightful simplicity and purity, such as *"Du lieber Heiland, Du,"* and "Golgotha," with the two deep oboes (clarinets at this performance), the *St. Matthew Passion* has an abundance.

Secondary, and yet of great interest, are the epic parts of the work. The recitatives of the Evangelist have a vitality and a keenness of declamation which admit even of occasional violence and angularity. The easy narrative flow of the classic Italian recitative was foreign to Bach, who stressed descriptive significance above all, even at the cost of beauty. For our times, the high *tessitura* in which the Evangelist is made to declaim seems questionable; the lower orchestral pitch of Bach's time is not an entirely adequate explanation. He must have had a tenor capable of declaiming distinctly, with uncommon ease, in the highest tenor range—a kind of *haut-contre*, as the French called that now extinct species of alto-like high tenor.

Can anyone have failed to notice the inspired device of surrounding every utterance of Christ with long-sustained tones of the violin, as if to suggest a transfiguring light, or halo, while the recitatives of the Evangelist, the Apostles, etc., are supported only by short notes in the bass? The dramatic element is felt immediately in the statements and replies of the leading characters; but it is most decisively felt in the brief choral exclamations of the Jews in the second half. What powerful and, at the same time, unlabored effects! It is the more remarkable in view of the fact that the strengthening and refinement of dramatic expression is the musical element which a later artistic epoch carried on with the greatest success. No one will dispute the debt Mendelssohn's most effective choruses owe to these Bach models.

As a whole, the *St. Matthew Passion* makes a deep and unique impression, a deeper impression, indeed, than I should have predicted from a mere study of the score. All those details which, in the course of the work, may strike the listener, despite himself, as strange or inadequate vanish in the grandeur or originality of this over-all impression. It is a supreme manifestation of a type of artistic expression which we recognize and respect as exalted, even though it is not our own. One feels that this work is unique, as its creator was unique. And for precisely that reason the listener is not tempted to make comparisons. They would be of little use and, at the same time, prejudicial to the work. In comparing the *St. Matthew Passion* and Beethoven's still vividly remembered *Missa Solemnis*, a listener's subjective preference, his individual attitude, might well prevail; an objective basis for comparative appraisal could probably not be found.

The respective approaches to religion of Bach and Beethoven are as far removed from one another as the characteristics of their musical imagination. That Beethoven's work finds an immediate response in a greater number of listeners is neither to be denied nor regretted. It is musically and religiously a product of the modern mind and spirit. One can say of Beethoven, as has been said of Shakespeare, that he is everywhere and nowhere religious. Only the first can be applied to Bach. No one will compare him with Shakespeare, but he often reminds us of Milton, although the latter was certainly a lesser genius. Just as Milton's poetry flowered from English Puritanism, so Bach's church music flows directly from the great Pietist movement of the seventeenth century, the word being used, of course, not in a derogatory sense, but rather in the sense of historical characterization. It would require faint perception, indeed, to overlook Bach's relationship to German Pietism. One need only consider the texts of his cantatas, motets, and Passions, the utter devotion of his music, and the sense of transfiguration so intimately associated with that devotion.

The tendency to translate everything into terms of inner experience so characteristic of Pietism, and the parallel tendency to seek out and contemplate that which has been felt, find an analogy in Bach's music. This is to be distinguished from pure piety. There is also deep religious feeling in Beethoven's *Missa Solemnis*, but it is modified and enriched by a thousand cultural elements which Beethoven had absorbed and which he was far from disavowing in what he wrote for the church. But we need not go as far as the distant Beethoven to grasp the distinction; we need only call upon Bach's great contemporary, Handel, whose *The Messiah* treats the same material as the Passion. Every note of *The Messiah* breathes genuine piety, and yet everything is freer, brighter, more spirited. The moments of consolation, rapture, and liberation are incomparably more numerous with Handel, and he stays with them longer and gives them greater emphasis. Throughout the whole *St. Matthew Passion* there is a compelling and profound but almost uninterruptedly gloomy, constrained piety which seems unable to free itself from the contemplation of sin and which lies upon the work like heavy mourning. That Bach was able, without undue effort, to exclude all worldly and fleshly elements and still absorb the listener in an area of human sensation so rigorously circumscribed is the supreme

100

testimony of the strength of his genius and of his feeling.

It was a pleasure to observe that the large audience followed Bach's earnest and demanding masterpiece with unflagging attention. The full enjoyment of such a work is vouchsafed, of course, only to those who come to it well prepared and who are able to appreciate the fathomless depths of the technical accomplishment. This freedom and artistry in the handling of polyphonic movement is a gold mine of musical knowledge for the working student. Only with the proper historical perspective can one enjoy the significance of the whole work and avoid being led astray by disturbing details. And, indeed, in musical matters, the public appears, with every passing year, to acquire more of this historical sense, the most precious heritage of our time. It knows how to isolate the modern, individual tendencies and customs from the monuments of a great past, and if, now and then, it bruises its feelers, it no longer yields to the instinctive impulse to draw them in again.

SCHUBERT'S
"UNFINISHED" SYMPHONY

———— •—•—•• ————

[1865]

AMONG the so-called "Friends of Schubert" par excellence,
one can distinguish two characteristic groups: the grasshoppers and the squirrels; or, to put it in terms of physics,
the centrifugals and the centripetals. The first calmly let
Schubert's manuscripts be scattered to the winds; they know
about some opera or symphony (they watched its creation!),
but they are not disturbed when these treasures fall for a
few florins to an American collector or, still cheaper, to a
cheesemonger. The squirrels, or centripetals, having
managed to get hold of two or three jewels of Schubertiana,
keep them locked in a trunk and take the key to bed with
them; whether this is out of friendship for the deceased or
contempt for the living is immaterial.

As of yesterday [1] we can no longer count Schubert's
friend Anselm Hüttenbrenner [2] among the latter. He yielded,
at last, to the artful persuasion of Herbeck, who had gone to
Graz expressly to get one of Hüttenbrenner's own compositions for the Society of the Friends of Music concerts, and
brought back a long-looked-for Schubert manuscript. Which
of the two compositions was fish and which was bait has not

---

[1] December 17.

[2] (1794–1868). He was also a friend of Beethoven's and was present at
his death.

been divulged; it is enough to note that Schubert and Hüttenbrenner appeared, as in real life, in friendly communion on the program of the last Society Concert.[3]

Hüttenbrenner, who contributed much to the popularity of Schubert's *Erlkönig* with a number of *Erlkönig Waltzes*, opened the concert with an overture in C minor which cannot be denied some craftsmanship and a certain sense of form. Then followed the Schubert novelty, which excited extraordinary enthusiasm. It consisted of the first two movements (Allegro moderato, B minor, and Andante, E major) of a symphony long considered lost. The original score, all in Schubert's handwriting, bears the date 1822 and contains, in addition to the first movements, the first nine measures of the third, a Scherzo in B minor. It cannot be ascertained whether Schubert continued to work on it. It is possible that one of the "grasshoppers" knows the solution of this riddle, or that one of the "squirrels" has it under his pillow.

We had to be content, in any case, with the two movements which, as revived by Herbeck, brought a new life into our concert halls. When, after the few introductory measures, clarinet and oboe in unison began their gentle cantilena above the calm murmur of the violins, every child recognized the composer, and a muffled "Schubert" was whispered in the audience. He had hardly entered, but it seemed that one recognized him by his step, by his way of opening the door. And when, after this nostalgic cantilena in the minor, there followed the contrasting G major theme of the violoncellos, a charming song of almost *Ländler*-like intimacy,

---

[3] Modern researchers are less reticent about assuming that Hüttenbrenner's composition was bait. The accepted version of the story is that Herbeck was tipped off about the Schubert manuscript by Anselm's brother, Josef, and lost no time getting down to Graz and throwing Anselm a baited hook.

every heart rejoiced, as if, after a long separation, the composer himself were among us in person. The whole movement is a melodic stream so crystal clear, despite its force and genius, that one can see every pebble on the bottom. And everywhere the same warmth, the same bright, life-giving sunshine!

The Andante develops more broadly. A few odd hints here and there of complaint or irritation are interwoven in a cantilena otherwise full of heartiness and quiet happiness; their effect is that of musical thunder clouds rather than of dangerous clouds of passion. As if loath to leave his own gentle song, the composer puts off too long the end of this Andante. We know this peculiar habit of Schubert's, which weakens the total impression of some of his works. At the end of the Andante, too, his flight seems to lose itself in space, but one still hears the fluttering of his wings.

The tonal beauty of the two movements is fascinating. With a few horn figurations and here and there a clarinet or oboe solo, Schubert achieves, with the most simple, basic orchestra, tonal effects which no refinement of Wagnerian instrumentation can capture. This symphonic fragment may be counted among Schubert's most beautiful instrumental works, and I am especially happy to say so here because I have permitted myself more than once to speak warningly of overzealous Schubert worship and the adulation of Schubert relics.

RICHARD WAGNER'S CONCERT

[1872]

THE concert conducted by Richard Wagner [1] consisted of two parts, one devoted to Beethoven's *"Eroica,"* the other to Wagner's own compositions. Since the *"Eroica"* is one of the most hackneyed pieces of the Vienna concert repertoire, it is reasonable to assume that Wagner chose it, not to acquaint us with the work, but to show us how it should be conducted—and also to provide a kind of illustrative appendix to his essay, *On Conducting.* He refers repeatedly to the *"Eroica"* in this treatise, chiefly by way of demonstrating his favorite thesis that our conductors have no idea of tempo and that the Beethoven we have learned to know through public performances is a "pure chimera."

Wagner is recognized as a brilliant conductor. He has excellent intentions, and he is able, with his great authority, to communicate them to the players. His spirited reading of the *"Eroica,"* with its fine, individual nuances, was, on the whole, a real pleasure. And yet it would be sad, indeed, if it were just yesterday, and thanks only to his benevolent intervention, that we had first learned to know and under-

---

[1] On May 12, ten days before the laying of the cornerstone of the theater at Bayreuth. It was a benefit concert for the Bayreuth project, and the ticket prices were, accordingly, "fantastic." The Musikvereinssaal was, nevertheless, quickly sold out. Nature helped give the concert a mystic-festive character. During the playing of the "Magic Fire Music," a storm raged outside, and at the summoning of Loge the hall was illuminated by a flash of lightning. Wagner commented: "A sign of heavenly approval."

stand this work. Beethoven composed it, after all, right here in Vienna and conducted it himself. It would be an unpardonable ingratitude not to state that we have heard excellent performances of the *"Eroica"* by the same orchestra under Herbeck and Dessoff,[2] performances still remembered as excellent even after yesterday's performance by Wagner. One conductor's tempi are a little faster, another's a little slower; the one colors his contrasts between forte and pianissimo more vividly, the other more moderately. There will always be such distinctions as long as conductors are not machines. With serious conductors of superior cultivation and undisputed talent these distinctions are usually slight. None will take an adagio fast or an allegro slow, or make a pianissimo out of a forte. As for deviations within certain artistically fixed boundaries, they can be disputed, and only the composer can decide. Without Beethoven's personal assurance that Wagner's conception is the only right one and that what appears Wagnerian in it is really genuine Beethoven, we cannot grant to the man of the hour the right to call everyone else who conducts the *"Eroica"* an ass.

The novel element in Wagner's reading consists, to put it briefly, in frequent "modifications of the tempo" within a single movement. He uses this term and a second— "correct comprehension of the song (melos)," which should provide the key to the right tempo—to characterize the reform which he demands and which he himself undertakes in the performance of Beethoven symphonies. There are, indeed, movements where the "dynamic monotony" so detested by Wagner can be animated and interrupted to

---

[2] Felix Otto Dessoff (1835–1892), conductor at the Vienna Court Opera from 1860 to 1875.

Silhouette by Otto Boehler of Wagner on the podium.

advantage. Such a movement is the Finale of the *"Eroica."*
It is based essentially on the variation form, and each variation of the theme undoubtedly permits of a characteristic
"modification of tempo." A succession of variations, all
played in the same tempo, can easily degenerate into spiritless formalism. Wagner's tempo changes in this movement
achieved a charming effect. Elsewhere he seemed to carry

his "modifications" too far. After a very fast beginning of the first movement, for example, he takes the second theme (forty-fifth measure) conspicuously slower, thus disturbing the listener's hardly confirmed establishment in the fundamental mood of the movement and diverting the "heroic" character of the symphony toward the sentimental. He takes the Scherzo uncommonly fast, almost presto—a hazardous undertaking even with a virtuoso orchestra. The Funeral March was beautiful, particularly the gradual dying away of the main theme. The whole performance was extremely interesting, full of stimulating devices and effects; at the same time, hardly anyone will doubt that the origin of these "modifications" is traceable rather to Wagner than to Beethoven.

An original and intelligent personality can often accomplish a deviation from the rules in a manner so convincing that only the narrow-minded philistine can take offense. But there is nothing more dangerous than to generalize on the basis of mere intelligent perception and to attempt to establish purely individual points of view as exclusively valid laws. Were Wagner's principles of conducting universally adopted, his tempo changes would open the door to intolerable arbitrariness, and we should soon be having symphonies "freely adapted from Beethoven," instead of "by Beethoven," with a different physiognomy under every conductor. *Tempo rubato*, that musical seasickness which so afflicts the performances of many singers and instrumentalists, would soon infect our orchestras, and that would be the end of the last healthy element of our musical life.

Wagner approaches conducting as he approaches composition. What suits his individuality and his utterly exceptional talent must be accepted as the one and only universal, true, and exclusively authorized artistic law. From his highly personal poetic-graphic-musical endowment he evolved a new theory of opera which has led him to brilliant and original accomplishments, to compositions whose imaginative subjectivity is their own accreditation, and which are effective because they are Wagnerian. But not satisfied with that, he denounces all other opera styles as "colossal errors," overlooking the fact that his own, in the hands of any other composer, would be only a caricature. If all other opera composers were to write in the style of *Tristan und Isolde*, we listeners should inevitably wind up in the madhouse; and if Wagner's "tempo modifications" were to gain general ascendancy in our orchestras, then conductors, fiddlers, and wind players would soon be our companions in lunacy.

FRANZ LISZT

———•—•—•———

[1874]

AS SOON as it was known that Franz Liszt would play in Vienna—for the benefit of the Franz Josef Foundation—our entire musical community was gripped by feverish anticipation.[1] Almost thirty years had passed since his last appearance as pianist in Vienna. In the intervening period he had undergone the most astonishing transformation as artist and as man. He had ended his unexampled virtuoso career in 1848, unexpectedly and irrevocably. He once explained this universally regretted abdication to me in the brief but significant pronouncement: "Virtuosity requires youth!" Indefatigable as composer, he remained inexorable as virtuoso in his proud decision to depart the public arena at the height of his powers, preferring to leave behind him a thirst for more rather than the slightest suggestion of satiety. Thus it was that the mere announcement of his concert in Vienna set the town by the ears. In the younger generation was rekindled the hitherto nearly extinct hope of hearing the *"Wundermann,"* about whom they had known since earliest childhood. The older generation, those who

---

[1] As well it might be! The concert took place in the Musikvereinssaal on January 11. Liszt was the big attraction, but the program also included offerings by the Men's Chorus and Choral Society of the Society of Friends of Music and the Court Opera Orchestra. The conductors were Herbeck, Dessoff, and Brahms, the latter at that time Artistic Director of the Society of Friends of Music and conductor of the Choral Society.

had participated in his early triumphs, were none the less eager to refresh their most vivid musical recollections and to compare them with the new impression.

It was in 1846 that Liszt last charmed the Viennese in a series of recitals. The old Musikvereinssaal was the modest scene of these triumphs. Compared with our present large concert hall, it was about what the old walled city was to the Vienna of today. The gallery, with its roost-ladder staircase, was, curiously enough, considered the most elegant location; there the feminine leaders of society displayed their finery. Since Liszt always played alone, the space on the stage usually reserved for the orchestra was pressed into service to accommodate the inevitable overflow. There was always a lovely wreath of handsome ladies around the piano of the "incomparable," himself a connoisseur never wanting in tasteful appreciation of such surroundings. Liszt always gave an entire solo recital, without the incidental numbers —sung, fiddled, and declaimed—previously regarded as indispensable. His enormous repertoire covered everything from Beethoven sonatas to Liszt galops, from opera fantasies to his own transcriptions of Schubert songs. He played the part of the distinguished and gracious man of the house, chatted with the ladies, greeted his friends, and charmed everyone. His playing was sometimes uneven, alternately good and bad; but it was always Liszt, and that was sufficient. The fact that it was influenced by the mood of the moment raised it only the higher in the esteem of the public, which was tired of the correct and dependable playing of the virtuosos who had gone before. I remember one occasion when a bravura piece on Spanish tunes resulted in unending recalls. Liszt, in excellent form, finally seated himself at the piano, played the main theme again, and then plunged into

111

a short free improvisation teeming with astonishing difficulties. This was at one of the so-called night concerts, an
appalling institution (they began at 9:30), introduced by
Liszt to circumvent a law designed to protect the theaters

*Liszt, in his youthful days, charming a contingent of
contemporary bobby-soxers.*

by forbidding other public entertainment during theater
hours. He alone had the drawing power to fill the Musikvereinssaal so late at night.

In Liszt's apartment in the hotel "Zur Stadt London"
the younger musical generation of Vienna was in more or
less continuous convention. He himself sat talking and
smoking at the piano in a black velvet blouse, correcting
proof sheets, or writing down some composition or other,

112

the manuscript paper on his knee. If one were fortunate enough to be present when he played some novelty at sight, one had fresh occasion to marvel at his immense musical endowment. Ferdinand Hiller,[2] in his interesting book on Mendelssohn, tells how the composer met him one day and cried: "I have just seen a miracle! I was with Liszt at Erard's [3] and showed him the manuscript of my concerto. He played it at sight—it is hardly legible—and with the utmost perfection. It simply can't be played any better than he played it. It was miraculous!" To which Hiller added the perceptive observation that Liszt commonly played any given piece best at the first reading; it was only then that it sufficiently occupied him. At a second playing he had to elaborate in order to make it interesting. But to return to his recent concert:

Jubilantly greeted, Liszt appeared in the long robe of an *abbé*, seated himself at the piano, and began Schubert's "Wanderer" Fantasy, opus 15.[4] His playing is as perfect as ever, with more spiritual repose and greater moderation. It is not so stunning or so gripping as it used to be, but it is more unified, more solid. He was more brilliantly effective in his second number, the Hungarian Rhapsody for Piano and Orchestra. This original work—which begins in real gypsy style, with a free melancholy improvisation, and then goes off into a czardas-like orgy—seemed to awaken his youthful spirits. The Allegro offered many astounding

---

[2] (1811–1855). German pianist, conductor, and composer, founder (in 1850) of the Cologne Conservatory. The book referred to is *Felix Mendelssohn-Bartholdy, Briefe und Erinnerungen* (1874).

[3] Pierre Erard (1796–1855), nephew of Sebastian Erard (1752–1831), and his successor as proprietor of the firm of Erard, Paris, piano and harp manufacturers, founded by his uncle in 1779.

[4] In Liszt's arrangement for piano and orchestra.

effects exclusively associated with Liszt, such as the hammering with both hands on a single key and the characteristic imitation of the cimbalom. The way he reproduces the sound effects of this favorite and basic Hungarian instrument is quite inimitable.

His playing was free, poetic, replete with imaginative shadings, and, at the same time, characterized by noble, artistic repose. And his technique, his virtuosity? I hesitate to speak of it. It suffices to observe that he has not lost it but has rather added to it in clarity and moderation. What a remarkable man! After a life incomparably rich and active, full of excitement, passion, and pleasure, he returns at the age of sixty-two and plays the most difficult music with the ease and strength and freshness of a youth. Not only does one listen with breathless attention to his playing; one also observes its reflection in the fine lines of his face. His head, thrown back, still suggests something of Jupiter. Sometimes the eyes flash beneath the prominent brows; sometimes the characteristically upturned corners of the mouth are raised even higher in a gentle smile. Head, eyes, and sometimes even a helping hand, maintain constant communication with orchestra and audience. Sometimes he plays from notes, at other times from memory, putting on and taking off his spectacles accordingly. Sometimes his head is bent forward attentively, sometimes thrown back boldly. All this has the utmost fascination for his listeners—particularly feminine listeners.

Liszt brought the Rhapsody to a conclusion in a storm of octaves. The audience applauded, shouted, cheered, rose to its feet, recalled the master again and again, indefatigably. The latter, in turn, with the quiet, friendly, gracious bearing

114

of the habitual conqueror, let it be known that he, too, was not yet tired. For the Liszt of today it was a great accomplishment; and yet he went about it as if it were nothing, and he himself still the Liszt of 1840. A darling of the gods, indeed!

"DIE MEISTERSINGER"[1]

[1874]

THE management of the Vienna Court Opera came in for some criticism in Wagner's famous essay on Jews,[2] where he stated that the management had revealed by its tricks "that it strove not only to avoid a performance of *Die Meistersinger* but also to prevent its performance in other theaters." The Vienna Court Opera answered this incredible accusation in 1870 with a brilliant production of the opera. The public met *Die Meistersinger* more than halfway, with that close attention which every new Wagner opera has a right to expect.

Friends and foes are well aware that a new opera by Wagner means something extraordinary, something to occupy the fantasy and the intellect in all respects. *Die Meistersinger* is, indeed, a remarkable creation, uniquely consistent in method, extremely earnest, novel in structure, rich in imaginative and even brilliant characteristics, often tiring

---

[1] This is the version of Hanslick's essay prepared for the Collected Works. Essentially it is identical with his review of the Munich *première* of June 21, 1868, although with some important moderations noted in subsequent footnotes. These moderations were embodied in Hanslick's review of the Vienna *première* at the Court Opera on February 27, 1870. For his review of this performance, Hanslick simply reprinted his Munich review, with the moderations previously mentioned and with a new lead. This new lead he reprinted in the version here given, merely changing "has now" to "in 1870." This lead ends with the words "dull or disagreeable music." It is characteristic of Hanslick's disregard of "news" that he makes no mention of the riotous demonstration staged by an anti-Wagnerian faction during the singing of Beckmesser's Serenade at the Vienna *première*.

[2] See page XII, note 3.

and exasperating, but always unusual. It is of compelling interest, if only as a phenomenon; whether one is pleased or repelled depends upon one's conception of musical and dramatic beauty. Its virtues cannot be denied—nor its faults; there are scenes which rank among Wagner's most fortunate musical inspirations, surrounded by long, unrewarding stretches of dull or disagreeable music. And as a theatrical spectacle alone it is worth seeing.

If we give the synopsis, as can be done in a few words, it will be difficult to understand how an opera longer than *Le Prophète* or *Les Huguenots* could be made of it. Its greatest fault is in the over-elaboration of a small, meager plot which, with neither intricacies nor intrigue, is continually at a standstill and would normally offer barely enough material for a modest two-act operetta. One can hardly give an apt description of the tenacious verbosity of the dialogue, with all the domestic altercations and dry instruction. Everything is composed in the same monotonous manner and in a slow tempo, Wagner having made the momentous discovery in his latest leaflet, *German Art and Politics*, that the andante is the specifically "German" tempo!

Let us sketch, as well as possible in a few lines, the dramatic and musical synopsis. The overture is hardly calculated to win the listener. All the leitmotives of the opera are dumped consecutively into a chromatic flood and finally tossed about in a kind of tonal typhoon.[3] It is a contrived

---

[3] In his Munich review, Hanslick went on to say, ". . . and must excite in the uninitiated the impression that the Nuremberg Mastersingers were predominantly concerned with cyanide. The only thing which prevents me from declaring it to be the world's most unpleasant overture is the even more horrible Prelude to *Tristan and Isolde*. The latter reminds me of the old Italian painting of that martyr whose intestines were slowly unwound from his body onto a reel. The Prelude to *Die Meistersinger*, at best, goes about it quickly, with spirit and a club."

piece, brutal in effect and painfully artificial. It leads immediately into the first scene, the interior of St. Catherine's Church in Nuremberg. The congregation sings a hymn. Between verses, the orchestra depicts the tender emotions of a young knight who, standing in the foreground, follows a burgher's young daughter with his eyes. The service ends; the Knight, Walther von Stolzing, rushes to the unknown beautiful maiden: "Fair Maiden, say, are you betrothed?" With the electrical swiftness and energy characteristic of all love affairs in Wagner's operas, Eva Pogner replies: "To you, or else no one!" The wooer must only meet the terms stipulated by her father: namely, win the Mastersingers' prize. Eva leaves, accompanied by her nurse, Magdalena. Walther remains behind in the church, where arrangements are made for the meeting of the Mastersingers. A fussy apprentice, David, with devastating thoroughness, instructs the knight in the rules and regulations of the "Singers' Court" and the poetic rules of the *Tabulatura*, enumerating forty to fifty different "tones and tunes." It sounds like an extract from a volume by Wagenseil [4] set to music.

Despite laudable cuts in this scene—simply intolerable without them—it is dry and boring. At long last the masters arrive, converse a while, and then answer to the roll call read by Kothner, the baker. The meeting opens with an address by the goldsmith, Pogner, in which he promises his daughter and all his valuable properties to the man who, tomorrow, on the Feast of St. John, shall win the Mastersingers' prize. The monologue penetrates the overwhelmingly boring, dreary musical mist like a sunbeam. Its heartfelt emotion.

---

[4] Johann Christoph Wagenseil (1633–1708), German librarian and musical historian, author of *De sacri Rom. Imp. libera civitate Nurembergensi commentatio. Accedit de Germaniae phonascorum origine*, etc. (1697), which included a 140-page treatise on the Mastersingers.

its melodious, beautifully harmonized main theme, make it one of the culminating points of the opera. Pogner's proposal is accepted after a lengthy debate. Walther appears and is asked to sing. Beckmesser,[5] the town clerk, a mischievous old fool, has the office of censor; he sits behind a curtain and chalks up the singer's mistakes. But first the rules are read to the singer, a procedure which the audience, satiated already with learned explanations, might be spared. Walther answers the questions with some impressive, well-made stanzas (*"Am stillen Herd in Winterszeit"*), which we prefer to the subsequent "Spring and Love" Song. The latter, despite clever and graceful details, is not fully effective, largely due to the restless accompaniment and excessive modulation. Walther has not finished singing when Beckmesser springs from the censor's booth, his tablet full of chalk marks. With the single exception of Hans Sachs, the other masters, too, are indignant at the irregularity of his song, which they denounce as "vain cacophony." There follows a raving tumult of all voices, ending with the judgment that the knight has failed. The total impression of this act is tiring, despite the two sunbeams (Pogner's and Walther's songs). Handled lightly and easily, the material would make an effective introduction; stretched to an entire lengthy act, it becomes an awkward burden.

The scene of the second act is a street in Nuremberg; in the foreground, on the right, is Pogner's neat house; to the left is Hans Sachs' cobbler shop. Between them, in clear perspective, one sees the whole length of the street, set with plastic movable scenery and offering a picturesque view in the light of the full moon. The act opens with the

---

[5] Called "Veit Hanslich" in the third draft of the text, completed in Vienna in 1861.

apprentices singing and making merry in anticipation of the Feast of St. John and teasing their comrade, David, who is in love with Magdalena. Pogner and Eva come along, singing a most uninteresting conversation, after which Eva, alone, goes to Sachs to find out how her knight fared at his audition. Sachs reports on the unfavorable result. The duet (if one can call this interminable dialogue a duet) strikes a hearty and charming tone here and there and has some pretty details. The whole, nevertheless, is painfully monotonous and clumsy. With a proper duet, perhaps at the end of the conversation, this could easily be remedied, but in Wagner's works people may sing only one after the other, never together. The latter is not genteel; it might even be agreeable.

Walther comes to Eva. Despite the enticing verses, "'Tis my true love! Yes, my own love!" etc., we have again no setting for two voices; each separately sings his own thoughts, contrived and without musical charm. The lovers are ready to flee, but must hide, first from the night watchman and then from Beckmesser. The latter plays on his lute the prelude to a serenade in front of Eva's window, but Hans Sachs anticipates him with a cobbler's song ("Jerum, Jerum! Holla, Holla ho!") ostensibly comical but actually reminiscent of a peevish hyena [6] rather than of a merry cobbler. At Beckmesser's pleading, Sachs promises at last to keep quiet but reserves the right to mark every fault of declamation or melody with a blow of his hammer on the sole of the shoe he is working on. This joke is overworked to the point of bad taste. Beckmesser begins his serenade in character, but it all too soon becomes artificial. Sachs

---

[6] "Roaring tiger" in the Munich original.

hammers once or twice in each measure. Beckmesser protests; Sachs quiets him. Beckmesser resumes his song, and Sachs his hammering. In the end, they quarrel so loudly that the neighbors look out of their windows and complain about the nocturnal disturbance. David grabs Beckmesser and beats him up. The street fills with people, screaming, shouting, and scuffling, until the din is truly satanic. The effect is probably unique in the annals of the lyric theater.

A study of the score had led me to expect more of this finale. Wagner has constructed the tumult with truly refined skill, now with single voices, now with whole choral groups opposing each other, eagerly taking the words out of each other's mouths. Strange to say, the composer's sharp practical eye has deceived him. Nothing, nothing at all, is discernible of subtle musical disposition; one hears nothing but brutal shouting and screaming. It was a good idea, however, not to close the act with the tumult on the street, but to disperse the crowd and let the noise abate. We see the night watchman walking alone on the empty moonlit street —one of those poetic, picturesque effects which Wagner understands so well. The second act is closed. We have heard engaging details, but little that could continuously give us pleasure or excite our sympathies.

Finally, the third act, the longest but the best of the opera. At first, however, it continues in the tasteless, long-winded declamatory style of the second. There is a philistine introductory scene between Sachs and his apprentice, who sings a legend of St. John and congratulates his master on his name day. There follows a long monologue in which Sachs philosophizes about folly. Were it not for a charming instrumental picture (*"Glühwürmchen"*) amidst the unctuous singsong, one would be tempted to seek refuge in

Cartoon by André Gill showing how many contemporaries thought Wagner's music affected the public ear in 1869.

slumber. Walther enters with harp arpeggios, and Sachs asks him to relate his dream. Walther's song (*"Morgendlich leuchtend"*) begins with an uncommonly beautiful, tender melody which, fortunately, does not lose itself in infinity after the third measure. It even has a quiet, simple accompaniment. The melody makes a good impression, a fact of which the composer is only too well aware, and which seems to have made it impossible for him to tear himself away from it. The many stanzas and later repetitions damage it beyond repair.

While Walther sings, Sachs writes down the poem. Beckmesser, who overhears the scene, trys to steal the paper. Sachs gives it to him and allows him to perform it as his own at the contest. The conversation between Sachs and Beckmesser (who, in his joy, sings as barbarically and unnaturally as he has sung previously in his anger) is again a test of the listener's patience. Fortunately, Eva appears in festive costume and lets Sachs take her shoe and widen it. Walther enters suddenly in his silken doublet. It is a matter of course that the two (like Senta and the Dutchman) should stand and look at each other for several minutes, as if in a trance. Walther again sings a stanza of his song "The glorious morning dream's true story" (*"Morgentraumdeutweise,"*) as Sachs, summoning David and Magdalena, solemnly christens it. We could easily forego this rather childish solemnity were it not for a highly surprising and agreeable circumstance developing from it: nothing less than a melodic, harmoniously rounded vocal quintet, whose melodious upper voice is sung first by Eva alone. For three hours one has heard hardly anything but declamatory solo singing above wavering "infinite melody" or noisy choral tumult. Now, quite unexpectedly, we have this melodious

123

quintet, and the audience is delighted to hear what would hardly have attracted so much attention in another opera. That is one of the secrets of our modern Mastersinger.

The scene changes to an open meadow before the gates of Nuremberg. It is the Feast of St. John. The various guilds are drawn up in festive array with bands and flags. The cobblers, the tailors, and the bakers sing the songs of their guilds with the poetic and musical sturdiness appropriate to the situation. A fresh, realistic character pervades the whole. A little waltz, melodically simple but exquisite in instrumentation, enlivens the scene. Trumpets herald the arrival of the Mastersingers' guild. It is a lively and historically accurate picture.

Beckmesser is the first to contend for the prize. He begins by decking himself out in borrowed plumes. But, confused and nervous, he forgets the text, makes nonsense out of every sentence, and has to retire amidst jeers and laughter. Sachs states that the poem was originally excellent but that it has been clumsily mutilated. At his behest Walther then sings the same song and is received with enthusiasm. What we cannot understand is how the same Mastersingers who, the previous day, jeered Walther's singing as "vain cacophony" are now so enthralled that they vote him the prize and Eva's hand. Enough said; the loving couple is united, and the opera ends with picturesque final grouping.

Apart from the tiresome way Wagner has handled it, the plot indicates progress toward a better and healthier attitude. Contrary to his theory (which accepts only mythology as a proper source of plots), but following a good instinct, Wagner has returned from his abstruse submarine and superterranean legends to the real theater. At long last he has turned his back on his dwarfs, giants, and Valkyries.

He has set foot in the midst of the real world and given us lively pictures of the life of the German people of the Middle Ages. These artisans of Nuremberg, with their simple, philistine adventures and plain doggerel verses, are preferable to the ecstasies and bombastic, stuttering alliterations of *Tristan and Isolde* or *Das Rheingold*. In the colorful description of the national festival on the Nuremberg meadows, Wagner has had a particularly fortunate poetic inspiration. It is also the first time that he has stooped again to the term "opera"; in *Tristan and Isolde*, he still saw fit to ennoble the subject with the vague term "action."

Aside from the description of medieval national life, it is the conflict between free poetry, spontaneously inspired, and spiritless, pedantic versification which constitutes the intellectual and emotional core of the work. Walther represents the one, the guild of the Nuremberg masters the other. A poet of genius against a dozen pedantic masters who cannot understand him and yet dare to judge him. Do you get it? Actually, the superiority of the genius who creates his own laws is fervently defended in each act—and all too long-windedly—against the strait jacket of scholarship. These sneers and innuendos recall Hebbel's *Michelangelo*,[7] with its hidden and yet unmistakable personal bias. Wagner's safety valve is Hans Sachs who, as an unprejudiced third person and intermediary, stands between the two parties. Brought up on the school rules of the singers' guild, and suddenly enlightened by Walther's "free poetry," he is a kind of

---

[7] Friedrich Hebbel (1813–1863), German poet and playwright. *Michelangelo* was a two-act play (1850) in which Hebbel has his hero make a statue of which he buries all but one arm. The statue is duly discovered and acclaimed as an antique masterpiece by the critics. Whereupon Michelangelo presents the missing arm as proof of his own identity as the sculptor—to the great confusion and consternation of the critics.

converted Mozartian who dares deliver a special vote on behalf of the "music of the future."

For a comic opera—and that is what *Die Meistersinger* is, according to its exposition and its two pronounced buffo parts—Wagner's talent seems inadequate, particularly with respect to humor. The conversational tone which dominates the first two acts is never easy and fluent. Quite the contrary, it is expressed through an awkward, contrived, continuously restless music, with a noisy and complex instrumentation. The most trivial questions and answers, commonly expressed in normal tones, are shouted above the tumult of the orchestra. To this false coloring is added a false design by a declamatory style characterized by leaps contradictory to all rules of diction. In comedy Wagner's music is even less successful; it is stilted, profuse, even repulsive. With the horrible dissonances in which the "funny" Beckmesser scolds or complains, one could accompany the most hair-raising scenes of a thriller. When David speaks of "bread and water" the orchestra plays of gallows and rack. If peaceful citizens and artisans express their disapproval of a poem in such irate tones as in the first and last act of *Die Meistersinger*, what resources are left the composer who would treat the French Revolution? Not to speak of the unfunny and vulgar riot finale of the second act.

One is reminded of Laube's [8] melancholy exclamation at the performance in Munich: "Bless you, lighthearted Rossini!"—and of the finale of the *Barber*, so harmonious and graceful despite its frenzy. It is true: music has only limited means for comedy effects. In the majority of cases it must be content to support and heighten a comical text on

---

[8] Heinrich Laube (1806–1884), German playwright, long-time director of the Vienna Burgtheater.

the light waves of merry, facetious melodies. But humor, repose, and unconstrained cheerfulness are lacking in Wagner; like his Italian counterpart, Verdi, he is always emotional. The oases in the drab desert (Pogner's speech, Walther's songs, the quintet in the third act) do not belong to the comical, but exclusively to those parts of the opera animated by emotion.

In *Die Meistersinger* Wagner has remained true to the musical reforms dominating the larger part of *Lohengrin* and the whole of *Tristan and Isolde*. This consistency lends the work an imposing sense of security and conviction. Wagner knows what he wants; every note of the score speaks of intentions fully realized. Nothing is left to chance, but neither is there anything of those intriguing coincidences which lend an ultimate charm to the creations of fantasy and nature. One must respect the consistency with which he sticks to his peculiar principle; but, no more than any of his other operas, has *Die Meistersinger* converted me to it. It consists of the intentional dissolution of every fixed form into a shapeless, sensually intoxicating resonance; the replacement of independent, articulate melody by vague melodization. One may confidently use Wagner's dry technical expression, "infinite melody," since everyone knows by now what is meant. The "infinite melody" is the dominant, musically undermining power in *Die Meistersinger*, as in *Tristan and Isolde*. A small motive begins, and, before it can develop into an actual melody or theme, it gets twisted, pinched, set higher or lower by continual modulation and enharmonization, enlarged and reduced, repeated or echoed, now by this instrument, now by another. Anxiously omitting every conclusive cadence, this boneless tonal mollusk floats on toward the immeasurable, renewing

127

itself from its own substance. Afraid [9] of the "profanity" of perfect or deceptive cadences, Wagner falls prey to another, and certainly not superior, pedantry: he becomes monotonous through the continual use of dissonant chords when the ear expects a concluding triad.

What a surprisingly agreeable effect is created by the two fully resounding C major chords which precede Walther's Prize Song in the third act, if only because the listener has been longing for three hours for just such a simple, healthy triad! If one surveys larger parts of the opera, one will observe everywhere the same monotony, together with a continuous nervous unrest and interruption in detail. Only in those few spots where the text offers a lyrical resting place (Walther's songs, Hans Sachs' second-act monologue), is the singing concentrated for a while in an independent melody. Throughout the whole dramatic sequence, in the monologues, dialogues, and ensembles, the thread of melody runs, not in the voices, but in the orchestra, where it is "infinitely" unwound as in a spinning mill. This melody-spinning orchestral accompaniment actually forms the integral and independent tone picture. The voice accommodates itself to this accompaniment by weaving its half-declamatory, half-melodic phrases into it.

It is obvious that his method of composition is diametrically opposed to that used by all the older masters. Vocal melody was ever their first and decisive consideration; the accompaniment (free or complex) was subordinate. To a given melody one could usually approximately anticipate the accompaniment, or at least an accompaniment; the ac-

---

[9] From here to "interruption in detail" was added to the Munich draft in the review of the Vienna *première* in 1870.

companiment alone, however, was dependent. In *Die Meistersinger* the vocal part alone is not only nonindependent, it is nonexistent! The accompaniment is everything, an independent symphonic creation, an orchestral fantasy with an accompanying vocal part. Given the text and the orchestral accompaniment, a good musician, well versed in Wagner's music, would be able to insert suitable vocal parts in the empty spaces, just as a sculptor can restore the missing hand of a statue. But one could as little restore the lost orchestral accompaniment to Hans Sachs' or Eva's vocal parts as create the whole statue with only the single hand to go on. The natural relationship has been reversed: the orchestra is the singer, bearing the guiding thoughts; the singers are merely complementary.

Far from pointing up character, this method tends rather to level and generalize. Thus, in order to achieve characterization and to establish an aural anchor in the ocean of melodic infinity, Wagner employs the so-called memory or "leitmotives," i.e., themes which recur in the orchestra when a certain person appears on the scene, or when a certain event is mentioned. The masters' guild has its own marchlike theme; the apprentice David has fussy figures in sixteenth notes, and Walther and Beckmesser have each his theme—musical uniforms, so to speak, with which one can recognize people in darkness or twilight. These reminders accompany both persons and things. When someone speaks of the Feast of St. John or of the song contest, the Pogner motive from the first act is heard. Walther's motive accompanies not only his person but also every allusion to him, to Eva's love, to true poetry in contrast to the guild poetry, etc. Since the facts to which the motives

129

refer constitute more or less the whole plot, and since, moreover, the motives are the most fortunate melodic inspirations of the whole opera, we hear them all evening, singly or together, now from one instrument, now from another, in lighter or darker color.

The listener at first enjoys these little melodies. They occupy his mind, if nothing else. But the more they pitch and toss, the more uncomfortable he feels. For the musician, able and inclined to enjoy essentially technical details and to forget for a time the disagreeable impression of the whole, the orchestral accompaniment has an indisputably compelling charm. Of all the many instruments working at the same time, each is actually playing solo. The skill with which Wagner fits the different leitmotives into the orchestra, modulates them, weaves two or three of them together, is unquestionably admirable. It is only a pity that this "dramatic polyphony," as one could describe it in contrast to musical polyphony, is but a product of cerebration. The magic power of the "unconscious," which should play the first role in the conception of every work of art, recoils from such absolutism of the intellect.

$\mathcal{L}$ The performance will remain a memorable artistic experience for every music lover who heard it, although the opera is not one of those whose beauty is a lifelong source of pleasure and elevation. It is hardly to be regarded as a creation of profound originality or lasting truth and beauty, but rather as a lively experiment, astonishing in the tenacious energy of its execution and its indisputable novelty. In a word, it belongs among the more interesting musical abnormalities. If such abnormalities should become the rule it would mean the end of music, but as an exception they are

130

more stimulating than a dozen run-of-the-mill operas by numerous "correct" composers in Germany, who are honored by a half too much when one calls them half-talents.[10]

---

[10] In concluding his Munich review, Hanslick went on to say: "It is not the creation of a real musical genius, but rather the work of a clever speculator who—an iridescent amalgam of half-poet and half-musician—has fashioned a new system from a talent superficially brilliant but fundamentally spotty. This system is erroneous in principle and, in its consistent implementation, unbeautiful and unmusical."

JOSEFFY

[1874]

IN Raphael Joseffy we have made the acquaintance of a brilliant virtuoso. A pupil of Tausig, and thus a Lisztian of the second generation, he also follows the not especially commendable example of his teachers in giving an entire solo program without assisting artists. The Tausig school is unmistakable in his well-rounded and consummate technique, in the sharply chiseled phrasing, and in the rich nuances of touch—also in a number of secondary matters, more showmanly than pertinent, such as the emphasis upon a single note; the rolling of the wrist where the finger alone and a hand at rest could accomplish what has to be done, without this waste of energy; the mannered pianissimi; etc.

Everything he does is technically perfect and worked out to the finest detail. In passage playing, he is the equal of the great virtuosos; in strength, he is surpassed by many. The secure repose with which he tossed off the *Perpetuum mobile* of Bach's florid music excited general admiration, and the paraphrase of the Spinning Song from *The Flying Dutchman* glistened with elegant perfection. He similarly overcame the technical difficulties of several pieces by Chopin and Schumann with the utmost ease.

But the poetic treasure, particularly in Schumann's character pieces, remained generally obscured. Does he lack the secret resonance of the spirit, or is it the pure pleasure

132

of virtuosity which thus constrains him? He played Schumann's *Traumeswirren*, one of the composer's most gracious little poems, as if it were an *étude* whose objective was the utmost velocity and the ultimate degree of pianissimo—almost in the manner of a musical clock. Even the wonderful middle movement, that characteristically veiled, misty center of the dream, was overexposed to morning sunlight. It was the same with Schumann's wonderful Novelette in D, opus 21, No. 4; we saw the ballroom but not the touching love story enacted there. With the virtuoso everything is worked out and established down to the smallest nuance; not the slightest impulse is left to the inspiration of the moment. There are few pianists today whose technical accomplishments so excite our admiration, but there are also few who leave us so cold.

BRAHMS' SYMPHONY NO. 1[1]

[1876]

SELDOM, if ever, has the entire musical world awaited a composer's first symphony with such tense anticipation—testimony that the unusual was expected of Brahms in this supreme and ultimately difficult form. But the greater the public expectation and the more importunate the demand for a new symphony, the more deliberate and scrupulous was Brahms. Inexorable conscientiousness and stern self-criticism are among his most outstanding characteristics. He always demands the best of himself and dedicates his whole strength to its achievement. He cannot and will not take it easy.

He hesitated a long time over the composition of string quartets, and more than one symphony was consigned, as a study, to the oblivion of a desk drawer. To the urging of his friends he used to reply that he had too much respect for his forerunners, and that one cannot "fool around" these days with a symphony. This severity with himself, this care for detail, is evident in the admirable workmanship of the new symphony. The listener may, indeed, find it rather too evident. He may miss, in all the astonishing contrapuntal art, the immediate communicative effect. And he will not be wholly wrong. The new symphony is so earnest and com-

<hr>

[1] The Vienna *première*, at a concert of the Society of Friends of Music, conducted by Herbeck, on December 17.

plex, so utterly unconcerned with common effects, that it hardly lends itself to quick understanding. This circumstance, although not necessarily a fault, is a misfortune, at least for the first impression. Subsequent repetitions will make it good. Grillparzer's [2] statement, "I strove for effect, not on the public but on myself," could stand as motto for Brahms' symphony.

Even the layman will immediately recognize it as one of the most individual and magnificent works of the symphonic literature. In the first movement, the listener is held by fervent emotional expression, by Faustian conflicts, and by a contrapuntal art as rich as it is severe. The Andante softens this mood with a long-drawn-out, noble song, which experiences surprising interruptions in the course of the movement. The Scherzo strikes me as inferior to the other movements. The theme is wanting in melodic and rhythmic charm, the whole in animation. The abrupt close is utterly inappropriate. The fourth movement begins most significantly with an Adagio in C minor; from darkening clouds the song of the woodland horn rises clear and sweet above the tremolo of the violins. All hearts tremble with the fiddles in anticipation. The entrance of the Allegro, with its simple, beautiful theme, reminiscent of the "Ode to Joy" in the Ninth Symphony, is overpowering as it rises onward and upward, right to the end.

If I say that no composer has come so close to the style of the late Beethoven as Brahms in this finale, I don't mean it as a paradoxical pronouncement but rather as a simple statement of indisputable fact. It is high praise, but it does

---

[2] Franz Grillparzer (1791–1872), Austrian poet and playwright, enthusiastic and gifted musical amateur, friend of Beethoven and Schubert. The quotation is from Grillparzer's diary.

not necessarily attribute to a composer every virtue, least of all every virtue in the highest degree. One-sided greatness is bought at the expense of other virtues. Mozart would not have been Mozart, and Weber would not have been Weber, had they possessed, in addition to their own peculiar charm, the exaltation and the profundity of Beethoven. The latter, on the other hand, lacked the tender fragrance, the melodic enchantment, the delicate intimacy by which Schumann and Mendelssohn are so directly and simply charming—and they are most conspicuously lacking in his greatest last works. In Schumann's little Symphony in D minor, and in Mendelssohn's "Italian" Symphony, there is a sweet enchantment, an intoxicating floral fragrance rarely —and then almost surreptitiously—in evidence in Brahms' symphony. But neither Mendelssohn nor Schumann approaches the late Beethoven. Beethoven's third period is not a prerequisite for their symphonies. Mendelssohn and Schumann incline rather to the point of view of Haydn's and Mozart's musical philosophy—and carry it further. Brahms' quartets and the symphony, on the other hand, could not have been were it not for Beethoven's last period.

This outlook is congenial to Brahms by nature, and he has made himself at home in it. He doesn't imitate, but what he creates from his innermost being is similarly felt. Thus, Brahms recalls Beethoven's symphonic style not only in his individually spiritual and suprasensual expression, the beautiful breadth of his melodies, the daring and originality of his modulations, and his sense of polyphonic structure, but also—and above all—in the manly and noble seriousness of the whole. It has been said of Beethoven's music that one of its chief characteristics is an ethical element that would

136

rather convince than charm. This distinguishes it conspicuously from all "entertainment" music—which is not to say that the latter is artistically worthless. This strong ethical character of Beethoven's music, which is serious even in merriment, and betrays a soul dedicated to the eternal, is also decisively evident in Brahms. In the latter's newest works there is even a good deal of the late Beethoven's darker side. Beethoven's style, toward the end, was often unclear, confused, arbitrary, and his subjectivity frequently descended to mere querulous bad humor. The beautiful clarity, the melodic charm, the estimable popularity of his first and second periods vanished. One could reverse the Goethe motto [3] and say: "What Beethoven wanted in old age (or what one might have wished him) he had in abundance in his youth."

Brahms seems to favor too one-sidedly the great and the serious, the difficult and the complex, and at the expense of sensuous beauty. We would often give the finest contrapuntal device (and they lie bedded away in the symphony by the dozen) for a moment of warm, heart-quickening sunshine. There are three elements—they all play a great role in the most modern German music—for which Brahms has a conspicuous predilection: syncopation, retard, and simultaneous employment of counter-rhythms. In these three points, and particularly with regard to syncopation, he can hardly go further than he has recently gone.

---

[3] Motto of autobiography, *Aus Meinem Leben: Dichtung und Wahrheit* (1811–1833):

> *"Was man in der Jugend sich wünscht,*
> *"Hat man im Alter die Fülle."*

("What you wish for in youth
"You'll have aplenty in old age.")

And so, having relieved myself of these minor reservations, I can continue in the jubilant manner in which I began. The new symphony of Brahms is a possession of which the nation may be proud, an inexhaustible fountain of sincere pleasure and fruitful study.

RICHARD WAGNER'S STAGE
FESTIVAL IN BAYREUTH

———.•.•.———

Bayreuth, August 12, 1876

"IF THE theater at Bayreuth, built at the direction of Richard Wagner solely for the production of his works, and financed by private contributions, should become a reality, as now seems likely, that fact alone may be counted one of the most remarkable events in the whole history of art and the greatest personal success of which any composer ever dreamed."

How well I recalled these words, with which I closed a study of *Das Rheingold* many years ago, when I first saw Wagner's completed theater on the eve of the first festival performance of *Der Ring des Nibelungen*.[1] An extraordinary theatrical experience, and much more! This four-evening-long music drama is a remarkable development in cultural history, not to mention the construction of a special theater solely for its production, and the pilgrimage of thousands of persons from half of Europe to this remote, half-forgotten little town whose name is now indelibly recorded in the history of art. Whether or not the work meets all the expectations of the Bayreuth pilgrims, there is one thing in which all will be of one mind: in admiration of the extraordinary energy and capacity for work and agitation

---

[1] On August 13, 14, 16, and 17.

of the man who, on his own, conceived this phenomenon and carried it through to fulfillment.

The *Ring* represents almost twenty-five years' work, an undertaking to which Wagner returned with redoubled enthusiasm after each interruption (*Die Meistersinger* and *Tristan and Isolde*). As long ago as 1848 he sketched the draft of a *Nibelungen Drama;* shortly thereafter he began the working out of *Siegfrieds Tod.* In 1853 he completed the poem, consisting of four separate dramas, and in the same year he began the composition of the music. Twenty-two years later, in the summer of 1875, he directed the first rehearsals in Bayreuth. And now, a year later, we are witnessing the complete production.

It may be well to preface this report with certain remarks by way of orientation. First, Wagner's poetic material is the Nibelungen saga. This is more easily said than understood, for this saga cycle has assumed many forms in a wide variety of times and places and is extant in widely diverse versions. It has been said of the Germans often enough—and even to the point of injustice—that they are more familiar with Roman and Greek mythology than with the old German, a circumstance which has only slowly and partially been corrected by the praiseworthy efforts of philologists, historians, and poets in the past few decades. In the meantime, the public has become more familiar with the Nibelungen saga through three plays, Raupach's [2] *Nibelungen Hort,* Geibel's [3] *Brünnhild,* and Hebbel's [4] *Nibelungen.*

---

[2] Ernst Benjamin Salomo Raupach (1784–1852), German playwright.
[3] Emanuel Geibel (1815–1884). *Brunnhild* was written in 1858.
[4] Hebbel's trilogy *Die Nibelungen* was written in 1862.

He who expects to find the same treatment in **Wagner's** "Stage Festival" has fallen into the first error. Even the term *Nibelungen* has, for **Wagner**, a different connotation. In the German epic, not only the dwarfs (*Niflungen*), but also the Burgundians are known as *Nibelungen*, and only the latter are referred to when one speaks of *Nibelungenlied* ("Song of the Nibelungs"), *Nibelungennoth* ("Distress of the Nibelungs"), and *Nibelungen Rache* ("Revenge of the Nibelungs"). And it is in this sense that the term has been employed by our modern poets. Wagner, on the other hand, limits it to the race of dwarfs dwelling in the caverns of Nibelheim. His poem recognizes no Burgundians; it simply omits everything historical and treats the whole story as something sagalike, a timeless fairy tale.

There is nothing in Wagner to suggest the impact of Christianity, which runs through the medieval epic like a new geological stratum, and which is employed with such genius in Hebbel's tragedy. Wagner retains hardly more than a few names, and even these are not always similar. Kriemhild, for instance, he calls by her Nordic designation, Gutrune. She, along with Gunther and Hagen, appear first in the fourth drama, almost as minor characters. Whereas our modern dramatists have sought to exploit the purely human elements, the eternally valid and compelling— Siegfried's faithful love for Kriemhild, Hagen's blind loyalty, and, finally, Kriemhild's revenge—we find in Wagner that human beings are intentionally relegated to the background and the stage given over to gods, giants, and dwarfs. Brünnhilde appears not as the much-courted Queen of Iceland but as the superhuman Valkyrie, the favorite daughter of the god Wotan; Kriemhild (Gutrune) does not

141

appear as the revenger, nor Hagen as the unselfish, devoted vassal. Wagner sticks to the older, sterner, more remote, and uncongenial tale of the *Edda*.

In the three initial dramas (*Das Rheingold, Die Walküre,* and *Siegfried*), the full emphasis is upon the super- and subterranean. We shall see that this conception serves Wagner's most brilliant musical specialty—the description of the wonderful through ultimately sublimated tone paintings—although to the disadvantage of the drama, in which we seek to find human beings in human relationships, sharing with them their joy and their sorrow. Not until the fourth evening do we finally meet the human figures familiar to us from the German *Nibelungenlied*, but it is characteristic that this drama, which Wagner originally called *Siegfrieds Tod*, he now calls *Götterdämmerung*, thus laying the full weight not upon the destiny of the participant mortals but upon that of the gods.

If one regards the poem as a whole, without pausing to examine many details, some tiresome, some offensive, one must admire the clever plan of the dramatic action. A character of greatness and austerity, a strong suggestion of natural forces unleashed, runs through the whole. The climaxes are prepared with a sure and experienced hand and presented in the most vivid light. But only the maddest of Wagnerites can regard the *Ring* as a self-sufficient drama capable of standing on its own feet as a dramatic piece, or masterpiece, without musical assistance. If they were spoken rather than sung, these stammering and stuttering alliterations would excite general irritation not unmixed with mirth. Nor did Wagner intend it to stand alone, despite the fact that he published the text long before the score, with assurances that it "could be subjected to the same critical

142

judgments which we are accustomed to apply to a piece written for the legitimate stage." Had Wagner seriously believed this, he would not have written the music. More credible is the author's other assurance, that "this dramatic poem owes its existence entirely to the possibility of a complete musical realization." From the musical point of view, one must acknowledge the disturbing effect of many unconscionably long, often utterly prosaic dialogues, but one must also admire many imposing situations, conceptions of real theatrical genius, which challenge the ultimate of musical exertion.

With regard to the basic conception and substance of the work, I have already stated my principal objections: the exclusion of the purely human factor in favor of gods, giants, dwarfs, and their various magic arts. This tendency is most disturbing in *Das Rheingold*, where it prevails exclusively. It is dominant in *Die Walküre* and *Siegfried*, and fortunately and significantly relaxed in *Götterdämmerung*, by far the most poetically successful of the four episodes. The "moral elevation" and the "purifying ethical effect," so highly praised by Wagner's interpreters, are hard to find. The motives at work in *Das Rheingold* are exclusively deceit, prevarication, violence, and animal sensuality. Even the gods are characterized by covetousness, cunning, and breach of contract. Not a single ray of noble moral feeling penetrates this suffocating mist. *Die Walküre* stands out among the four episodes by virtue of its great dramatic and musical beauties; but we will never overcome the moral repulsion of so ecstatic a revelation of incest. Wagner's predilection for such scenes and problems is well known. Here the offense is even more blameworthy because so utterly unnecessary. Why make Siegmund and Sieglinde brother and sister?

Because it is so written in the old songs of the *Edda?* That does not obligate the dramatist, who can alter as he chooses in the interests of his poetic purposes. Not everything is permissible in the theater which can be found in the epics; our moral views are other than those which prevailed in the eleventh century. Dramatically weakest is *Siegfried.* The two principals, Mime and Siegfried, border on caricature, and the fight with the dragon on comedy. Only the third act, the release of Brünnhilde by Siegfried, reaches significant dramatic heights. *Götterdämmerung* surpasses the three preceding dramas, if only because it has many genuine musical situations. It has, moreover, a forceful exposition and a steady increase of tension and suspense right to the end. The human element comes to the fore; the ghosts of the *Edda* fade away before the heroes of the *Nibelungenlied.*

How far, however, even here, did Wagner depart from the German epic and degrade its characters! How repugnant is the motive, introduced by Wagner, whereby Siegfried, in the service of another, subdues his own beloved bride and, having tamed her, turns her over to him! In this moment we lose all sympathy for Siegfried and hardly regret his violent end. The mitigating device of the magic draught of forgetfulness makes the proceedings no less ugly and distasteful. He who gets around his hero's sensibilities in a physical manner by recourse to potions may be a good druggist but he is a bad poet. Even in *Tristan and Isolde,* the fact that love is solely the effect of a magic potion, a mechanical circumstance, has something repugnant about it. But in *Tristan and Isolde,* at least, Wagner lets his patients off with the one medicine. The unfaithful Siegfried, in his last hour, is given a memory potion to counteract the effects of the previous one, in order that he may, with pretty senti-

144

Wagner lecturing Hanslick as other pro-Wagnerians wait. (In the foreground, from left to right, they are Lindau, Kalbeck, and Speidel.)

mentality à la Werther, breathe a tender address to his beloved. This is not a hero but a puppet. A magic potion by which some simpleton suddenly becomes aware of all the stupidities he has committed in his state of enchantment (or intoxication) is a subject better suited to a farce. In tragedy, where a moral will must dominate, it becomes an absurdity. Whether these magic potions belong to the oldest sagas matters little. We read in the program, indeed, "Poem by Richard Wagner." Who compelled this modern dramatist to incorporate the repugnant and the absurd in his drama? Hebbel and Geibel knew their myth as well as Wagner, but how differently do they both treat the Siegfried tragedy! They discard as unnecessary precisely that which Wagner's predilection for the morally offensive makes the main subject. When we recall Hebbel's tragedy, particularly the plaint of Kriemhild at the bier of Siegfried, how base is Wagner's conception by comparison! Wagner, with his poisonous prescriptions, has robbed the pure, noble figure of Kriemhild (Gutrune) of all its beauty. Hagen, the very model of rough, selfless vassal devotion, becomes a greedy common blackguard. Brünnhilde remains the only sympathetic figure of the lot.

The dramatic action is interwoven with, and interrupted by, scenes pointing back to the stories of the gods in the earlier pieces and intended to establish the interrelationship and continuity. This involvement with the mythological past is a misfortune for the tragedy, because it is arbitrary and unmotivated and remains unintelligible to the listener. The transformation of the original title, *Siegfrieds Tod*, into the present, *Götterdämmerung*, tells all. It shows plainly how Wagner subsequently distorted and confused the original simple and clear relationships of the Siegfried tragedy. In the second volume of his *Collected Writings*, he tells of the original conception of his tragedy, *Siegfrieds Tod*; there was at this time no talk of a *Götterdämmerung*. Actually, Siegfried's death has nothing whatever to do with the twilight of the gods, which runs through the German mythology as a mysterious prophecy. The arbitrariness and willfullness with which Wagner insists on the ring as the driving and unifying motive of all four dramas is avenged in the impression made by the whole. The supernatural presuppositions have unnatural and unintelligible consequences. The poet himself appears now and again to have gulped down a draught of forgetfulness. Of the much-sung power of the ring, which gives dominion over the world to its possessor, there is nothing to be heard from any of its respective possessors, from Wotan and Fafner to Brünnhilde. And Siegfried, having drunk the potion which should rob him of all recollection of Brünnhilde, promptly finds his way back to her and addresses her, as she approaches him, as "Brünnhilde!" Wagner wrote the exposition scene for *Götterdämmerung* not for dramatic reasons but out of "profound" primeval mysticism: the three Norns (daughters of Erda) toss the cord from one to another, symbolizing the warp and woof of the world's destiny. The confusion between the laws of the epic and the laws of the theater, between the merely symbolic and the scenically portrayed, is here conspicuous enough.

An undertaking like that at Bayreuth, based on the unique and the utterly new, challenges every prevailing standard of criticism. But since the form of the dramatic trilogy exists in ancient Greek as well as in modern German literature, one cannot resist the analogy or the pertinence of Grillparzer's words when (in his autobiography) he comments on his treatment of the Medea legend. "The trilogy, or the treatment of any dramatic material in multiple parts," he says, "is in itself a bad form. The drama is ever of the present and must contain within itself all that pertains to the action." Thus he finds the form of Schiller's *Wallenstein* faulty, regardless of the fine quality of the poesy. This is true of the *Ring* to a far greater extent.

ii— THE THEATER

Bayreuth, August 14, 1876

And why, of all places, Bayreuth?

Wagner had not originally intended the construction of a new theater in this town.[1] He thought first of using the old Bayreuth opera house, a stately monument of former feudal magnificence. But the more he considered the necessary alterations, the less did it seem that the house could suffice. Wagner soon recognized that, reforming from scratch, he would have to build from scratch, and that a new operatic genre would require a new theater. But he stuck to tiny, out-of-the-way Bayreuth in order that listeners might not be distracted from his work by urban disturbances. In this he counted upon the festive mood of an audience predisposed in his favor. According to the unanimous statements of numerous festival guests, he appears to have miscalculated.

A little town like Bayreuth is in no way prepared for the reception of so many visitors. Not only are there no luxuries; often enough there are not even the necessities. I doubt that the enjoyment of art is furthered by being uncomfortably housed for a week, sleeping badly, eating wretchedly, and, after a strenuous five or six hours' per-

---

[1] Actually, he first considered building his theater in Munich.

formance of opera, being uncertain of securing a modest snack. Even yesterday I saw many who had arrived in the flush of enthusiasm crawling up the hot, dusty street to the distant Wagner Theater in a considerably more sober frame of mind. The participating artists, too, have expressed fully justified reservations. How easily, they say, could many a deficiency, which came to light only at the dress rehearsals (inadequate casting of minor roles, etc.) have been corrected in a big city, while here a change is no longer possible. A distinguished member of the orchestra arrived with a cello half-ruined on the journey. In any larger city it could have easily been repaired; Bayreuth, however, has no instrument maker. There is no need to go any further with this chapter, which, under the heading, "He who never ate his bread in Bayreuth," is better fitted for humorous treatment. I only wish to state my increased conviction that a major artistic undertaking belongs in a major city.

As to the purpose of the Wagner Theater, one is often asked, "Does it really exist for the *Ring* alone?" Wagner's initial answer was: "This new institution should represent nothing other than the geographically fixed meeting place of the best theatrical talents of Germany for the exercise and execution of their art in a superior and original manner" —thus, model performances as such. In a "final report," Wagner narrows the circle and observes that the Bayreuth performances may embrace "in ever-widening compass every type of dramatic work which, because of the original- ity of its conception and its truly German character, could lay claim to a particularly correct production." That such works do not include original Italian operas, such as *Don Giovanni*, or French, such as *Armide*, or operas with spoken dialogue, such as *Der Freischütz* and *Fidelio*, will be understood by everyone well versed in Wagner's writings. And, indeed, it would be madness to travel all the way to Bayreuth solely to hear operas by Mozart, Beethoven, and Weber which are given quite satisfactorily in our court theaters. There is no longer any doubt that the theater erected for the *Nibelungen* will henceforth belong exclusively to the *Nibelungen*. But this leads inevitably to the dilemma: either the *Ring* is really performable only in this Festival Theater—in which case Wagner's enormous exertion is in no proportion to a fleeting success—or it can and will be given in other major theaters—in which case the erection of so costly a private theater would seem to be a singular luxury. However inexorably Wagner may condemn our theaters, with which he "wishes to have no further traffic," everything points to the second assumption, and Wagner himself will hardly be able to resist. Every serious work of art requires repeated hearing; it achieves its full effect and appreciation only through a repeated and periodically renewed impression. To wish to limit the greatest work of his career to Bayreuth suggests a kind of artistic suicide. The number of wealthy Bayreuth pilgrims is not, by far, what Wagner must desire for his work; least of all do these "patrons" represent the German people, for whom, indeed, the *Ring* was intended. If Wagner does not intend to please merely a handful of persons in one place, and once and forever, but rather therewith to take root in the nation, then he must consign it to the cursed "opera houses." Germany's leading theaters will unquestionably be able to present it in a satisfactory manner, scenically and musically. Should it prove unable to survive in Vienna, Munich, Berlin, and Dresden, simply because the tinted steam is less abundant or because the swimming machines move more slowly, then something must be wrong with the main factor, the musical core of the work. The more genuine and strong the inner poetical force of a dramatic work, the more easily does it bear imperfections of performance and staging. *Don Giovanni* and *Der Freischütz*, *Egmont* [2] and *Die Räuber* [3] are effective even in modest provincial theaters. And Wagner's operas, those to which he owes his fame, his popularity, and the possibility of the whole Bayreuth undertaking—*Tannhäuser*, *The Flying Dutchman*, *Lohengrin*— have won him his greatest following on small stages. The brilliant success of the *Ring* in Bayreuth—it was practically assured—is still no true test of the worth and effect of the composition. Bayreuth must travel to Europe for that, now that Europe has traveled to Bayreuth.

The Wagner Theater itself is one of the most interesting and instructive of curiosities, not for its exterior, which is rather meager, and impressive only because of its situation, but rather because of the ingenious novelties of its interior arrangement. Even the entrance to the auditorium is surprising: rows of seats rising in the style of an amphitheater in a semicircle, behind them a low gallery, the Royal Box. Otherwise there are no boxes in the entire house; in their place are columns right and left. There is no chandelier, no prompter's box. Vision is equally good from every seat. One sees the proceedings on the stage without obstruction— and nothing else. At the beginning of a performance the auditorium is completely darkened; the brightly lighted stage, with neither spotlights nor footlights in evidence, appears like a brilliantly colored picture in a dark frame. Many scenes have almost the effect of transparent pictures

---

[2] By Goethe.   [3] *The Robbers* by Schiller.

or views in a diorama. Wagner claims "that the scenic picture should appear to the spectator with the inapproachability of an apparition in a dream."

Most noteworthy of all is the invisible orchestra, the "mystical abyss," as Wagner calls it, "because its mission is to separate the real from the ideal." The orchestra is set so deep that one is reminded of the engine room of a steamship. It is, moreover, almost entirely hidden by a kind of tin roof. The musicians haven't the slightest view of the stage or of the public; only the conductor can see the singers, and not even he can see the audience. Wagner's inspired idea of sparing us the disturbing spectacle of the musicians' fiddling and puffing and pounding is something to which I gave my blessing long ago and for which, following the Munich example, I have even campaigned. The lowering of the orchestra is one of the most reasonable and enduring of Wagner's reforms; it has already taken hold in the legitimate theaters (where its necessity is even more obvious), and it has become a blessing of our Burgtheater. And yet, it seems to me that Wagner has gone too far, or to put it better, too deep; for in the whole of *Das Rheingold* I missed, if not the precision, at least the brilliance of the orchestra. Even the stormy passages sound muffled and dampened. This is, of course, a boon for the singers, but at some cost to the role of the instruments, to which, especially in this work, is assigned much of the most significant and the most beautiful. From this muffled sound hardly anyone would have guessed the numerical strength of the orchestra, whose eight harps sound like two or three. But not only in important matters, such as the position of the orchestra, but also in secondary matters, Wagner has been at pains to rearrange things so as avoid as much as possible

152

any resemblance to our "opera houses." Thus, the signal at the beginning of each piece and each act is given not by a bell but by a fanfare of trumpets; the curtain, instead of being rung up and down, is parted in the middle, etc.

III— THE MUSIC

Bayreuth, August 18, 1876

Yesterday we had *Götterdämmerung* as the finale of the whole cycle. With the Bayreuth program now completed, the music of the future has become a force of the present— outwardly, at least, and for the moment. The critic indulges in prophecies about art with as little eagerness as the serious astronomer in prophecies about the weather. But this much is highly probable: the style of Wagner's *Ring* will not be the music of the future; it will be, at best, one style among many, possibly only a yeast for the fermentation of new developments harking back to the old. Wagner's most recent reform does not represent an enrichment, an extension, a renewal of music in the sense that the art of Mozart, Beethoven, Weber, and Schumann did; it is, on the contrary, a distortion, a perversion of basic musical laws, a style contrary to the nature of human hearing and feeling. One could say of this tone poetry: there is music in it, but it isn't music.

To raise one point immediately for the temporary orientation of the reader: through four evenings we hear singing upon the stage without independent, distinct melodies, without a single duet, trio, ensemble, chorus, or finale. The exceptions vanish as fleeting moments in the

153

whole. This alone demonstrates that the knife is applied not to an outward form but to the living roots of dramatic music. Opera lovers who do not know *Tristan* and the *Ring* are prone to suspect that the opponents of these late works are Wagner opponents altogether. They think only in terms of *The Flying Dutchman* or *Tannhäuser*, which are as different from this newest music as two things can be within the same art. One can regard *Tannhäuser* as one of the most beautiful of operas and think the opposite of the *Ring*; and, indeed, one must. For what made the fortune of Wagner's earlier operas, and continues to make it, is the firm bond of the descriptive, specifically dramatic element with the charm of the comprehensible melody, the alternation of dialogue with ensembles, choruses, and finales, musically conceived and formed. In the *Ring* Wagner has removed all trace of anything reminiscent of these virtues. Even *Die Meistersinger*, in which separate vocal melody occurs less frequently but, for all that, in certain magnificent examples, seems by comparison a musically charming and popularly comprehensible work.

The *Ring* is, in fact, something entirely new, something essentially different from all that has gone before, a thing alone and apart. As such, as an imaginative experiment, inexhaustibly instructive for the musician, it has its enduring significance. That it will ever become popular in the way that Mozart's or Weber's operas are popular appears improbable. Three main considerations distinguish this music in principle from all previous operas, including Wagner's: first, the absence of independent, separate vocal melodies, replaced here by a kind of exalted recitative with the "endless melody" in the orchestra as the basis; second, the dissolution of all form, not just the usual forms (arias, duets, etc.) but of symmetry, of musical logic developed in accordance with laws; third, the exclusion of multiple-voiced pieces, of duets, trios, choruses, and finales, not counting a few odd passing entrances.

Let us hear the master's words on his new musical methods. He has, says Wagner, "elevated the dramatic dialogue itself as the main substance of the musical production, whereas in the real 'opera' the moments of lyrical dalliance imposed upon the action specifically for this purpose have been regarded as sufficient for the only kind of musical production heretofore considered possible. It is music which, while independently awakening our sensibilities to the motives of the action in their widest ramifications, makes it possible to present just this action with drastic precision; since the protagonists do not, in the sense of conscious reflection, have to inform us of their motivations, the dialogue gains a naïve precision which constitutes the life of the drama."

It reads well enough, but Wagner's objective has, in the implementation, in no way been attained, and the complete amalgamation of opera and drama remains an illusion. The ostensible equality of word and tone renders impossible the full effectiveness of either. It is natural to tone that it broaden out and extend the duration of the word. That is why continuous dialogue belongs to the drama, and sung melody to the opera. The separation of the two is not unnatural; on the contrary, it is Wagner's method of uniting them that is unnatural. The artificial *Singsprechen* or *Sprechsingen* of the *Ring* is an adequate substitute neither for the spoken word of the drama nor for the sung word of the opera, if only because with most singers one doesn't understand the text anyway, and even with the best only here and there. And, since the auditorium of the Festival Theater is entirely darkened, there is not even the possibility of consulting the libretto. Thus we sit there, helpless and bored, amid these endless dialogues, thirsting equally for articulate speech and intelligible melody. And what dialogue! Never have human beings spoken to one another in this fashion, probably not even gods. Jumping here and there in awkward intervals, always slow, always glum, exaggerated, one dialogue is essentially like another!

Since, in the "music drama," the people involved are not distinguished from one another by the character of the vocal melodies assigned them, as in the old-fashioned "opera" (Don Giovanni and Leporello, Donna Anna and Zerlina, Max and Caspar),[1] but are identical in the physiognomy of their *Sprechton*, Wagner has sought to fill the gap with the so-called leitmotives in the orchestra. He had already employed this musico-psychological aid rather extensively in *Tannhäuser* and *Lohengrin;* he overdid it in *Die Meistersinger*. In the *Ring* he has carried it to the point where it becomes an actual arithmetical problem. It is easy to retain the few melodically and rhythmically pregnant leitmotives of *Tannhäuser* or *Lohengrin*. But how does Wagner proceed in the *Ring?* The answer is given in a brochure by H. von Wolzogen,[2] *Thematic Guide*, a musical Baedeker without which no respectable tourist here dares to be seen and which is on sale everywhere in Bayreuth. Anywhere but in Bayreuth one might well find such a book funny. The serious and sad thing about it is simply that it

---

[1] In *Der Freischütz*.

[2] Hans Paul Freiherr von Wolzogen (1848–1938), one of Wagner's most ardent disciples and onetime editor of the *Bayreuther Blätter*. The book referred to is *Thematische Leitfäden durch die Musik von Richard Wagner's Festspiel "Der Ring des Nibelungen"* (1876).

is necessary. Wolzogen cites no fewer than ninety separate and distinct leitmotives which the hapless festival visitor should impress upon his memory and recognize wherever they turn up in the tonal mass of four evenings. Not only persons but also inanimate objects have their leit- or *leib*-motives,[3] which bob up here and there and everywhere, and in the most mysterious relationships. Thus we have the "ring" motive, the motives of "subjugation," of the "threat," of the "gold of the Rhine," of "the tired Sieg-mund," of the "sword," of the "giant," of the "dwarf," of the "curse," of the "dragon," and of "revenge"; the motives of Alberich, Siegfried, Wotan, and so on, to No. 90. This rich musical wardrobe in which the heroes share is changed, however, only at their feet, in the orchestra; on the stage they have no melodic finery whatsoever.

The leitmotives are, with few exceptions (the "Ride of the Valkyries," the "Valhalla" motive, the "arrival" mo-tive, Siegfried's horn call), of meager melodic and rhythmic substance, made up of only a few notes, and often very much alike. Only an extraordinary ear and memory can retain them all. And supposing that one has actually accomplished it and has recognized that the orchestra is alluding here to the giants, there to the gods, and somewhere else to the giants and gods together, has anything really great been achieved? It is simply a matter of comprehension, a conscious process of comparison and association. Full enjoyment and reception are impossible when understanding and memory must be ever on the alert to catch the wary allusion. This mystico-allegoric tendency in the *Ring* is reminiscent in many respects of Part II of Goethe's *Faust*, whose poetic

---

[3] A play on words, *Leib* meaning body, and personal, if used as a prefix.

effect is diminished by just this habit on the part of the poet of indulging in "hidden inner meanings" which torture the reader as riddles. Whether a given composition derives from the depths of musical sensibility or from the result of imaginative contrivance cannot—as evident as it may appear to the individual—be proved scientifically.

In the old pre-*Nibelungen* "opera," the composer followed the universal rules of musical logic, fashioned a succession of individual organisms, each intelligible in itself. In "opera" the masters gave us music understandable in its unity, pleasurable in its beauty, and dramatic in its inner identification with the action. They have demonstrated a hundred times that the "absolute melody," so despised by Wagner, can also be eminently dramatic and, in multiple-voiced pieces, particularly in finales, can energetically compress and complete the progress of the action. To abolish the multiple-voiced song, duet, trio, and chorus as ostensibly "undramatic" is to ignore the most valuable accomplishments of the art of music and to go back two hundred years to the musical kindergarten. It is the most beautiful property of music, its most characteristic charm, its greatest advantage over the drama, that it permits two and more persons, even whole masses, to speak out at once. This treasure, for which the poet must envy the musician, Wagner heaves out of the window as superfluous. In the *Ring* there may be two, three, or six persons standing together on the stage, but, aside from insignificant and fleeting exceptions, they never sing together; they speak, instead, as in court proceedings, one after the other. Only he who has experienced it can fully appreciate what a torture it is to follow this musical goose step for a whole evening. But since Wagner continues the tyranny of this monodic style through four evenings in a row, he compels us, with almost suicidal pointedness, to attack the nonsense of his method and to long for the much-abused old-fashioned "opera."

On top of that is the incredible and iniquitous length of the individual scenes and conversations. I do not overlook the new element of greatness and exaltation which Wagner gives to his work by limiting each act to only two or three episodes, each unfolding in serene breadth, often appearing, like plastic pictures, to stand still. The *Ring* is most advantageously distinguished from the restless change of scene and surplus action in our "grand opera" precisely through this simplicity. But an epic breadth must not be permitted to jeopardize the whole drama. It is hard to understand how so theater-wise a dramatic composer should suddenly lose all sense of proportion and fail to sense that conversations such as Wotan's with Fricka, with Brünnhilde, with Mime, etc., try the listener's patience to the utmost. One seeks in vain a dramatic or musical justification for the unheard-of length of the "Valhalla" scene in *Das Rheingold*, of the dialogues in the second act of *Die Walkure*, of the six questions in *Siegfried*, etc.

An eloquent and imaginative advocate of Wagner's, Ludwig Ehlert,[4] suggests in his critique of *Tristan and Isolde* that in order to assure the opera's survival every episode might be considerably shortened. Now one may well ask: Where has there ever been a real dramatic composer in whose operas any piece might be cut at will without damage? But in listening to the *Ring* I felt that every scene could stand not only the most extensive cuts but also the most extensive expansion. The new method of "dialogue music

---

[4] (1825–1884), German pianist, composer, and critic, a pupil of Mendelssohn.

drama" does, indeed, reject every thought of musical proportion; it is the formless infinite. Wagner, to be sure, protests that his "stage plays" should not be criticized from the standpoint of music. But then why does he write music, and a lot of music at that—four whole evenings of it?

In many places, indeed, one is confronted with musical beauties, brilliantly effective, strong as well as tender. It is as if the new Wagner were recalling the old. It is hardly necessary to cite these fine moments specifically: the song of the Rhine Maidens in the first and last works, Siegmund's "Spring Song," the "Magic Fire Music," the "Ride of the Valkyries," the "Forest Murmurs," among others. In the Bayreuth performances, one could note how each such flower of blooming melody was remarked with visible pleasure by the listeners and literally pressed to their hearts. When, after two hours of monodic steppe, there appears a bit of multiple-voiced song—the closing chords of the three Rhine Maidens, the group singing of the Valkyries, the few triads at the close of the love duet in *Siegfried*—one can see in the faces of the listeners a joyous thrill, as if they had been released from long imprisonment. These are noteworthy symptoms. They bear eloquent witness to the fact that the musical nature of human beings cannot be denied or suppressed, that Wagner's new methods are not a reform of outlived traditions but an assault upon musical sensibilities inherent within us and cultivated by centuries of education. Let the assault be undertaken with the most brilliant weapons of the intellect—nature resists it and throws the besieger back at will with a few roses and violets.

The descriptive powers of Wagner's fantasy, the astonishing mastery of his orchestral technique, and many musical beauties exert a magic force to which we surrender

160

readily and gratefully. These beautiful details, which some-how sneak in behind the back of the system, do not prevent the system itself, the tyranny of the word, the tuneless dia-logue, the dreary monotony, from poisoning the whole. The strange coloristic splendor of the *Ring*, the fascinating fra-grance of the orchestra, surround us with a demoniac charm. But as Tannhäuser longed for the familiar and loved sound of the bells of earth, so we soon long with all our hearts for the melodic blessing of our old music.

iv— THE PRODUCTION AND THE OVER-ALL IMPRESSION

Bayreuth, August 19, 1876

Were the impression which Wagner's *Ring* made upon the audience predominantly concerned with the music, it would have to be described as depressing. But Wagner's versatility, certainly the most brilliant aspect of his talent, allows him to work simultaneously with the special talents of the musician, the painter, the librettist, and the stage director, and he often achieves through the latter three that which the first could not have effected alone. The painter's fantasy is inexhaustibly at work in the *Ring*, and from it appears to have stemmed the initial impulse for many scenes. If one studies the photographs of the sets so poetically de-vised by Joseph Hoffmann, one cannot escape the thought that such scenes must have first appeared in Wagner's im-agination and inspired the appropriate music.

Thus it is with the first scene of *Das Rheingold*. The

161

Rhine Maidens, singing and swimming in the Rhine, encompassed for a hundred and thirty-six measures by no more than the diffused chord of E-flat major, provide a tableau which achieves a predominantly visual effect. But this scene, unquestionably the best of *Das Rheingold*, is essentially musical in conception. From that point on, the musical charm of the work declines rapidly, and since, at the same time, the listener's sensibilities, taxed for almost three hours without interruption, wear thin, he leaves with the impression of utter monotony. I shall waste no words on the indigestible German stammered in *Das Rheingold* and offered as poetry. It would, indeed, be a misfortune if familiarity with this *Nibelungen* style, together with indiscriminate admiration for everything that comes from Wagner, were gradually so to dull public perception as to render it impervious to the ugliness of such diction.

The second drama, *Die Walküre*, begins very impressively with the entrance of the fugitive Siegfried into Hunding's house. The tedious breadth of the scene at the table (Siegmund, Hunding, and Sieglinde) is compensated for, gradually, in the course of the love duet between Siegmund and Sieglinde, in which the B-flat major episode, *"Winterstürme wichen dem Wonnemond,"* enters like long-missed sunlight. Here we are revived by a ray of melodious, sustained song.

The second act is an abyss of boredom. Wotan appears, holds a long conversation with his wife, and then, turning to Brünnhilde, gives an autobiographical lecture covering eight full pages of text. This utterly tuneless, plodding narrative, in slow tempo, engulfs us like an inconsolable broad sea from which only the meager crumbs of a few leitmotives come floating toward us out of the orchestra. Scenes like

162

this recall the medieval torture of waking a sleep-crazed prisoner by stabbing him with a needle at every nod. We have heard even Wagnerites characterize this second act as a disaster. It is entirely unnecessary, since with two cuts both episodes could be done away with, painlessly. *Die Walküre* has, indeed, a very loose relationship with the action of the whole; it tells nothing of the fateful ring which we haven't already learned in *Das Rheingold*, and only Brünnhilde's punishment is important for the progress of the drama.

In the third act, there is a return to music of significant force and fullness, first through the Valkyries, whose wild and disordered ensemble enlivens the scene advantageously. The "Ride of the Valkyries" and the "Magic Fire Music" are two brilliant specimens of daring tone painting, abundantly familiar from concert performances. Taking their dramatic connotation into consideration, I had, in my reviews of them, predicted a much greater effect than they actually seemed to have had in Bayreuth. There are two possible explanations: first, the "mystic abyss" of the Bayreuth Theater offered nothing like the brilliance and verve of a freely exposed concert orchestra; second, both pieces occur toward the end of the opera and are thus heard by an audience exhausted and dulled by what has gone before.

Contrary to all expectations, *Siegfried* had a greater effect than *Die Walküre*. It was not an entirely inexplicable surprise. A fresh tone is felt in the first act, something realistic, a boyish naturalness. This is dissipated, to be sure, in the disproportionate length of the scenes and musical episodes, but the effect is refreshing after the stilted progress of the first two evenings. But what can one say of Wotan's long scene with the dwarf? Each gives the other three questions, and each answers with the detailed precision of a well-tutored candidate at a school examination. The whole scene, utterly superfluous from the dramatic point of view, is an oppressive bore. The listeners are abandoned to the diversion of hunting hidden leitmotives in the orchestra ("Where is the cat, where is the bear?"). Generally speaking, one can be certain that with the appearance of so much as the point of Wotan's spear, a half hour of emphatic boredom is in store. Should this "exalted god," who never knows what is needed or does the right thing, who yields in the first drama to a stupid giant, in the second to his domineering wife, and in the third to an impudent youth— should this unctuous pedant be revered as the godly ideal of the German people?

For the illustration of the forging of the sword, the orchestra provides admirable tone painting. Siegfried's much-praised "Forge Song" is more funereal than joyous. Wagner simply is not acquainted with naïve, natural joyousness. He has just as little knack for the comical, as we know from Beckmesser. In the characterization of Mime he has been totally unable to distinguish between the comical and the tedious.

The second act introduces us to a forest near the cavern of the *Lindwurm*. Following a scene between Alberich and Wotan, a model of forced, anti-lingual declamation, comes the high point of the whole score, the "Forest Murmurs." Siegfried reclines under a tree, listening to the rustling of the leaves and the song of the birds. Here Wagner's virtuosity as a tone painter enjoys its most genuine triumph, derived, as it is, from natural materials and imbued with purely human impressions. Here, as in his concert piece, *Siegfried Idyl*, he portrays the song of the birds with a fidelity to nature achieved neither by Haydn in *The Creation* nor by Beethoven in the "Pastoral" Symphony.

Now Siegfried comes face to face with the giant Fafner as the *Lindwurm* (dragon), roaring and spitting fire. Wagner has composed the scene in deadly earnest, but the effect is comical, particularly at the end, when the croaking *Lindwurm* becomes sentimental and offers his murderer confidential information. A woodland bird, whose language Siegfried now understands, shows him the way to Brünnhilde. The song of the bird is an illuminating example of how much better Wagner can make an orchestra sing than he can the human voice.

The third act brings Siegfried to Brünnhilde. First, however, we have two heavy scenes to survive. Wotan appears in a rocky cleft and summons Erda from below. He asks her weighty questions, but she, the "fountain of knowledge," knows absolutely nothing, and disappears. It seems unlikely that ten persons in the theater were quite in the clear about this "Erda." I was not among them. Enter Siegfried. A dispute, expressed in rather uninhibited language, develops between him and Wotan, who attempts to bar his way to Brünnhilde. Finally, Siegfried smashes Wotan's spear, whereupon this divine night watchman slinks away, more helpless than ever. An orchestral interlude of tumultuous forces, conjuring up the motives of the "Ride of the Valkyries" and the "Magic Fire Music," conducts us at once through fire and glowing smoke to Brünnhilde's resting place. The scene between Siegfried and Brünnhilde is of exhausting length. Brünnhilde's awakening is tenderly depicted, and in the E major section of the love duet, *"Ewig bin ich,"* the melody blossoms more freely and expressively. The duet falls off lamentably toward the end through the inexplicable introduction of a stiff theme in descending fourths (C major, *alla breve*). These exalted accents, of which Wagner is so proud—the passionate groaning and moaning, crying out and collapsing—border offensively on the ultimate limits of a flaming, insatiable sensuality. The textual excesses become sheer nonsense (*"Göttliche Ruhe ras't mir in Wogen,"* etc.—"godlike repose is plunged into tempest"). The poet and composer of this scene has a fine right to poke fun at the "high-flown Schumann"!

Götterdämmerung strikes me as the most successful, dramatically, of the cycle; here we move about again on our own earth and among our flesh-and-blood fellows. We even have a real plot, although the intrusion of the "draught of forgetfulness," which affected me so unpleasantly in prospect, proved even more repulsive and incomprehensible in performance. Executed with truly beelike industry, even more carefully than in the preceding dramas, the music of *Götterdämmerung* is noticeably inferior. The first three dramas may seem sterile and unnatural in their musical method, sometimes violent and abstruse, but they are animated by quicker, warmer blood and a more original invention. This is possibly due to their earlier origin. *Götterdämmerung*, on the other hand, is oppressed by a singular exhaustion and fatigue, something like the approaching affliction of middle age.

Someone has said—and not unjustly—that the action in *Götterdämmerung* is distinct from the other three dramas, while the music, on the whole, is the same. The music is constructed predominantly upon the leitmotives of the first three: thus, from the same material and according to the same familiar method. The essential musical distinction consists in the presence—albeit sporadic—of multiple-voiced song. The unexpected concession of a real male chorus, in particular, must come as a pleasant surprise to listeners so long subjected to monodic discipline. I attribute the pleasure afforded by the mad merriment of Gunther's men to simple delight in the long-denied sound of men's voices in concert. Of incomparably more beautiful invention is the charming glimmer of the song of the Rhine Maidens in the third act. Neither the first nor second act is without beautiful, melodious moments, but they all possess, like Siegfried, a Tarnhelm under which they quickly disappear or change at will into something else.

In the first act, the parting of Siegfried and Brünnhilde makes the deepest impression. Studying single phrases of the great duet individually and separately, one finds them full of substance and passion; taken as a whole, this declamatory song, continually goading itself on to ecstasy, resembles a succession of expressive interjections making no cohesive speech. At first excited, the listener gradually gives way to fatigue and finally to distraction; with the best of intentions he can no longer remain attentive. The subsequent orchestral postlude, with the horn fanfare of the departing Siegfried, makes a nice effect. The piece has the utmost musical charm and cohesiveness, particularly by virtue of the attractive contrapuntal ornamentation surrounding that vigorous horn call.

"Siegfried's Death" is much less satisfactory. What the dying man sings with astonishing lung power seems almost superfluous in the dazzling fluctuation of the orchestra, which—with four harps, trombones, kettle drums, and the most piercing high tones of the violins—excites acute nervous irritation. More significant and more gripping than Siegfried's Death Song is the Funeral March, now intoned for the departed hero. It is an instrumental necrologue assembled from earlier Siegfried motives, and rather a work of imaginative reflection than of immediate creative force. Brünnhilde's monologue at Siegfried's bier is simply colossal. She sends the ravens home and hurls the torch into the pyre. The way in which the croaking birds and their upward flight are pictured by the muted trumpets and whirring figurations in the violins, and the way in which the crackling of the flames is represented by the most delicate and ingenious handling of the brass and percussion—all this belongs among the most distinguished accomplishments of a master unrivaled in this kind of painting. Brünnhilde's song rises to the height of exaltation, continuously in the extreme upper range and under the most violent strain, soaring above the hurricane of the orchestra. Then, for a moment, the orchestra subsides in deference to a tender passage for Brünnhilde, and we are touched as by a supernatural revelation. Now, following Brünnhilde's death, comes the *"Götterdämmerung,"* the end of the world; with a mighty crash, Wagner releases all the demons of the orchestra and so overwhelms us that we are hardly capable even of admiring the technique with which it is all accomplished.

The best things in *Götterdämmerung* made an uncommon, intellectually stimulating, sensuously dazzling impression, but not a profound or enduring one. The music has, at best, the fascination of a magic charm; it does not have the faculty of making the heart rejoice, which is the essential characteristic of a work of art. One must certainly admit its incomparable objectivity and its dazzling richness of color. One has only to read the text to admire Wagner's painter's eye and his genius for theatrical effect. How wonderfully it is all thought out and how vividly it is all seen! How Siegfried rides through the flames to the Rhine after taking leave of Brünnhilde! How the latter, at Siegfried's bier, springs upon her horse and leaps into the flaming pyre! These are pictures such as have never before been offered upon the stage. In keeping with this mission, Wagner's music is first and foremost graphic and decorative. The orchestra, in the utmost refinement of sound, is the essential element. The singing voices alternate between monotonous declamation and explosive outbursts of unbounded passion. One can listen to this incoherent ardor amidst the fluctuations of deafening and nerve-racking orchestral effects for only a short time without relaxation. The majority of listeners were already more or less exhausted after the second act. Who could endure four consecutive evenings of this exaltation?

The musical style is familiar from the preceding parts; it is completely stereotyped. Wagner is mannered; an inspired genius, but still a mannerist. His eccentricities of declamation, modulation, and harmonization are imposed on every kind of material. In this style he could probably write ten more operas without undue effort or inspiration. Although the element of passionate exaltation never seems to achieve satiety, it is often difficult to believe in its truth and necessity. It is reminiscent of many of Victor Hugo's poems, products of inner coldness which imagine themselves glowing and inspired. The music to *Götterdämmerung* characterizes its author anew as a brilliant specialist, rather adjacent to music than of it. It is unthinkable that his method shall be, as he contends, the only valid opera style from now on, the absolute "art work of the future." When an art arrives at a period of utmost luxury, it is already on the decline. Wagner's opera style recognizes only superlatives; but a superlative has no future. It is the end, not the beginning.

From *Lohengrin* on, Wagner broke a new path, dangerous to life and limb; and this path is for him alone. He who follows will break his neck, and the public will contemplate the disaster with indifference.

I have given here only a fleeting impression of the four *Nibelungen* dramas; there can be no thought of an intensive analysis. Nor can there be any thought, as I have said before, of a purely musical impression. Wagner felt, indeed, that the pleasure of listening would be insufficient for so long a period of incarceration in the theater, and he has provided much to occupy the eye as well. Never before has such an accumulation of scenic wonders been offered in an opera. Devices heretofore held impossible—or, more accurately, unthought of—follow one on top of another: the Rhine Maidens swimming deep in the water; the gods strolling over a rainbow; the transformation of Alberich, first into a serpent, then into a toad; the magic fire; the twilight of the gods, etc. In all this, the poet has given the composer the widest possible scope for his brilliant virtuosity—tone painting. But should it be the highest ambition of the dramatic composer to make music for a succession of magic contrivances?

Actually, the *Ring* has much in common with the genre of magic tricks and fairy tales. These utterly material effects are in direct contradiction to the pure idealism which Wagner claims for his works. He strives everywhere for the strongest sensual impression, and with every available means. The mysterious heaving of the invisible orchestra gives the listener a mild opium jag even before the rise of the curtain; he is subjected to the enduring impression of a magically lighted fairy-tale scene before anyone on the stage has opened his mouth. In the numerous night scenes, a dazzling electric light plays upon the figure of the principal character, while tinted steam undulates upon and above the stage. This steam, which in *Das Rheingold* even takes the place of a change-of-scene curtain, constitutes the most powerful weapon in Wagner's new dramatic arsenal. As a formless, fantastic, sensually fascinating element, it has a special affinity with Wagner's musical principles. He himself compares the music emanating from his invisible orchestra with the "steams rising up from under Pythia's tripod," which "introduces the listener to an exalted condition of clairvoyance." From here it is only a step to the artful employment of certain smells and odors—psychology recognizes them, indeed, as particularly stimulating and exciting.

We are quite in earnest. Who does not know from children's fairy tales that fairies are encompassed by a sweet smell of roses, while the devil regularly makes off in a stink of sulphur? The principle of allowing all atmosphere-promoting stimulants to co-operate in the heightening of certain sensations and images should draw upon the sympathetic and pleasurable faculties of the olfactory nerves. Wagner has utilized all the modern advances of applied science. We have seen with astonishment the colossal machinery, the gas apparatus, the steam machines above and below the stage at Bayreuth. Wagner could as little have composed the *Ring* before the invention of the electric light as without the harp and bass tuba. Thus it is that the element of color in the broadest sense disguises the paltry design in his newest works and usurps for itself an unheard-of self-sufficiency. It is through its sensually fascinating magic that this music, as a direct nervous stimulant, works so powerfully upon the audience and upon the female audience particularly. The professional musician's interest in this highly advanced orchestral technique has rather to do with "how it is all accomplished." I underestimate neither the one nor the other; but neither is entitled to violent domination. Neither the conductor's technical gourmet's interest, nor the hashish dream of the ecstatic female, fulfills the nature and benediction of genuine musical composition; both can, and often do, exist independently of the soul of music.

With whatever hopes and fears one may have made the pilgrimage to Bayreuth, we were all united at least in our anticipation of an extraordinary theatrical event. But even this expectation was only partially fulfilled. I have duly acknowledged Wagner's imaginative innovations in the arrangement of his theater, including, as regards the mechanical side, the scene of the swimming Rhine Maidens in *Das Rheingold*. From there on the course is a gradual descent. That the very first change of scene failed mechanically, that everything went generally awry, is not something to which I attach much importance. That sort of thing can happen in any theater, although it would have been better had it not happened in this widely heralded and elaborately prepared "model production" at Bayreuth. There were examples aplenty of incorrect and deficient mounting, and in decisive places. The rainbow, over which the gods proceeded to Valhalla, was set so low that one could have taken it for a painted bridge in a flower garden. The struggle between Siegmund and Hunding, and Wotan's intervention, took place in such remote darkness that none of the listeners got any idea of what was going on. The Valkyries never appeared on horseback. They simply moved across the horizon in ineffective and indistinct "dissolving views." In Munich they had young stable boys dressed as Valkyries jumping back and forth on thick carpets; their riding, uncannily rapid

172

and noiseless, was remarkably effective. What was possible for such a humble court theater should certainly be possible for the model stage at Bayreuth. The wall of fire which should surround Brünnhilde was visible only behind her; on three sides she was perfectly free and approachable. The Munich Theater, years ago, showed how this, too, should be done.

I shall pass over Fricka's ludicrous team of rams and the aging nag which Brünnhilde didn't ride but which was led by the bridle and held fast by a cord beneath the stage; likewise, the many unsuccessful scenic effects. I shall mention only the final scene of *Götterdämmerung*, in which the scenic art of the Wagner Theater should have reached its height. Who could not have looked forward eagerly to the moment when Brünnhilde, according to the explicit assurances of the libretto, would "leap impetuously upon the steed and with one impulse vault into the flaming pyre"? Instead of this she led her miserable Rosinante calmly off into the wings. There was no thought either of leaping or vaulting. Hagen, who should throw himself as if crazed into the river, strolled into the wings on the right and turned up a few seconds later in the middle of the Rhine. And finally the Rhine, which should "burst its banks in a mighty flood," wobbled—with its badly daubed and visibly sewn up waves —like the Red Sea in a provincial production of Rossini's *Moses*. If in such a principal scene a performance cannot achieve what Wagner expressly prescribes in the libretto and promises to the spectator, then there is little further occasion to speak of a "model production." By far the most successful were the sets by Joseph Hoffmann, as well painted as they were original in conception; with faithful execution and more purposeful lighting they could have been even more effective. The painter of the scenery can account for only a half of the total effect; the other half rests with the lighting, which corresponds to the instrumentation of a musical idea. This second half was not fully carried out in Bayreuth, and Hoffmann's ideas appear more melodiously conceived in the photographs than they sounded in the Festival Theater.

That the vast majority of the Bayreuth pilgrims broke into jubilant applause after each of the four dramas was to be expected; they came for that purpose. The conviction I expressed in my first report, that the durability of Wagner's newest works and their effect on the public will be definitively proved only on other stages, still stands.

BRAHMS' SYMPHONY NO. 2

[1878]

THE novelty was a great, unqualified success.[1] Seldom has there been such a cordial public expression of pleasure in a new composition. Brahms' Symphony No. 1, introduced a year ago, was a work for earnest connoisseurs capable of constant and microscopic pursuit of its minutely ramified excursions. The Symphony No. 2 extends its warm sunshine to connoisseurs and laymen alike. It belongs to all who long for good music, whether they are capable of grasping the most difficult or not.

Among Brahms' compositions, the closest to it in style and mood is the Sextet in B flat, the most popular of his instrumental works—so popular, indeed, that subsequent complicated quartets have subsisted on its popularity. The new symphony is radiant with healthy freshness and clarity. It is readily intelligible, although it offers plenty to listen to and think about. There is much that is new, and yet nothing of the unfortunate contemporary tendency to emphasize novelty in the sense of the unprecedented. Nor are there any furtive glances in the direction of foreign artistic fields, nor any begging from poetry or painting. It is all purely musical in conception and structure, and purely musical in effect. It provides irrefutable proof that one (not everyone,

---

[1] The world *première*, at a Philharmonic Concert on December 30, 1877, Hans Richter conducting.

175

to be sure) can still write symphonies, and, moreover, in the old forms and on the old foundations.

Richard Wagner and his disciples go so far as to deny not only the possibility of writing symphonies after Beethoven but also the justification for the existence of purely instrumental music altogether. The symphony is alleged to have become superfluous since Wagner transplanted it into the opera. The utmost concession is to admit the contemporary viability of Liszt's "symphonic poems," in one movement and with specific poetic programs. This nonsensical theory has been cooked up for the domestic requirements of the Wagner-Liszt household. If any further contradiction is needed, there is none more brilliant than the long succession of Brahms' instrumental works, and particularly this Second Symphony.

Its essential characteristics can best be defined as serene cheerfulness, at once manly and gentle, animated alternately by pleased good humor and reflective seriousness. The first movement, begun by a darkly tender horn theme, has something serenadelike in its mood, which becomes more pronounced in the Scherzo and Finale. This first movement, an Allegro moderato in three-four time, envelops us like a clear melodic wave on which we toss joyously, undisturbed by two lightly intruding Mendelssohn reminiscences. It is followed by a broad, songlike Adagio in B major, whose thoughtful preparation strikes me as more significant than the theme itself. For this reason it is less effective than the other three movements. Charming is the Scherzo, in minuet tempo, twice interrupted by a Presto in two-four time, which brightens up the surroundings like a fleeting spark. The Finale is rather more lively, but still comfortable in its ruddy good cheer. It is a far cry from the stormy finales of the modern school. Mozartian blood flows in its veins.

The D major Symphony is to the C minor both companion and counterpiece, even in its effect upon an audience. In listening to the First Symphony, an audience may often have the feeling of reading a scientific book, full of profound philosophic thought and secret presentiment. Brahms' tendency to veil or dampen anything which might have the appearance of "effect" makes itself felt in the C minor Symphony to a questionable degree. The listener cannot possibly comprehend all the motives and parts of motives which sometimes seem like buds slumbering beneath the snow and sometimes seem to appear as distant specks above the clouds. The Symphony No. 2 has nothing to offer such as the great emotional outpouring of the Finale of the Symphony No. 1; but, by way of compensation, it has, in its uniform coloring and its sunny clarity, a virtue not to be underestimated. This time Brahms has managed to suppress his imposing, but dangerous, art of hiding his ideas in a polyphonic web or exposing them to contrapuntal frustration. If the thematic elaboration is less astonishing, the themes are more fluent and fresh, their development more natural and transparent, and therefore more effective. I cannot adequately express my pleasure in the fact that Brahms, having given such forceful expression to the emotion of a Faustian struggle in his First Symphony, has turned again to the spring blossoms of earth in his Second.

VERDI'S REQUIEM

———— •◆•◆• ————

[1879]

IN JUNE of 1875, Verdi directed four performances of his Requiem in Vienna, scoring a series of triumphs over a hostile combination of summer heat and high admission prices. The public received the work with unwonted enthusiasm; our best connoisseurs and laymen, among them many a sworn anti-Verdian, participated unreservedly in the applause. Verdi, already so ill-considered as an opera composer in German countries, must have been prepared for the bitterest opposition as a church composer, the more so since it is one of the delights of the German critic to dampen the public's pleasure by merciless fault-finding in trivial and superficial matters. But in these days of *succès d'estime*, a real, genuine success is so rare that the critic, too, is disposed to share in the general enthusiasm, even if the festivity is not without certain improprieties and some of the enthusiasm unnecessarily boisterous.

Verdi's Requiem is a sound and beautiful work, above all a milestone in the history of his development as a composer. One may rate it higher or lower as one pleases; the cry, "We never expected this from Verdi," will never end. In this sense it is a companion piece to *Aïda*, which still seems more significant both in invention and execution. How far it is from *Ernani* or *Il Trovatore!* And yet it is unmistakably Verdi, wholly and completely. The study of old Roman church music shines through it, but only as a glimmer, not as a model.

To be sure—and this must be stated at the outset—the theater has greater need of Verdi than has the church. If he has shown in the Requiem what he can do on foreign soil, he remains, nevertheless, far stronger on his home ground. Not even in the Requiem can he deny the dramatic composer. Mourning and supplication, awe and faith—they speak here in language more passionate and individual than we are accustomed to hear in the church.

The "unchurchliness" of the Verdi Requiem is the first of its qualities to invite criticism. And yet there are few subjects about which it is so risky to pass judgment. The subjective religiousness of the artist must be left out of the question; criticism is not inquisition. At the same time, a composer's faith is no guarantee for the religious dignity of the work, and vice versa. Can one doubt the piety of Mozart and Haydn? Certainly not. And yet a good deal of their church music strikes one as very, very worldly. Compared with the festive country-fair atmosphere of many a "Gloria" of these masters, and the operatic flourishes of many a "Benedictus" and "Agnus Dei," Verdi's Requiem sounds holy. It is the same with the church music of many famous old Italian composers, whose "classicism" in faith and devotion is passed along from decade to decade with less and less critical examination. What antiquated ornaments and tender opera melodies did Pergolesi,[1] Lotti,[2] Jonmelli,[3]

---

[1] Giovanni Battista Pergolesi (1710–1736), now remembered almost solely for his *Stabat Mater* and his comic opera *La Serva Padrona*.
[2] Antonio Lotti (1667–1740).
[3] See page 56, note 4.

Salieri,[4] and many another not inject bona fide into church compositions! To get to the untarnished, unworldly purity of Catholic church music we would have to go back to Palestrina, or even to the Gregorian Chant—for Palestrina himself is not above reproach from the strict churchly point of view. The essential factor remains: the composer, with due regard for his mission, must remain true to himself.

One must grant Verdi this testament of sincerity: no movement of his Requiem is trivial, false, or frivolous. He proceeds incomparably more earnestly, more sternly, than Rossini in his *Stabat Mater*, although the kinship of the two works is not to be denied. Both composers have hitherto worked exclusively in the opera idiom. That Rossini's special field was comic opera, while Verdi's has been the serious and the tragic, is to the latter's advantage in his Requiem. In sweet melodic charm the *Stabat Mater* is superior to Verdi's Requiem, if one may say "superior" where "inferior" would be more pertinent. Verdi, following the better Neapolitan church music, has denied neither the rich artistic means of his time nor the lively fervor of his nature. He has, like many a pious painter, placed his own portrait on his sacred canvas. Religious devotion, too, varies in its expression; it has its countries and its times. What may appear so passionate, so sensuous in Verdi's Requiem is derived from the emotional habits of his people, and the Italian has a perfect right to inquire whether he may not talk to the dear Lord in the Italian language!

We should be satisfied with a piece of modern church music if it expresses honest conviction and sincere beauty.

---

[4] Antonio Salieri (1750–1825), Italian composer and conductor; teacher of Beethoven, Schubert, and Liszt; rival of Mozart. He was associated with Vienna for the greater part of his long career.

The question of specific churchly qualifications grows daily more dubious and immaterial. It is time to clarify the matter. In regard to sacred music we tend nowadays to listen to and appraise it as art. What the church finds in it to praise or blame is a matter of indifference. The interest of the church will always be the subordination of the artistic expression to the dogmatic; it will demand that the composer not call attention to himself through the independent beauty of his work and thereby distract the attention of the congregation from the churchly proceedings. We children of our time, on the other hand, see in the *Stabat Mater*, the Requiem, even in the text of the Mass, a poem hallowed by content and tradition, but still a poem at the service of the composer as material for his work. What he makes of it is, for us, a work of free art, whose right to exist is embodied in its own artistic greatness and beauty, not in its usefulness to the church. In a word, we think of the concert hall rather than the church, and so do the masters. It used to be otherwise. It never occurred to Haydn and Mozart that their Masses would ever be performed elsewhere than in the church.

It was Beethoven who opened the new era by permitting the performance of three movements of his *Missa Solemnis* in the Kärntnertortheater in Vienna.[5] He had originally intended the Mass for the great church festival, but the musical richness of the composition carried him so forcefully beyond the churchly frame that he himself sought refuge in the concert hall. And like Beethoven's *Missa Solemnis*, a few sacred compositions by renowned modern masters have found their home in the concert hall: Rossini's *Stabat Mater*, Liszt's *Graner* Mass, the Requiems of Schu-

[5] On May 17, 1824, on the same program which introduced to the world the Ninth Symphony.

mann, Brahms, and Verdi. For every twenty performances of these works in concert halls there is perhaps one in a church, and this rather for music lovers than for parishioners.

In the degree in which the church has lost its leading position in life and seen its authority limited to an ever-decreasing circle, so—possibly unconsciously—has the conviction developed among artists that they should awaken in their sacred compositions an aesthetic rather than a churchly devotion. The church, which has always used music as its most important cultural medium, can naturally not be satisfied to have the faithful confuse aesthetic with religious devotion. But art labors ever more sparingly for the church. The time is past when every great composer required the church in order to count as a finished artist. No one deceives himself these days either with the notion that the church needs composers of genius or vice versa. It is assumed that the church has a sufficiency of older music and, by way of novelty, a sufficiency of respectable, commonplace, even run-of-the-mill contemporary music. Those who write specifically for the church are music teachers and journeymen, choirmasters, cathedral organists, and other half-ordained musical bureaucrats whose small talent is insufficient for the general public. Our leading composers do a piece of sacred music now and then, but not essentially for the church.

Even Verdi, after the first performance of his Requiem in the Cathedral at Milan,[6] took it on tour, so to speak. In the concert halls of Paris, London, and Vienna, he introduced it to the congregation for which it was really intended—the musical community. The best parts of the work are those in

---

[6] On May 22, 1874.

which he imposed the least constraint upon his emotions and his talent. The weakest are those which represent a strict observance of certain churchly traditions: the contrapuntal episodes and the fugues. Of these there were originally three: the first, on the words *"Liber scriptus,"* was withdrawn by the composer in favor of the effective solo for mezzo-soprano, much to the advantage of the work as a whole. The other two fugues, the "Sanctus" (for double chorus) and the *"Libera me"* (the Finale), are conspicuous among the other movements for their thematic insignificance and the stiffness and dryness of their development. They never achieve a free, fresh fluency or an imposing climax.

It is not surprising that an Italian opera composer who never thought of a fugue before he was sixty should approach the task of writing one with some anxiety and find himself stopping every four measures and debating, "What comes next?" This constraint is perceptible in most modern fugues, in contrast to those of Bach and Handel, which almost always reveal an inspirational freedom at the very outset, in the invention of the theme and in the compelling strength and naturalness of the development. The fugal style was their natural manner of speech (just as the most difficult verse forms came naturally to many of the older poets), and they could think and compose in it with sovereign freedom. He who thought and invented polyphonically wrote good fugues. It has more recently tended to become a mere form, but in church music it remains the composer's solemn duty, although it has nothing at all to do with the religious service (as Jahn [7] demonstrated nicely in his Mozart biography).

---

[7] Otto Jahn (1813–1869), German scholar and musical historian. The book referred to is his *Life of Mozart* (1856–1859).

Even Mendelssohn, who handled the devices of scholarly music with greater mastery, or at least with more clarity and spirit than most modern composers, always seemed to lose something of the specific gravity of his talent when he wrote extended fugues. Speaking of his five-voiced B-flat major fugue in *Paul*, Mendelssohn himself said that he had written it "because in an oratorio the people wish to hear a decent fugue and believe that if the composer doesn't write one it is only because he can't." Verdi certainly wrote the fugues in his Requiem for these reasons, but they are less successful than Mendelssohn's.

These little sandy stretches in Verdi's Requiem exist, fortunately, amid a garden of blooms. The A minor movement at the very beginning, *"Requiem aeternam,"* is uncommonly beautiful in its expression of mourning, calm and composed. The A major motive, *"et lux,"* strikes in upon it like a soft ray of sunlight. The *"Dies irae,"* effective in its rather garish coloring, is reminiscent of the celebrated frescoes in the Campo Santo at Pisa, which portray all the horrors of Judgment Day, Purgatory, and Hell with such merciless clarity. The idea of realizing the *"Tuba mirum"* through the exchange of trumpet and trombone calls from instruments posted at the four corners of the orchestra is something Verdi had from the Requiem of Berlioz. Credit is due him, however, not only for having treated it self-sufficiently but also for having exercised reasonable moderation: Berlioz's Requiem, in seeking the same effect, employs four separate brass orchestras and eight pairs of kettle-drums.

From the rumbling thunder of the *"Rex tremendae majestatis"* rises the heartfelt, pleading melody of the *"Salve me,"* an effect of rare loveliness. Then follows the duet,

"*Recordare*," made wonderfully appealing by the enchanting sound of the two female voices, a stream of harmonious sound, even if it does flow close to operatic banks—and finally the flames of the "*Dies irae*" roar upward once more. A tenor solo, "*Ingemisco*," with its vacillation between perfect and diminished fifths in the accompaniment, recalls similar passages in *Aïda*. This innocent harmony was the only passage in the Requiem which struck me as reminiscent of that opera. The two works are about as self-sufficient and individual in relation to one another as any two works by the same composer could very well be.

It remains to cite the four-voiced offertory, "*Domine Jesu*," with its simple and yet rhythmically quickening middle section, "*Quam olim Abrahae*," as a movement of beautiful architectural plan and uncommon tonal beauty; then the "*Agnus Dei*," whose rather psalmodic soprano melody is given a most atmospheric semi-darkness by the accompaniment of the alto in unison an octave lower; finally the touching soft close of the whole work on the ever more softly intoned "*Libera me!*"

Alongside its many beauties, Verdi's Requiem has many weak passages, even some downright ugly ones (as, for instance, the obviously intentional parallel fifths in the bass solo, "*Confutatis*"); but they are outweighed by the favorable impression made by the work as a whole. Despite them, this Requiem remains a genuine and beautiful example of Italian art. In the physiology of this art, and in the character of its Catholicism, there is a certain overload of the sensuous and of ardent southern emotionalism. It is sufficient that in Verdi's Requiem the spirit is not suffocated in the flesh, as has happened in so many Italian sacred compositions, including some highly celebrated ones. Italy may

185

well be proud of this work, and we may share in the pride—without, however, indulging in such exaggeration as: "This Requiem is the most significant musical composition of the century!" It is not even the most significant sacred composition of the decade! For certainly no one will be so childish as to place it on an equal level with Brahms' *A German Requiem*. Fortunately, nothing compels us to indulge in such comparison, and we may honor both composers, each honestly and significantly creative in his own style.

ADELINA PATTI

[1879]

THAT enthusiastic admirer of Italian art, W. Heinse,[1] once wrote: "The Italians are quite right in paying a Gabrielli [2] or a Marchesi [3] five or ten times as much for singing an opera as they pay a Sarti [4] or a Paisiello [5] for writing it. The finest composition is a mere skeleton if the melodies are not animated and made beautiful by such voices." Although this assertion is questionable, especially if it were to lead to the general assumption that the interpretive artist takes precedence over the creative, there is much to be said for it, particularly as regards Italian opera.

I have often thought of it when Patti charmed me in operas which I would ordinarily have gone considerably out of my way to avoid. When extraordinary natural gifts are combined with consummate artistry, the person thus endowed is capable of offering an utterly individual pleasure almost independent of the composition at hand, of being both artist and poet in a work whose author was neither. If we go today to hear operas such as *Linda, Sonnambula, I*

---

[1] See page 73, note 2.
[2] Catarina Gabrielli (1730–1796), one of the foremost Italian sopranos of her time, famous both for her virtuosity and her beauty.
[3] Luigi Marchesi (1755–1829), a famous Italian castrato.
[4] Giuseppe Sarti (1729–1802).
[5] Giovanni Paisiello (1741–1816), composer of "*Nel cor più non mi sento.*"

187

Puritani, etc., we do it not to hear the works themselves—all dull— but to hear Patti. It is her talent and her voice which breathe new life into these empty and ineffectual melodies.

The aural image of such intoxicating vocal accomplishments fades all too swiftly; unlike a score, they cannot be recalled at home by reading. Thus, it is well to establish the characteristics of great singers while the memory of them is still fresh. In my personal contacts with Adelina Patti I had occasion to record numerous observations which will, I believe, be of interest to a wide circle of music lovers and add illustratively to her story. From the parquet alone one cannot determine just how much is attributable to natural gifts and how much to the labor of learning and the profit of instruction. That can be determined only in the singer's studio. And in Adelina Patti I have learned to know a musical organization perfect beyond all others—I may, indeed, say: a musical genius.

Nature endowed her with three assets in uncommon degree: refinement of hearing, quickness to grasp and to learn, and a secure memory. The infallible purity of her intonation is common knowledge. But a recent example may serve to demonstrate the extent to which the impression of the correct interval has become an integral part of that ever-compliant instrument, the throat, quite independently of any auxiliary devices. The occasion was the Patti benefit performance of Gounod's *Faust*.[6] Following the "Jewel Song," there was prolonged applause and then a riotous ovation. Wreaths flew from the boxes. Gigantic bouquets and even whole baskets of flowers were brought up from the

---

[6] At the Court Opera on May 1, 1877.

188

orchestra, all acknowledged by innumerable bows. Finally, just as the spectacle seemed to be subsiding, there came even more fervent shouts demanding a repetition of the aria. Without giving any signal to the orchestra, Patti attacked the trill on the B-natural. The orchestra entered in the next measure—and all was precisely in tune. The noisy, tiring interruption, lasting some quarter of an hour, had not disturbed her certainty in the free attack on the correct pitch. It is understandable that she finds the false intonation of others painful. She is unusually considerate in her judgment of her colleagues, and the only expression of disapproval I ever heard from her concerned out-of-tune singing —which is, unfortunately, not uncommon at the Vienna Court Opera.

Patti's memory borders on the miraculous. She learns a new part completely by singing it two or three times *sotto voce*, and what she has once learned and sung publicly she never forgets. Of the operas she has sung often, she had neither the vocal nor the piano score with her in Vienna. Of all of the operas she sang during her last visit, she reread only *Semiramide* prior to the performance, and this only because she had sung it rarely and, in the last two years, not at all. In the final performance of *Don Pasquale*, I visited her in her dressing room after the first act. In the course of the conversation she asked to see a piano score of the opera. She opened it to the second act, sang two measures *sotto voce*, and laid the book aside, continuing with the conversation. "What was it?" I asked. "Nothing," she answered. "I know the opera by heart all right, although I sang it last a year ago. But I sang *Linda* day before yesterday, and I just remembered that a certain part in *Linda* starts exactly like a part in the second finale of *Don Pasquale*.

189

I just wanted to make sure that I would not fall into the wrong theme."

This is the only case I know of where she experienced a moment of uncertainty. It seems to speak as much for her memory as for her musical presence of mind. She once sang me a mazurka of Strauss's which I had played for her some ten years before and which she had not heard again. Her voice, schooled from earliest childhood and treated with an instinctive security—as we treat the most ordinary gesture —hardly requires systematic exercise. She practices solfeggii for half an hour every day, normally *mezza voce*. She does not run through her roles. She never practices facial expressions before the mirror. "That leads only to mugging," she says.

Patti first came to Vienna early in 1863,[7] appearing with her opera troupe at the Carltheater. She stayed until May. I was not especially anxious to make her personal acquaintance, since she was said to be unfriendly, but in the end I complied with the repeated requests of her brother-in-law, Strakosch,[8] and went with him one morning to visit her. I can still see her before me, a small, pale, slender figure in a red wool Garibaldi blouse, seated in an armchair at the window, caressing her dog, Cora. I was soon on good footing with both, with the dog because I coaxed and with Adelina because I didn't. With her father, her brother-in-law, and her faithful companion, Louisa,[9] she had rented a

---

[7] When Patti was twenty.

[8] Maurice Strakosch (1825–1887), teacher, pianist, and impresario; brother of Max Strakosch, and husband of Adelina's sister Amalia.

[9] Louisa Lauw, a German girl who was Patti's companion from 1863 to 1877. In 1884 she published a book *Fourteen Years with Adelina Patti* (*Vierzehn Jahre mit Adelina Patti*), which contains a highly partisan and rather uninhibited account of Patti's affair with the tenor Nicolini (1834–1898), which broke up her marriage to the Marquis de Caux and culminated in her

small private apartment where she lived simply and quietly during this first year in Vienna. She had no fondness for parties, visits, or flirtations, and this coincided with the tastes of Strakosch, who took good care of her. Apart from

BETTMANN ARCHIVE

Contemporary caricature of Adelina Patti receiving homage from a pit conductor.

myself, there were few visitors. The manager and conductor of the Italian opera [10] called now and then, as did the family of the banker Julius Fischof, in-laws of Strakosch.

Adelina was a child of nature, half timid and half wild, what the French call *sauvage*, good-humored and violent, inclined to sudden, quickly passing fits of temper, directed

---

marriage to Nicolini in 1886. Louisa Lauw sided with the Marquis and left Patti shortly before her husband decided to do likewise.

[10] Eugenio Merelli.

usually against Strakosch, who tried to appease her. She had not yet learned to restrain herself, to be amiable with people for whom she did not care—an art which she later learned to perfection. Even today, as a French *grande dame*, she has not lost her kindness of heart, but the American child of nature of 1863 was more stimulating and appealing. When I happened in at mealtimes, which were frequently changed, I had to join them without demur. Hardly another "diva" can have eaten more simply or in a more bourgeois manner. After meals, I would play waltzes by Strauss and Lanner, which she loved to hear. Sometimes she would impulsively push tables and chairs aside, Strakosch (an excellent waltz player) would take over at the piano, and we would dance as a single, enraptured couple around the room. It was highly comical when Strakosch, worried about her voice, would plead with us to stop. "For heaven's sake, Lina," he would cry, "you must sing tonight." "Leave that to me," she would answer, laughing, and the waltz would go on. How often in later years did she remember these serene, peaceful days.[11]

I also had occasion to become acquainted with her marked talent for languages. One day I said something in

---

[11] Louisa Lauw wrote (in her *Fourteen Years with Adelina Patti*): "Shortly after her Vienna debut, Adelina made the acquaintance of Dr. Hanslick, of whom she stood in considerable awe. She found him 'not at all so stern and ferocious' as she had feared he might be. Indeed, with the first small talk with which conversation began, she found him most gracious. He soon became a daily guest and found pleasure in catering to the whims of his little friend by playing her the most popular Strauss waltzes, which Adelina loved. Adelina would have liked, if only as a joke, to find fault with the playing of a man whose judgment was so decisive for her success in the Austrian metropolis, but Hanslick's splendid playing quite took the wind from her sails. He had to pay dearly, however, for this friendly admiration, for when he had played until he was too tired to play any longer, Strakosch would be harnessed to the piano, and Hanslick would have to dance with us, willy nilly."

German to Strakosch which I did not want her to understand. In mock anger she suddenly began speaking in broken German. She had understood everything, although she had lived in Vienna only four weeks and had never heard or read a German word before. At home she spoke English, which she described as her mother tongue, but she also commanded a full knowledge of Italian and French.

The young Patti was preoccupied in those days solely with music and the theater. Such energetic singleness of purpose bears secure fruits, but it also has its disadvantages. I have never found in Adelina the slightest concern for higher questions of humanity, for science, politics, religion, or even for literature. A book was always the rarest item in her apartment. We professors, however, cannot restrain the desire to make such charming beings also a bit literary, and thus I urged her, in this first year, to read something. She agreed to try a nice English novel. I brought her one of the later novels of Dickens, which I deemed suitable because of its fortunate mixture of comic and tragic elements.[12] The book starts with a tale about an old woman who, deserted by her bridegroom on her wedding day, goes insane from the shock. She dresses in her faded bridal dress, sits before her half-petrified wedding cake, and waits for her lover.

When I asked Adelina, a few days later, how she had liked the novel, she answered excitedly that she had started it but did not intend to continue. "It's nothing but lies which nobody will make me believe. That an old woman wouldn't give up her old bridal dress and her old wedding cake can't be true and isn't possible. I am no longer a child to whom one can give such things to read." The simplicity of her

---

[12] *Great Expectations.*

attitude was charming, but it restrained me from further literary attempts. It may be that her horizon has broadened in this respect with the passage of years. I don't know.

Patti's repertoire at that time consisted exclusively of naïve or half-serious roles. Even now, when her voice and her dramatic talents have developed and become intensified, she seems most perfect to me in parts like Zerlina in *Don Giovanni*, Norina in *Don Pasquale*, or Rosina in *The Barber of Seville*. These parts blend most naturally with her artistic individuality and her appearance—considerations whose sovereign importance is not always sufficiently appreciated by the critics. At that time (1863), she sang these naïve parts, if not better, at least with more pleasure and youthful exuberance than today, when her full sympathy belongs exclusively to expressly dramatic parts. Life, too, has made her more serious. She had a strong affection even then for dramatic roles, but she was wisely told to wait for the future. She did not like to hear the naïve parts described as her particular domain. She once replied, tossing her head, "I am no *buffa*." Once, after a performance of *Don Giovanni*, she said, ignoring my praise of her Zerlina: "I should prefer to sing Donna Anna, and I shall sing her yet!"

Her first role in Vienna was *Sonnambula*. In order to reproduce conscientiously this first impression, I should like to quote a part of my review of that performance:

"If Patti's singing, acting, and personality are regarded as a whole, one must confess to having hardly ever met a more charming individual on the stage. I have heard greater artists as singers, and more brilliant voices. I recall more sophisticated actresses, and more beautiful women. But Patti's charm consists in making one forget them. What she offers is so completely hers, so harmonious and lovable, that

194

one allows oneself to be captivated and accepts capitulation with pleasure. When this slip of a girl steps lightly on the stage, inclines her childish face, radiant with artless pleasure, and regards the audience, intelligently and good-naturedly, with her big, shining doelike eyes, she has already conquered. When she begins to sing and act, both eye and ear are happy to say yes to the rash judgment of the heart. What a youthful fresh voice, ranging evenly and effortlessly from C to the F above the staff! A silver-clear, genuine soprano, it is wonderfully pure and distinct, particularly in the higher tones. The middle register has a suspicion of sharpness, but the impression is rather of brisk morning freshness. The lower register still lacks force. The voice is not extraordinarily soft and warm, and its strength is impressive only in relation to the singer's slight frame. It seems hardly capable of big climaxes or great dramatic effects, but it is advisedly never extended to the limit of what it can master completely. Her bravura is considerable, more brilliant in leaps and staccati than in legato. Over all, however, is immeasurable charm."

The author of this certainly very measured praise was attacked as an enthusiast by an anti-Patti faction of the Viennese press. Several papers then would have liked to represent her as a flash-in-the-pan, of whom nobody would speak a few years later. Time has furnished conclusive proof to the contrary.[13]

Patti's Lucia came in for particularly adverse criticism

---

[13] Louisa Lauw wrote (in her *Fourteen Years with Adelina Patti*): "When some of his friends suggested to the serious and conscientious critic that he might have been swayed in this judgment by his own enthusiasm, he attended, contrary to his custom, the second performance of *Don Giovanni*, in order to test the justification of this suggestion. Never was he so gay and enthusiastic as after this performance, and he replied to his friends that he would not alter so much as the dot of an 'i' in his review of Patti's Zerlina."

in that first year. I, too, was not as enthusiastic about this role as I was about her Rosina or Norina. One had only to see her to be persuaded that she was better suited for naïve parts than for tragic or heroic ones. But what is there of the tragic or heroic in this Lucia of Donizetti? She is a charming, weak, rather spoiled creature, who promises everything to her lover in the first act, can refuse nothing to her brother in the second, and has no recourse other than insanity in the third. Patti does not play her in "grand style," but there is no place for "grand style" in this opera. What has been criticized as lack of greatness rests more or less in her slight physique. The slender figure cannot possibly stride imposingly; the arms cannot make full sweeping gestures or present plastic studies for a Niobe. In a word, Patti is prevented by her appearance from lifting Lucia from the atmosphere of Donizetti into something higher and more imposing. Of the singers I have heard, none has sung the role with greater mastery.

Most perfect and most charming, however, were the cheerful parts, especially Zerlina. Mozart himself, in his fondest dreams, can hardly have seen a more natural and charming embodiment of this creature of his fantasy, with whom, according to Oulibischeff,[14] he seems to have fallen in love himself. Patti's Zerlina creates the illusion of a beautiful natural phenomenon, perfect, artless, inexplicable, and incapable of reproduction, even through the ultimate devices of art. Nature is the superior and decisive device which she possesses for this role, and it is just about the only one she applies. The whole accomplishment is replete with the inborn serenity of a perfectly attuned personality,

---

[14] Alexander von Oulibischeff (1795–1858), Russian nobleman and musical amateur, author of a three-volume biography of Mozart.

with a grace at once natural and individual. The majority of Zerlinas lapse either into false sentimentality or open flirtatiousness. Patti's Zerlina borders neither on the one nor on the other. When she encounters Don Giovanni she is a cheerful young girl, somewhat thoughtless and vain, but harmless and inexperienced. And it is with the curiosity of surprised childish vanity, not with the repulsive sophistication of coquetry, that she listens to his blandishments. In her precious *"andiam!"* there is neither an assumption of passion nor a suggestion of eager acquiescence. There is nothing, indeed, but the unthinking impulsiveness of a flattered peasant girl who, as soon as she realizes the danger, finds her way back with the instinct of innocence. Thus, Patti, more through instinct than reflection, not only overcomes the dubious in Zerlina but even evokes the beautiful image as if there were nothing dubious about it. I need hardly add that she sings the part not only according to the spirit but also according to the letter of the score.

Similar accomplishments, coupled with brilliant virtuosity, animate her Rosina and Norina. Her Sonnambula and Lucia may be wanting in warmth and depth of feeling, but it is impossible to imagine a Rosina or Norina more graceful, more brilliant, or more natural. The song is clear, strong, and fresh as a lark's trill; the acting inspired with delightful wit and the most graceful realism. Rosina offers perhaps the best material for an appreciation of her miraculous technique. She is the only contemporary singer who has a thorough command of the traditions of the Rossini style. She furnished new proof of this in *Semiramide*, the last new part she sang in Vienna. Granted that even she can restore to this faded work only an illusion of life, I still enjoyed the rare opportunity of hearing it from the only singer presently capable of singing it with complete mastery. The dean of European music critics, W. von Lenz in Petersburg,[15] has named her the "Paganini of vocal virtuosity." He was prompted not only by her comparable virtuosity but also by a comparable sense of disembodiment of tone. "No other violinist," he wrote of Paganini, "achieved such physical identity with the instrument. Once he began, he seemed, so to speak, to continue. When I first heard Patti, I was struck at once with the fact that she launches a tone in a manner characteristic only of great instrumentalists. She attacks the first note with a security and an exactness of intonation which the majority of singers achieve only in the course of a cantilena."

I first saw Patti again in the spring of 1867, in Paris. She was doing nothing new. The repertoire of the Opéra Italien was the most commonplace in the world, but the public crowded the theater whenever she sang, regardless of the role. New, however, was her social progress. She had an elegant apartment on the Avenue de l'Impératrice. There were visitors galore and even brilliant parties, where I met a number of celebrities. I made the acquaintance, among others, of the gifted illustrator Gustave Doré and of that famous sportsman the Marquis de Caux, both of whom were infatuated with her. She treated them both with the same friendliness and impartiality—and without a thought of serious involvement. The consistent endeavors of the Marquis were, however, eventually successful. They were married in London, in 1869.

Those who observed Adelina in the company of the Marquis—before, as well as after, their marriage—were

---

[15] Wilhelm von Lenz (1808–1883), Russian musical historian and authority on Beethoven.

aware that she did not marry for love. She had no knowledge of love in the sense of *la grande passion*. Thus, she was able to believe that she could marry a man without this unknown element, a man in whom she saw an accomplished gentleman and whom she knew to be her enthusiastic admirer. Aristocratic society was open to her as a queen in her own right even before she became a marquise, but the title and the exalted connections of her suitor may have flattered her childlike mind.

She returned to Vienna in the spring of 1872, after an absence of nine years, to fulfill an engagement at the Theater an der Wien. Since then she has returned every year, singing three years ago in the newly built house of the Comic Opera,[16] and last year and the year before in the Court Opera. Each year, despite the frequency of her appearances, she has been a charming novelty, and we critics have been subjected to ever greater embarrassment in our efforts to write something new about a phenomenon so perfect. To the operas which she had sung here before were added: *Il Trovatore* and *Rigoletto* of Verdi; *Dinorah* and *The Huguenots* of Meyerbeer; *Romeo and Juliet* and *Faust* of Gounod; *Linda di Chamounix* of Donizetti; *I Puritani* of Bellini; *Martha* of Flotow; and *Semiramide* of Rossini.

---

[16] The Komische Oper on the Schottenring was opened on January 17, 1874, with the American mezzo-soprano, Minnie Hauk, appearing as Rosina in *The Barber of Seville*. Its *raison d'être* was the new Opera House on the Opernring, into which the Court Opera had moved from the Kärntnertortheater in 1869. The new house was ill-suited to the performance of operas in the lighter genre, and thus the Komische Oper was conceived—in imitation of the Opéra Comique in Paris—as a means of filling the gap. Patti and Pauline Lucca, in addition to Minnie Hauk, sang there in the seventies and gave it a considerable luster, but it fell upon bad days toward the end of the decade and was closed. It was reopened in 1880 as the Ringtheater and was the scene of the Vienna *première* of Offenbach's *The Tales of Hoffmann* on December 7, 1881. It burned down the next night, with a considerable loss of life, and was not rebuilt.

The reunion was artistically most pleasing. The homage she had received in Europe had not turned her head. She never considered herself an infallible "diva." She strove conscientiously for perfection. Her natural charm has remained unspoiled, but, at the same time, her art has ripened to a marvelous fruit. If, in 1863, we had to warn enthusiasts against regarding as a phenomenon of the art of perfect singing what was, indeed, a phenomenon in its totality, we must now recognize in her the greatest of singing artists. The irresistible charm which so surrounded her first appearance, and her pure joy in singing and acting, have not been lost with her youth. Graced by God with talent, she is, at the same time, one of the happiest of His creatures, simply by virtue of her inexhaustible joy in her vocation. This doesn't always go hand in hand with success. Her sister Carlotta longs for the day when she need no longer sing.[17] For Adelina, singing and acting are vital requirements. Such passionate artistic natures quickly establish a magnetic relationship with the public. She has grown not only musically but also dramatically. Her understanding seems to have deepened, her acting to have gained in refinement, her ever-attractive pantomime to have become exemplary. Such expressive, delicately detailed acting as her farewell to Alfredo in the second act of *La Traviata* was still beyond her grasp in 1863. Her voice, too, has gained strikingly; one enjoyed especially the greater fullness and beauty of the low notes. They sounded immature nine years ago; now they remind one of the dark tones of a Cremonese viola.

Of her new parts the most effective was that of Leonora in *Il Trovatore*. Especially admirable was her singing of the

----

[17] (1840–1899), a celebrated coloratura.

two big arias. The slow movements she sings broadly and expressively. The dubious triviality of the allegros she overcomes by two devices. First, she gives free rein to a brilliant virtuosity which completely overshadows the composer. One must have experienced the silver-clear impact of this infallible voice, which toys with the most astounding difficulties and attacks the most distant pitches, the highest notes, with a security rare even among instrumentalists. And she knows how to soften the coarseness of these allegros, to ennoble them by musical phrasing, by facial expression and gesture. The effect of a look or a gesture is not everything, but it may contribute a lot. Not every singer can make such characteristics her own, just as not every singer can have that sharply profiled, marble-pale face with the two black flames which glow with every upward surge in the music.

Her *La Traviata* is equally good. It is even more convincing and attractive, because the part and the whole opera are superior to *Il Trovatore* in naturalness, feeling, and musical charm. *La Traviata* represents considerable progress from the stylistic violence of *Il Trovatore*, and its origin in an effective, cleverly made play is a dramatic advantage. The character and the plot of *La Traviata* develop before our eyes. They are understandable and compel our participation more or less, while the persons and situations in *Il Trovatore* arrive on the stage as if shot from a pistol. The events leading up to the tragedy in *Il Trovatore* are, moreover, so unintelligible that few manage to grasp which of the two young men was kidnaped and burned and which wasn't. Patti's Violetta has one fault—a fault which I would rather praise than condemn. She is no Traviata, no *Dame-aux-Camellias*. The piquant *haut-goût* of the demimonde, which

Désirée Artôt,[18] the sophisticated French singer, bestowed on this figure with so much elegance, is completely wanting. When Patti enters in the first scene, bubbling with child-like gaiety, the camellias in her corsage seem transformed into lilies. Her rendering of the first aria resembles a shower of flowers, and in the last act she finds the most touching accents. Such delicate shading from piano to expiring pianissimo, as in the death scene, such remarkable transitions from *mezza voce* to fortissimo, as in her duet with Alfredo, I have never heard before.

A new part with which Patti surprised us was Dinorah —perhaps her most perfect achievement. I have always disliked *Dinorah* despite delicate, sophisticated musical details —disliked it nearly as much as I formerly disliked *La Traviata*, which I first heard in a very crude and bad performance. I must confess that Patti has made even repeated hearings of these operas pleasant and, when she is on the stage, downright enjoyable.

In conclusion I must mention two of Patti's roles which I cannot praise in the same degree—Valentine in *The Huguenots* and Marguerite in Gounod's *Faust*. She sings them both with passionate affection, but without realizing the limits of her dramatic talent and the contradictory characteristics of her individuality. Juliet, in Gounod's opera, is a transition to these two tragic roles. But in this part she offers in the first act such a perfect masterpiece, and in the second so much that is graceful and beautiful, that one can easily overlook the insufficient depth and passion in the second half of the opera. As Juliet, she possesses, above all, what the majority of singers are unable to bring to this

---

[18] (1835–1907), a pupil of Pauline Viardot-Garcia, one-time fiancée of Tchaikovsky.

exacting part: the credibility of her appearance. And her singing! Her rendering of the waltz aria in the first act is a little miracle in itself, the perfect art of singing combined with the purest taste and the most delightful naturalness. She sings the piece, which nearly all singers transpose one tone down, in the original key of G major. The ease with which her light silvery voice masters the high *tessitura* and the continually recurring A, B, C is as pleasant and refreshing as a sunny morning. Always rhythmically strict as regards measures, she treats the rhythm within each measure with individual freedom—nothing is dragged, nothing is rushed, and yet everything is animated right down to the softest vibrations of tone. With what delicate musical feeling she renders the thrice repeated appoggiaturas of the theme, not sharply and precipitously, but calmly as in a gentle breath! And later the ascending and descending chromatic scale, not like a vocal tempest, but with incomparable calm and purity, every step as if carved in marble, a fitting counterpart to the "Shadow Song" in *Dinorah!* In the one as in the other, there is the clearest precision in design, adorned with the most charming fragrance and melting sweetness of color. From both these classic melodies she effaces everything trivial and raises to pure beauty what are, at best, well-made show pieces.

As far as vocal achievement goes, her Valentine is perfect, too; it is always Patti who sings. But a certain striving to get the last ounce of power from the voice, an overeagerness to achieve the ultimate of forcefulness and dramatic expression, blemish her peculiar charm. She is primarily a musical temperament; the actress in her, although far beyond all her Italian rivals, comes only second. Although her acting never lacks dramatic life and characterization, she never transgresses the limits of agreeable musical sound. And the latter is usually sacrificed where dramatic expression is overemphasized. Our famous German singers are not ignorant of this axiom, but they exchange the values anyway and willingly sacrifice musical form and beauty to pointed "dramatic" characterization. Patti is the ideal embodiment of Italian music rather than of French or German music, whose frequently nebulous and vague manifestations cannot always stand the light of day and the clarity of the Italian sky. There is no space in Valentine for Patti's finest and most characteristic virtues. The part of the Queen would be better. Valentine offers nothing which she alone can do, and nothing which nobody else can do as well. The role demands effects derived from sheer weight of voice. To achieve them, Patti must summon all her strength. The energy with which she overcomes such obstacles deserves admiration; but, while we express this admiration by fervent applause, we attempt with the same applause to smother our regret that so sweet a voice and so charming an art should be exposed unnecessarily to such hazards. Not only the vocal tour de force but also the dramatic passion of this role, stretched to the breaking point, contradicts Patti's harmonious nature. She acts the part with great vitality and with telling details, but the effort to maintain a dizzy peak of passion leaves the impression of a mental tempest more contrived than genuinely experienced. The single tragic, touching scenes in *La Traviata, Linda,* and *Dinorah* are different. These characters progress from joy to suffering, Violetta even to death, but they are passive, removed from tragic heroism, from Valentine's uninterrupted conflict. *La Traviata* is to *The Huguenots* as a conversation piece to a historical tragedy. Patti's art approaches the latter, but nature did not create her for it. The artist who, only a few years ago, was satisfied with *opera buffa* or *semi-seria*, has energetically enlarged the boundaries of her art, and should be praised for it, as should every artist whose ambition does not go to seed in the comfort of possession and the indulgence of success. But, nevertheless, I shall always cherish Patti most in the gracious, which by no means excludes seriousness and feeling.

Her Marguerite, too, is less satisfactory than her other roles. The singing is magnificent; no one could surpass the simplicity of the "King of Thule" or the brilliance of the "Jewel Song." But it is always Patti who stands before us and not Marguerite. It would be shortsighted to blame her for something inseparable from her personality and her national sensibilities. I do not mean the black hair—which could easily be corrected with a blond wig—but rather the sharply cut features, which are always in passionate movement. This is in contradiction to our image of Marguerite. With the smallest expression of pain Patti's face takes on something violent, excited, and, with increasing passion, almost savage. The wide-open, burning eyes, the head arched forward, the corners of the mouth drooping—it is a perfect representation of blazing southern passion, but it is the opposite of Marguerite's calm, deep soulfulness. The expression of quiet, thoughtful ardor and half-hidden feeling is not Patti's to command. With her, just as in Italian music, every stimulus rises to the surface, becomes plastic and clear. As a genuine Italian, she also resembles Italian music in that both are seldom touching in a simple manner. There can be no doubt that Lucca [19] and Nilsson [20] surpass her as Valentine and Marguerite respectively, because not

---

[19] Pauline Lucca (1841–1908), Viennese soprano, who rose from the chorus of the Court Opera to be one of the most celebrated singers of her time.

[20] Christine Nilsson (1843–1921), Swedish soprano, who sang widely in America under the aegis of Strakosch, in 1870–1874 and 1884.

only their art but also their whole individuality coincides with the characters they represent. In parts which do not violate this boundary, Patti remains unrivaled and inimitible.

If I have taken up undue space with my topic, I have done so because I consider Patti the representative of the perfect art of singing, gifted with the most beautiful of voices and the utmost of musical talent. We in Germany have particular reason to cherish this art and to study it in such a singer. As far as general schooling goes, our German singers may well be superior to the Italians, but in the technical training indispensable for the artist they are far behind. Italians pursue their singing as an art, a difficult, serious art which must be studied. The Germans are usually satisfied with voice, talent, routine, and a noble disdain for vocal discipline. The last remnant of beautiful singing in Germany will be destroyed by Wagner's *Ring*. In Vienna one can annually compare German and Italian opera performances. The majority of our Italian guests are notable for the perfect schooling of their far from imposing voices, our German singers for powerful voices, less imposing than they would be had they been exposed to similar training and perseverance. With the Italians, one enjoys the utmost security and uniformity; with the Germans, a constant and unpredictable fluctuation between brilliance and mediocrity. Among the Italians, one hears aging tenors whose carefully schooled voices retain their youthful beauty of tone; among the Germans, young singers with voices prematurely brittle and insecure. With the French and the Italians, everything is worked out, complete and effective in itself; with the Germans, it is hit or miss.

Every younger singer should study Patti's tone formation, portamento, scales, and interpretive art right down to the smallest mordent. There is no more perfect model. She has also shown us how a voice can be preserved. She enjoys, of course, a rare gift of nature; her eternal youth borders upon the miraculous. The crystal-clear sound of her voice, her youthful appearance, her ease and endurance have not been affected by the passage of time. But above all is her incomparable sense of beauty in music. Virtuosity does not blossom exclusively in eminently musical natures, and the virtuoso who hastens from triumph to triumph for more than ten years usually suffers the loss of simple musical and dramatic feeling. He becomes sophisticated and artificial and tries to replace his lost innocence by contrived effects, overaccentuation, and lavish ornamentation. How often we have witnessed this distortion in brilliant stage talents whose "Journey Round the World in 80 Days" has cost them artistic achievements dearly won.

There is not a trace of such influence in Patti. Who has ever caught her in an unmotivated effect? Who has ever seen her trespass, even in the most dramatic situations, the white borderlines of the musically beautiful? She always sings in time and in tune. She always respects the composer's indicated intentions. She does not indulge in tremolo, nor does she blur or overstress. She possesses completely the nearly lost secret of good Italian singers: to project the tone widely and strongly without shouting. Her acting, too, has retained the full simplicity of a gracious nature. Satiety with roles sung a hundred times has never tempted her to stratagems of comedy or of novelty at any cost.

In many years of activity as a critic in Vienna I have suffered a world of boredom in Italian opera music. Often, when our German music suffered under it, I have wished that it might return to the land of its origin. Today the situation is different. The regime of equestrian Valkyries and singing dragons has established itself. Our singers will be busy for some years studying the four *Ring* operas. They may learn a lot doing it—but one thing they will certainly unlearn: what singing actually means. Under such conditions it would be regrettable if there were not in at least one German capital (Vienna) an excellent Italian company to remind us from time to time of the vanishing art of beautiful singing—*nota bene*, an excellent company with an artist like Patti at its head.

BÜLOW

[1881]

HANS VON BÜLOW is one of the most interesting and
gifted musical personalities of our time. His arrival in a
town is enough to quicken the hearts of all who want something more than merely pleasant musical entertainment.
One always learns something new. He is not interested in
the hackneyed and the well known, and what doesn't interest
him he won't talk about. His restless, brilliant mind and his
reckless energy blow like a northwind, brisk and refreshing,
through the stagnant complacency of our everyday musical
life. Neither productive nor important as a composer, he
is a born interpreter, one of the most remarkable I have
ever known. Nor are his revolutionary tendencies in this
respect confined to virtuosity alone. When it comes to
introducing the supremely difficult, Bülow is right on hand
and hard at work. I have known him as an eminent virtuoso
for thirty years. I made his acquaintance as a conductor in
Munich in 1868, when he directed the first performance of
Die Meistersinger. Let it be said in his favor that his enthusiasm for Wagner has not rendered him blind or unjust to
the virtues of other composers. He, whose close personal
relation to Wagner and Liszt could well account for a
predilection obstinate to the point of injustice, distinguishes
himself in this respect from the Bayreuth fanatics. While the
latter scorn every successful composer except Wagner, and

209

would like nothing better than the execution of every critic who is not exclusively Wagner-mad, Bülow has retained full independence of opinion and judgment. He has even praised publicly and enthusiastically the two most prominent anti-Wagnerian composers, Brahms and Rubinstein.

He fights not only with his pen but also with the baton. As court conductor of the ducal orchestra in Meiningen he consecrated this new position with a truly Bülowian experiment. He concluded a cycle of Beethoven concerts with a double performance of the Ninth Symphony. *Nota bene:* in one and the same concert, he played the whole Ninth Symphony twice. It is difficult to comprehend this paternal device for enlightening the masses on a great work, a drastic treatment not without danger for the patient. Bülow not only underestimates the sensibility of the listener; he also underestimates the effect of the symphony, which is too great to be assimilated more than once at a time even under the best of circumstances. One may, however, realize the fervent religious zeal with which he preaches the Beethoven gospel. He baptizes the infidels with a fire hose.

Bülow has just made his bow in Vienna with a more rational but similarly strange and daring experiment. He played the five last great Beethoven sonatas, one after the other, in a single recital. Nothing else. These are among Beethoven's most sublime works, difficult of comprehension and performance alike. It has only been within the past thirty years that anyone has dared to play one or another of them in public. Mortier de Fontaine, who made a name for himself with his (rather inept) performance of the great B major Sonata (1847), remained without a successor for a long time. Only recently have such authoritative artists as Clara Schumann and Brahms performed the individual sonatas publicly. To play all five at one sitting was considered an impossibility until yesterday. Bülow survived the adventure, and so did the public. Only one who has tried to master these sonatas with his own hands can appreciate Bülow's extraordinary achievement. It is difficult to determine which is more admirable, his memory, his physical stamina, his technique, or the elasticity of his mind. The whole performance lasted more than two full hours. The total impression was fatigue mixed with admiration. If I correctly read the faces of the listeners going home, they said: "Beautiful—but never again." Some chose to put it the other way around: "Never again—but beautiful."

This was not the last of Bülow's adventures. He topped it with a three-hour Liszt recital. He is obviously not content with little things or with things done before. He played fifteen pieces by Liszt, one after the other, and repeated four or five. The outward success was extremely brilliant, although I prefer, for the sake of Vienna's reputation as a musical community, to believe that the greater part of the applause was directed at the virtuoso. And for Bülow's sake, I prefer to believe that it was the human being rather than the musician in him that was prompted to such enthusiastic exertion.

" PARSIFAL "

[Letters from Bayreuth, July, 1882]

I

AND so we found ourselves once again in the friendly little
Bavarian town of Bayreuth, once famous for courtly splendor
and twice hallowed by the power of the spirit. Half a century
ago devotees of Jean Paul [1] made the pilgrimage one by
one; six years ago it was made in whole caravans by the
admirers of Richard Wagner.

Yes, six years have passed since the Festival Theater
was first opened to cast the spell of Wagner's four-day
wonder, *Der Ring des Nibelungen*. Since then, the odd theater in the mountains has been closed, the hot dusty road
leading up to it deserted. It had been differently planned.
Wagner had hoped for annual productions. He had even
expressed the intention of having his theater, in ever-ex-
panding scope, undertake "every type of dramatic work
which, because of the originality of its conception and its
truly German character, could lay claim to a particularly
correct production."

Nobody, of course, believed that he would ever produce
any but his own works at Bayreuth. And quite properly so,
for in order to hear a good *Fidelio* or *Don Giovanni* nobody
had to travel to Bayreuth, still less construct a special thea-

---

[1] Jean Paul Friedrich Richter (1763–1825), German poet, who died in
Bayreuth.

212

ter. More credible and reliable seemed the other promise: an annual repetition of the *Ring* cycle in Bayreuth. This was in keeping with Wagner's definite public pronouncement that he would not permit the production of the *Nibelungen* trilogy on any other stage. As sincere as this edict may have been originally, I doubted its durability from the start and predicted, back in 1876, that once Europe had traveled to Bayreuth, Bayreuth would have to come to Europe.

And so it has been—to the real advantage of the work and its creator. The *Nibelungen* trilogy has, in the past six years, traveled to every court and municipal theater worth mentioning. And the Wagner temple in Bayreuth has remained shut. Only now have its doors been reopened, and for a new work, *Parsifal*, to which Wagner has given a special significance by the term *Bühnenweihfestspiel* (Consecrational Stage Festival).

In the choice of material, Wagner has moved upwards in a twofold sense: genealogically from Lohengrin to his father, Parsifal, and metaphysically from myth to Christian mysticism. The soul of the piece is the Holy Grail, the miraculous cup or vessel in which Joseph of Arimathea is believed to have caught the blood of the Crucified, and which is guarded by the Knights of the Grail on Montsalvat. As early as *Lohengrin*, the Holy Grail, as an invisible, remotely effective force (*"Mich ruft der Gral"*—"the Grail calls me") brought on the catastrophe. In *Parsifal* the Grail is the visible center and supreme will of the drama. Only a person of utter purity, who does not seek to find it, can reach it and be accepted into its knighthood. Parsifal is this innocent, unworldly youth, the *"reiner Tor"* ("guileless fool"), who first neglects his higher calling in order, after severe tests and increasingly intensive moral purification, to fulfill it.

As is generally known, the knightly minstrel Wolfram von Eschenbach commemorated Parsifal at the beginning of the thirteenth century in an epic, lengthy as it was profound and colorful, based on the poem of Chrétien de Troyes,[2] uniting in it the saga of the Holy Grail with that of the Knights of King Arthur's Round Table. Eschenbach, who—the exact opposite of Wagner—could neither read nor write, has served the latter as a preferable if not exclusive source. It is a nice coincidence that the newest Parsifal, the Wagnerian, should reappear in the same country, Bavaria, and even in the same Frankish county where, six hundred years ago, Wolfram had his home. Eschenbach lies southeast of Ansbach, not far from Bayreuth. Wolfram had his house in Wiedenberg, presumably Wehlenberg bei Ansbach, and lived there with his wife and child, poor but content. He died in his late fifties, about 1220, and was buried in the Frauenkirche at Eschenbach. Thus, the Bavarian north country, which also includes Bayreuth, is a direct reminder of the unsurpassed first poet of Parsifal. Probably only the scholars, the literary historians, and the Germanists will have immersed themselves in his poem. A much larger circle knows of Wolfram and his *Parzival* from older works of literature, most recently, perhaps, from Wilhelm Hertz's [3] careful biography, or from Wilhelm Scherer's [4] admirable *History of Literature.* A third group is the considerable minority who know Wolfram von Esch-

---

[2] Chrétien de Troyes, French poet of the Middle Ages, who started the epics revolving around the Holy Grail. *Perceval, ou Conte de Graal* was his last work, probably written about 1180.

[3] Wilhelm Hertz (1835–1902), poet and literary historian, who devoted his work and researches to medieval epics such as *Parzival, Tristan and Isolde,* etc.

[4] Wilhelm Scherer (1841–1886), German philologist and literary historian.

enbach as the melodious singer of the "Evening Star" in *Tannhäuser*. Even this should suffice for the understanding of the "Consecrational Stage Festival," since a properly made drama, spoken or sung, should explain itself without reference to scholarly preparation.

Anyone acquainted with Wagner's theatrical genius will derive the impression of an effective stage piece from a review of the text alone. It is a skillfully contrived drama with completely new, sometimes brilliant, situations. With respect to form, it has undeniable virtues, and surpasses the poem of the *Nibelungen* trilogy by virtue of its more compact narrative and effective climaxes. It represents, moreover, a welcome advance (or healthy retreat) in diction. It is certainly not wanting in tortuous word and sentence structure, in pretentious obscurities and bombastic ornamentation, but we are free of the childish jingle of alliterative verse. Compared with the linguistic mayhem of *Siegfried* or *Tristan and Isolde*, the language of *Parsifal* is simple and natural—insofar as Wagner is capable of speaking simply and naturally.

He has made some essential changes in the Eschenbach narrative, to the disadvantage of the dramatic motivation. At the same time he has pursued the practical purpose of excluding everything that might interfere with the unity of his plan, such as the knightly figure of Gawain, who, as an enamored adventurer, offers the contrasting companion piece to Parsifal, and the whole Round Table of King Arthur, this worldly companion piece to the spiritual association of the Knights of the Grail. Through this exclusion of everything episodic and unessential, Wagner has achieved a calmly, steadily developing dramatic plan, distributed in three acts, comprising six graphic tableaux, two to each act.

The born composer for the theater betrays himself in every scene of the libretto, so vividly is everything foreseen exactly as it must work out on the stage. And what a richness of scenic wonders and novel effects! The Transformation Scene and the Holy Communion in the first act; the living flowers, the miracle of the spear and the sinking enchanted garden in the second; and, at last, the obsequies for Titurel and the whole final scene—these are all surprising new proofs of Wagner's inexhaustible theatrical fantasy. Wonder follows wonder in this strange and perplexingly vibrant drama. The listener who is sufficiently naïve to conceive of the Wagnerian *Parsifal* as a kind of superior magic opera, as a free play of fantasy reveling in the wondrous, will catch the best aspect of it and salvage the least troubled pleasure. He will have to defend himself only against the false notion that beneath it all lies an unfathomably profound, holy meaning, a philosophic and religious revelation. Unfortunately, it is upon this alleged deep, moral significance, upon the Christian-mystical element in Wagner's poem, that the greatest weight is laid. And about this aspect of the new "Consecrational Stage Festival" and its dramatic physiognomy I have grave reservations.

Just as in most Wagnerian works the dramatic kernel, clothed in brilliant raiment, is sickly and meager because the characters behave less according to their own free will than according to the will of supernatural powers, so it is in *Parsifal*, and even more so than in any of Wagner's earlier works. In everyone involved there is wanting precisely that which makes for dramatic character: free self-determination in good or bad. Neither the virtuous hero, Parsifal, nor his diabolical counterpart, Klingsor, nor even Kundry, helplessly torn between one and the other, is good or bad—or dramatic—to say nothing of the enlightened Society of the Grail. Parsifal himself, his guilt and his subsequent moral purification, are unintelligible in Wagner's conception. Parsifal is the inexperienced, good-natured youth at the awkward age, a favorite character of countless medieval stories, whom Wolfram von Eschenbach first transfigured by a profounder conception. In Wagner's first act he is quite in character, a kind of tractable Siegfried. In his youthful ardor for hunting he shoots a swan, and it never occurs to him that there may be anything wrong about it. He answers, "I don't know," to every question, and allows himself to be conducted to the Mount of the Grail, where he dumbly regards all the wonders and the curious persons he sees about him. All this is perfectly understandable. But perfectly un-understandable is the fact that in the second act the same "guileless fool" suddenly recognizes himself as a terrible sinner. This is where Wagner pays for his departure from the Parsifal saga and Wolfram's narrative, a departure which nearly invalidates the psychological motivation of the hero and the logical development of the action.

According to both the saga and Wolfram's narrative, the ailing King Amfortas is to be delivered by an innocent youth in accordance with a revelation of the Grail—a youth who will involuntarily find his way to the Mount of the Grail and there put to the King the question, "What ails you, Sir?" By this mere question Amfortas is to be healed and the questioner made king in his stead. But since a point has been made of impressing upon young Parsifal that he mustn't ask questions, he fails at first to do so. Only when Kundry, at King Arthur's Round Table, denounces him as a traitor for having frustrated Amfortas' delivery by his silence does he realize what he has done. Disgusted with himself, confused, and in doubt, he comes at last to an old hermit, Trevrizent, who becomes his teacher and redeemer, explaining to him the mysteries of the Grail and his own inner spirit. Penitent, and reconciled with God, Parsifal retraces his steps. After long wandering and severe trials, he finds his way back to the Grail. He appears before Amfortas and asks, "What ails you, Sir?" The ailing King rises, healed, and hands him his crown.

Thus Wolfram relates the story. The solution is poetic and understandable. But since Wagner omits the motive of the question, we are left to wonder wherein Parsifal has sinned. In Wolfram's version the utterance of the Grail is quite clear; in Wagner's it is more obscure than we are accustomed to expect even from oracles: *"Durch Mitleid wissend, der reine Tor:—Harre sein, den ich erkor."* [5] I must frankly admit that I do not understand it. In vain we ask how it happens that Wagner's Parsifal, who has never been enlightened as to his guilt and is himself conscious of none, should suddenly be overcome with remorse and contrition during the love scene of the second act and be transformed from a pure fool to a pure saint. Without a thought for the ailing king and without a shadow of guilt, he rides off in the second act "with boyish shouts," bent on adventure, and arrives in Klingsor's magic castle among the seductive maidens. Kundry, transformed into a beautiful enchantress, gives him "the first kiss of love," and he jumps up, crying "Amfortas, the wound, the wound!" and falls, nonplused, to his knees. Let him make sense of it who can. Even Kundry seems unable to grasp it: *"So war es mein Kuss,"* she says,

---

[5] Made wise through pity, the guileless Fool—Wait for him, my chosen tool.

"der Welt-hellsichtig dich machte?" ("And was it my kiss this great knowledge conveyed thee?")

Psychological wonders multiply in the second act, as do dogmatic wonders in the third. Among the former, an ugly one: that the image of his dying mother should be used to excite Parsifal's sensual ecstasy. This mixture of the most holy feelings with the most unholy is the more offensive here because it is both unnecessary and unnatural. After the decisive kiss, he who has now become *"Welt-hellsichtig"* tears himself from Kundry and sets off to visit Amfortas, armed with the holy spear, for which he has not even had to fight. It has miraculously flown into his hand like a roast pigeon. This remote, ancient legend of a spear which alone can heal the wounds it has inflicted—Wolfram makes no reference to it—is an interpolation by Wagner, who probably thought to gain another miracle and a brilliant finale. Wagner's interpreters, often even more profound and unintelligible than Wagner himself, find in the spear "the curative faculty of compassion become conscious." My own reaction is that with this miraculous spear Wagner has pierced his own drama to the heart.

Not exactly wonderful, but certainly curious, is the fact that from Parsifal, the hero of the piece, we have not one spiritually or physically heroic act. At most there is the purely negative accomplishment of resistance to sensual temptation. With mounting astonishment we observe that in the course of the piece an ever larger halo crowns the head of the pure fool, until he becomes, as it were, the Redeemer of Mankind. In the scene where Kundry, as the penitent Magdalena, washes his feet and dries them with her hair, he merges actually with the figure of Christ. At the end, a white dove even settles upon his head as the incarnation of the Holy Ghost, while invisible voices chant: "Supreme Holy Miracle! Redemption to the Redeemer!" What the Wagnerian Parsifal has done to justify this distasteful identification with the Saviour, I leave to others to say; I also leave to them the decision as to whether the spirit of true Christianity is furthered by such spectacles. Confronted with moments from the life of Christ thus lightly represented, one can only ask why Wagner did not prefer to glorify Jesus himself in a "Consecrational Stage Festival." I mean this seriously. Something from the institution of the Oberammergau Passion Play—including its rare periodic repetition—seems to have caught the fancy of the founder of the Bayreuth Festivals. The person and life of the Saviour are, indeed, dramatic in the highest sense, and there is no reason why a qualified poet should not take up such a drama with the same devout spirit with which the painter Munkácsy,[6] for example, undertook a modern and realistic representation of the historic Christ. Friedrich Hebbel long entertained the plan of a Christ-drama, "the most prodigious of all tragedies," but he died before he put pen to paper. Wagner is certainly not inferior to Hebbel in artistic daring; and he could, today, dare more than Hebbel or anyone else. The "Last Supper" of Leonardo da Vinci would certainly offer a picture a thousand times more gripping—if rather less ostentatious—than the Eucharist of the Knights of the Grail in *Parsifal*, which is, after all, only a transparent masquerade of that "Last Supper." For truly Christian spirits the original would probably give less offense than the most earnestly intended parody.

---

[6] Mihály von Munkácsy (1844–1900), eminent Hungarian painter.

Just as Parsifal is motivated by supernatural powers and promoted quite unintentionally from an amiable bumpkin to "redeemer of the redeemer," so is Kundry a helpless tool, alternately in the power of the Grail and of Klingsor. In Wolfram von Eschenbach the wild "messengeress of the Grail" (Kundry), and the beautiful seductress of Parsifal (Orgeluse) are two entirely different persons; Wagner blends both into the single figure of Kundry. One may choose to call this figure novel and interesting, but it is not humanly intelligible, and what Wagner intends with all this hysterical nonsense is hardly to be divined without a learned commentary. A related figure is Klingsor, a curious fallen angel, cast out from the Knighthood of the Grail for self-mutilation and reduced to an evil sorcerer. He, too, is a bloodless abstraction and, like Kundry, confuses us with many contradictions and riddles. The ailing Amfortas remains a purely suffering figure, and there is so much talk about his searing pains, bleeding wounds, baths, and medicaments that our sympathy is clinical-pathological rather than tragic.

The further the plot progresses, the more arbitrary, mystical, and symbolical it becomes. We human beings finally lose all sense of identification with these occurrences bound up in holy miracles and with these abnormal super- and sub-beings who move as if dangled from celestial marionette strings. To which of them can one attach himself with a feeling of human warmth? Even in *Lohengrin* it is not until the final scene that our hero becomes the supernatural knight, the seraphic soldier who must blindly follow his commander, the Grail, and leave Elsa. Throughout the rest of the piece he behaves and feels like a human being, and the people about him likewise. In *Parsifal*, on the other hand, the Holy Grail is all, signifies all, and decides all.

What is the Grail to us? A legendary curiosity, a long-forgotten superstition, foreign both to popular and enlightened consciousness. The hysterical exaltation incessantly associated with the Holy Grail, the Holy Lance, and the Holy Blood in Wagner's *Parsifal* finds no response today in German minds and German hearts, and never will.

When Wagner's official interpreter, Wolzogen, declares that Wagner has "taken and deepened the universally human fundamental thoughts" from Wolfram's epic, it seems to me that rather the opposite is true. Wagner has taken the mystical-religious-symbolic and put it under a magnifying glass, suppressing the purely human elements of this lively, richly motivated poem. How beautiful and touching, in Wolfram's narrative, is Parsifal's constant thought of his wife! Not even the Grail is able to suppress this true love and the constant search for domestic family happiness. As soon as Parsifal asks the previously neglected sympathetic question of Amfortas and enters the kingdom, he is united with his wife, the gracious Conduiramur, and with his two sons, Lohengrin and Kardeiz. There is no trace of all this in Wagner, for whose Christian ideal celibacy is obviously a prerequisite. We are told that it is Wagner's greatest deed that he has glorified "the Grail, the supreme Christian-religious ideal." But for whom among us is the Grail a religious ideal? For whom has it ever been? The Christianity of our time is quite different from the miracle-seeking Christianity of the Knights of the Grail, and possibly not inferior. It has been well said of Shakespeare that he is nowhere and yet everywhere religious. The Christian ecstasy of *Parsifal* is the exact opposite of Shakespeare's poetic healthiness, and reminds us not infrequently of the versified devotional seizures of the German Pietists.

Is this really Wagner, one asks, the same Wagner who, in his famous book, *Art and Religion* (1850), fought so energetically against the lamentable effect of Christianity? Wagner then saw in Christianity a hostile counteragent to true art and to the sole natural development of human beings. Today he appears to be going to the other extreme, to be finding in the Christian mysteries the salvation of art. If, on the threshold of his seventieth year, he has become personally devout, it would not be the first example of such a transformation, and it would be none of anyone's business. "Religiosity," says Grillparzer, "is the fermentation of the mind in cultivation and the souring of the mind in decay." And we can almost sense a decaying mentality when a modern artist sees in the relic of the Grail and in sacred miracles the mission of German art, and proposes therewith to effect the regeneration of humanity.

Wagner's own utterances, and those of his associates and disciples even more so, speak for such a generalization of his newest ideal, just as Wagner's whole theory claims as a universal and exclusive fundamental of art only that which suits his own talent. Despite the efforts of a hundred Wagner associations to see the salvation of art in Christian mysticism, the present generation will hardly find it necessary to take up again Goethe's campaign against the "new German religious-patriotic art." We wish—as Scherer exclaimed with reference to the *Ring*—to continue to live and work in the spirit of Goethe, "unconcerned with the barbaric nonsense of half-understood Nordic mythology, which is being pressed upon us as a new evangelism." This newest art-evangelism, that of Christian mysticism, may well remain isolated in *Parsifal*, despite its brilliant embodiment. Like the resurrection of that extinct world of the gods, it would accomplish only retrogression, and would impoverish art rather than enrich it.

I know perfectly well that it is unfair to judge any Wagner opera from the libretto, detached from the music and the whole scenic representation. In having, nevertheless, attempted it, I have done no more than adapt myself to the claims of Wagner himself, who considers his libretti of value and significance as self-sufficient poems, and publishes them as independent dramas long before the appearance of the scores. For the *Parsifal* poem it was especially necessary to meet this claim, since it has been greeted in the Wagner camp with a transport of admiration.

II

The first performance of *Parsifal* took place on July 25. It was an unqualified success. It proclaimed in its grand outline, as well as in the smallest detail, the individuality of its creator. Like the Babylonian ruler who had his monogram burned into every single brick of new public buildings, so also has the author of *Parsifal* impressed an invisible R.W. upon every measure. Future researches will be able to recognize every torn-out page of the score.

Certain parts seemed strong and elevating, others indifferent and oppressive. Always, however, there is the spell of a forceful personality. The energy of a strong will, undisturbed by doubt, has an impressive effect in art as well as in life. It commands respect, if not always sympathy. Compared with the *Nibelungen* trilogy, *Parsifal* proves the advantage of compact form and, consequently, of unified impression. The mere circumstance that Wagner has discarded the dramatically false, unhappy form of the trilogy, or tetralogy—which made the artistic pleasure of 1876 a tortuous exertion—assures a cleaner effect for *Parsifal*, which will one day certainly be appropriated by the theaters of the world.[7]

The method of musical composition is essentially the same. It is in the style determined by the "endless orchestral melody," which Wagner first carried out strictly in *Tristan and Isolde*. In *Die Meistersinger* he enlivened it with flowering oases of melodic and multiple-voiced song, and in the *Ring* he imposed upon it a rigid conformity. This method, which purports to elevate opera to true drama, involves the exclusion of the old organic forms, assigning the leading role to the ceaselessly moving orchestra and leaving the voices to declaim rather than sing. The materials from which the orchestra spins its ever-changing, infinite web are the so-called leitmotives. In *Parsifal*, too, each character has his own special musical leitmotive, or rather several of them, according to the various dramatic references. Wolzogen's *Leitfäden* lists twenty-six such motives; another, by Heintz,[8] sixty-six; and a third, by Eichberg [9] (there is already a small library of such Bayreuth booklets), only twenty-three. These twenty-three, however, as the author points out, are especially suitable for memorization.

This explicit direction is characteristic. If the listener is to understand and enjoy *Parsifal* he must first have committed the leitmotives to memory. In the surging waves of

---

[7] The *Gralsraub* was committed by Heinrich Conried for the Metropolitan Opera House in 1903, despite the determined efforts of Cosima to have the performance stopped by court injunction. It has, since then, become available to all theaters, just as Hanslick predicted.

[8] Albert Heintz (1822–1911), German musical scholar and organist, author of a number of analytical works on the Wagner operas.

[9] Oskar Eichberg (1845–1898), German musician and critic, author of *Parsifal, Einführung in die Dichtung Wolframs von Eschenbach und Richard Wagners* (1882).

a restless orchestra, he is faced with the endless test of detecting the "Grail" motive, the "Love Feast" motive, the "Faith" motive, the "Promise" motive, etc. These are all connected with the Grail. There are, in addition, a number of Kundry motives ("Kundry's Wild Ride," "Kundry's Love," "Kundry's Laugh," etc.) as well as those for Parsifal, Klingsor, and others. These leitmotives, in ever-new combinations, variations, and instrumentations, provide a continuous symphonic web. He who has not already heard it from Wagner's intimate friends should be able on his own to detect that Wagner, as a rule, writes the orchestral accompaniment first and then sketches in the vocal parts; the integrated and integrating whole is the self-sufficient orchestra; what is sung to it are fragments whose sense is in the words, not in the tones. Thus, with the exception of a few conspicuous examples of melodious, intelligible song, *Parsifal* also offers the spectacle of a busy orchestra, rich in allusions and significance, in which float the flakes of an agitated song-speech.

A second essential characteristic of Wagner's later style is boundless freedom of modulation. In *Parsifal* there is no longer any real modulation but rather an incessant undulation, in which the listener loses all sense of a definite tonality. We feel as though we were on the high seas, with nothing firm under our feet. Wagner has got himself into a chromatic-enharmonic way of thinking quite his own, continuously twisting in and out of the most remote keys. *Parsifal* does have individual movements of tonal equilibrium. They are welcome exceptions, some of them even charming; but exceptions they are, and usually fleeting. The tyrannical domination of the leitmotives in the orchestra and the license of the modulations strike me as serious shortcomings in opera music; Wagner and his disciples prize them as the ultimate in progress. These are basic differences of opinion about which it is no longer possible to quarrel.

A simple, sustained, lengthy prelude, whose solemn dullness can have no other purpose than to set the mood,

Contemporary caricature of Hanslick lecturing Wagner.

introduces the first act and, at the same time, the three principal Grail motives. In the various leitmotives in *Parsifal*, I find neither charm nor any particular faculty of characterization. The model for a leitmotive and its application has been provided by Wagner in *Lohengrin: "Nie sollst du mich befragen!"* ("Never must you ask me!"). Proclaimed by Lohengrin like a dogma, the theme stands forth at the outset in all its full significance. It doesn't have to be looked for or guessed at; it cuts through the score like a bright sword. The leitmotives in the *Ring* and *Parsifal* have nothing like the same sharply etched physiognomy, nor the same striking effect, if only because there are too many of them. Where every little sequence of notes is supposed to lead somewhere and signify something there can be no guidance and no significance.

The "Grail" motives from the Prelude continue, as orchestral accompaniment, to color the restrained first scene, notable for a manner of expression conspicuously more natural than the Nibelung dialogues and much the better for it. Gurnemanz, the bass, for all his ceremoniousness, is an amiable old man compared to Wotan. By way of declamation, on which, of course, the main burden of the Wagner roles rests, he does some odd jumping around; one notes that he knows *Die Meistersinger*. He repeatedly declaims such words as *Linderung, lindern, schaden, hämisch*, with an intentionally false emphasis on the last syllable, with upward leaps, now of a sixth, now of an octave.

The episodes preceding Parsifal's entrance offer nothing outstanding, with the exception of isolated imaginative phrases and sound effects in the orchestral accompaniment; there is no want of these, indeed, in any page of the score. After these monotonous, attenuated episodes—and not a moment too soon—comes the wounded swan on the wing, a splendid bit of stage mechanics. The Knights and pages, dashing up in great excitement with the miscreant Parsifal, fill the stage with lively animation. It is a dramatic, masterfully composed picture, in which we greet a reference to the "Swan" motive from *Lohengrin* as a pleasant reminiscence. Parsifal's entrance has a sympathetic effect. The "stupidity" of the inexperienced boy is represented simply, without false pathos. It is a phenomenon, psychologically well founded, that we tend to admire in others those virtues which we do not ourselves possess. Wagner, the reflective, sharp-witted artist, loves to glorify naïve simplicity, but in his case even naïveté sounds much too calculated. One need only think back to the song of the sailors in *Tristan and Isolde*, the song of the cobbler in *Die Meistersinger*, the Forge Song in *Siegfried*—these most unnatural of all the singing children of nature. It is otherwise with Parsifal in the first scene; he is just what he should be. Kundry is something else again! She is, to be sure, just what the poet would have her—but that is exactly the unnatural, the contradictory. A psychological and physiological hybrid, she sings— or rather cries and stammers—brokenly and in the most hair-raising intervals, at the same time being required to accomplish unheard-of tasks in the art of pantomime.

Now comes the wonderfully effective Transformation Scene. This masterpiece of scenic art receives only stepmotherly musical support. Until their arrival in the Temple of the Grail, Parsifal and Gurnemanz march to heavy, tiresomely monotonous chords. From here on the composition gets under way and rises to significant realization, supported by the magnificent and original impressions of the setting. Admirable in their effect are the solemn unison song of the knights, the chorus of the young men, and finally, floating down from above, the promise: *"Durch Mitleid wissend, der reine Tor."* In this surprising blend of pure high voices, the "promise motive" makes exactly the desired impression; in itself the rather empty ascending theme in fifths would hardly appear original or interesting.

The Holy Communion of the Knights of the Grail in the vaulted hall, with the three singing groups of knights, youths, and boys (above in the cupola), with the heavy ringing of the bells, the strange, paintinglike walls, the solemn unveiling of the Grail—all this combines to make a wonderful picture. The finale belongs unquestionably among those dazzling musico-scenic achievements in which Wagner has no rival. It may be my fault, or the fault of too great expectations, but the fact remains that I found the effect less powerful and brilliant than I had imagined it in reading the text and the score. I expected, particularly, an extraordinarily dazzling brilliance from the orchestra and an almost overpowering impression from the chorus, a relentlessly cumulative crescendo of sound right to the finish. As a rule, he who reads the Wagnerian scores finds his expectations far surpassed in the actual performance; this time, for me at least, hopes were not fulfilled. The conspicuously slow tempi in this very long first act may have contributed to this disappointment, as well as the familiar structural peculiarities of the sunken and hidden orchestra in Bayreuth, which does not permit of a supremely brilliant sound effect. In any event, after a first half vocally declaimed and orchestrally swallowed, the second half of this act is a musical treat, bringing with it rhythmically ordered and melodically self-sufficient song, and multiple-voiced song at that. Only one thing disturbs this pleasure: each scene is so endlessly drawn out. This inability to stop is as damaging to *Parsifal* as it is to the *Ring*. Everything is endless, everything too long, from the largest to the smallest, from the solemn Holy Communion to Kundry's impossible kiss.

The evil sorcerer, Klingsor, opens the second act with his conjuring of Kundry. The demoniacal is represented by not uncommon, yet nevertheless gripping, means. The vocal line is again precipitate, jerky, and recitative; the orchestra a witches' cauldron of bubbling leitmotives; and Kundry a musical-dramatic convulsion. Did Wagner intentionally of-

fer here every kind of sulphuric vapor just to render us
doubly receptive to the fragrance of the flowers in the following scene? If so, he achieved his purpose to the utmost.
The poesy of these lovely flower maidens sinks in places to
questionable doggerel. But then, who pays any attention to
the words when they flow, charmingly sung, from the lips
of thirty pretty girls? Even their pell-mell entrance amidst
the swarming triplets in the violins is full of dramatic life;
and so is the second half of this scene, the appearance of the
maidens as flowers. Their A-flat episode, *"Komm', Komm',
holder Knabe,"* rather in the tempo of a slow waltz, melodically charming, piquantly and yet simply harmonized, belongs to Wagner's happiest inspirations. With what fine
calculation are the thirty voices grouped, alternated, joined
together, now and then making way for little solo passages!
This is something one must see and hear for oneself. Of all
the scenes in *Parsifal* I would rate this the highest, for it
achieves the purest and most certain effects through the
simplest means: charming, expressive melody. Among all of
Wagner's tone poems this chorus of the maidens, difficult as
it is to perform, stands out, almost unique, as the only large-
scale scene in a light, gracious genre, and at the same time a
masterpiece of that genre.

The Flower Maidens, or Maiden Flowers, finally disappear, laughing; Kundry, now young and seductively beautiful, calls Parsifal by name. There follows the great scene
in which she first tells him of his mother, and then, with
ever-increasing ardor and desire, presses herself upon him.
Her narrative begins simply and singably, one of those
promising melodic buds which, with Wagner, frequently
peep out, only to be broken off before coming to bloom.
From there on, the composition builds up ever higher in

forced emotionalism. The composer seems perpetually on the point of running out of breath. He who doesn't know his leitmotives by heart is helpless in the face of the raging orchestral ferment, and he who does is hardly better off. It is too much to ask of the listener that he keep up with all the unmotivated, frightful changes of mood in which Parsifal and Kundry are tossed about throughout the whole long scene: from tedious narrative to sensual ardor, from ardor to religious ecstasy, and always in flight from everything musically beautiful and moderate. In Wagner's music certain stereotyped phrases have evolved for just such scenes of ultimately passionate expression, and by now they have hardened into what is almost a mannerism. I am aware that the sworn Wagnerians accept these standard phrases as natural sounds of deepest feeling, and that they prize this scene between Kundry and Parsifal as the finest the master has written. It depends upon the point of view. To me, the whole scene appears fundamentally untrue, the music outwardly ardent but inwardly cold, like baked ice. Then, just as we are beginning to grow tired and distracted amidst this tumult of fruitless passion, Parsifal's hand grasps the Holy Spear and we are saved. The magic castle collapses under the weight of truly shattering music, and the curtain closes on Klingsor's realm.

The third act begins with a kind of religious idyl, composed with much affection, but also with the utmost breadth. It is a poetic, peaceful picture: Parsifal, in snow-white ecclesiastical robes, sitting by the Holy Well enjoying the beauty of the verdant scene, while Kundry washes his feet, and old Gurnemanz anoints his head. The scene belongs among those, quite characteristic of Wagner, which fascinate us as an atmospheric picture. But one can contemplate a painted picture longer than the most beautiful static tableau in a drama, where the situation soon presses for movement and development. In this case the author has seemed incapable of satiety in the plastic quiet of the scene; the music goes its bucolic way with impressive monotony. A fragrant surprise is Parsifal's lyric excursion on the beauty of the flowering meadow, but this, too, is soon lost in the quicksand of instrumental infinity.

Parsifal, Gurnemanz, and Kundry finally make their way to the Mount of the Grail. Here, according to the directions of the text and the score, another transformation scene, like that of the first act, should perform its pleasant office and charm the three stationary pilgrims through all kinds of landscape to their destination. Technical considerations, resulting from the experiences of rehearsal, persuaded Wagner that it would be better to pass it up, and thus, in the performance, we had only a simple curtain closing over the three pilgrims as they set forth. This is certainly more appropriate. The repetition of one and the same device of scenic magic, reminiscent of fairy tales and children's theater, appeared questionable from the very beginning, a testimony to the poverty of the author's fantasy. The third act brought a second and equally praiseworthy departure from the directions of the libretto: the dead Titurel, who is supposed to arise from the coffin to give his blessing, does not arise but remains at rest, as a corpse should. The introductory funeral music is too extended.

How badly the plot, after lengthy lyric contemplation, needs a moment of dramatic energy is apparent in the great effect of Amfortas' passionate upward leap against the Knights of the Grail crowding about him. Right from the words "My father," his song (over an expressive accompanying figure, first in the cellos and then in the violins) is gripping. The final scene is executed with the same extraordinarily brilliant material—the same, to be sure, which served the Grail Scene of the first act. The solemn sounds of the harp, the song of the boys sounding from the cupola, the bright radiance of the Grail, the appearance of the dove—all contribute again to a dazzling spectacle, similar to the first finale.

The third act may be counted the most unified and the most atmospheric; it is not the richest musically.

And Wagner's creative powers? For a man of his age and of his method they are astounding. He who can create music as charming as the "gambols of the flowers" and as vivid as the final scene possesses powers which our youngest composers may well envy. *Parsifal*, on the other·hand, does not consist solely of such lucid intervals. It would be "pure foolishness" to declare that Wagner's fantasy, and particularly his specifically musical invention, has retained the freshness and facility of yore. One cannot help but discern sterility and prosaism, together with increasing long-windedness. Are not the irresistible Kundry's attempts at seduction rather stiff and cool in comparison with the similar scene in *Tannhäuser?* And is the Prelude to *Parsifal* not of the same origin and intent as the Prelude to *Lohengrin?* It is the same tree, but in one case in full bloom and in the other autumnally leafless and chilly. Or compare the song of Gurnemanz in the "Good Friday Spell" to the melodically related description of the Feast of St. John in *Die Meistersinger*. Pogner's poetic song seems to have recurred to Wagner in the composition of the "Good Friday Spell," but where is the inner strength, the singing soul of the model? Even the most powerful episodes from the *Ring*, considered individually and apart, have no equal counterparts in *Parsifal*, always excepting the chorus of the Flower Maidens, which stands quite alone. When one considers that those great moments in the *Ring* are distributed throughout four full evenings, the comparison may, to be sure, show a favorable balance. And *Parsifal* has the advantage of a more effective libretto. Although utterly inadequate as a "dramatic poem," it is a better opera text. It is, in a word, more musical. If we regard it as a festive, magic opera, if we ignore, as we often must in any case, its logical and psychological impossibilities and its false religious-philosophical pretensions, we can find in it moments of artistic stimulation and brilliant effectiveness.

III

The question of whether *Parsifal* should really be withheld from all theaters and limited to an occasional (and, in the long run, very doubtful) revival in Bayreuth was naturally on all tongues. Wagner himself, in an open letter from Palermo (April 1, 1882), emphasizes the "thoroughly distinctive character of this work" and assumes that he has made any performance of it outside Bayreuth impossible in that he has, "with this poem, entered upon a sphere rightfully and eternally foreign to our opera houses." I fail to see the "impossibility" of it. I have already pointed out the odd, and even improper, aspects of the church scenes. But since when has impropriety been an obstacle to the performance of Wagner operas? I find the ardent love scene between Siegmund and his sister Sieglinde in *Die Walküre* a thousand times more offensive than the religious scenes in *Parsifal*. The letter may be irritating to confirmed Christians, but they are in no way so shocking to human sensibilities as the scene cited above, once characterized by Schopenhauer as "infamous!" I must observe here that the church scenes in *Parsifal* did not make the offensive impression upon me that I and others had been led to expect from reading the libretto. These are religious situations; but, for all their earnest dignity, they are not in the style of the church but completely in the style of the opera. *Parsifal* is an opera, call it a "stage festival" or "consecrational stage festival" if you will. It cannot even be called a "spiritual opera," as the term was used by Anton Rubinstein; [10] for in such an opera the voluptuous worldly second act of *Parsifal* would be impossible. The way in which the Wagner of the Venusberg, that splendid old theatrical devil, jumps out of the habits of the pious monk in this second act is simply too stimulating.

Why should *Parsifal* not be given in a theater? Is the Bayreuth Festival Theater, for which it was written, not a theater? Is it a church or a concert hall? No! It is a theater, and one in which *Parsifal*, like any other opera, is played by professional singers in costume, with the most brilliant operatic apparatus conceivable, and for a continuously changing, paying public. Why should a performance of *Parsifal* offend religious sensibilities everywhere but in Bayreuth? We do not doubt Wagner's earnest resolve to prohibit it in Europe; he may have ulterior motives for reserving it for Bayreuth. But so far as inner motives, derived from the work itself, are concerned, I am unable to grasp the impossibility of performing it on other stages. And I should sincerely regret the prohibition. Just as it would have been a pity for all the cost and effort of the *Ring*, which was also

---

[10] The reference is presumably to Rubinstein's "sacred operas," *Der Turm von Babel*, and *Das verlorene Paradies*.

supposed to have been expended "solely for Bayreuth," so also would it be a pity—and even more of a pity—for *Parsifal*. It is easier to produce than the tetralogy, more compact, and more effective. Its music (with the single exception of the Kundry scene) has more repose and nobility. Assuming expedient cuts to be indispensable, it may prove more valuable and successful for the world's stages. For the past quarter century we in Central Europe have been badly off for new operas capable of survival, and we seem to be growing poorer in this respect from year to year. One need not be a Wagnerite to complain in all sincerity of this threatened withholding of *Parsifal*. I know very well that Wagner is the greatest living opera composer and the only one in Germany worth talking about in a historical sense. He is the only German composer since Weber and Meyerbeer whom one cannot disregard in the history of dramatic music. Even Mendelssohn and Schumann—not to speak of Rubinstein and the newer ones—can be ignored without leaving a gap in the history of opera. But between this admission and the repulsive idolatry which has grown up in connection with Wagner and which he has encouraged, there is an infinite chasm.

According to all that has been said or intimated here, an annual repetition of *Parsifal* in Bayreuth appears to be no less than a certainty. And then what? And if, even for Wagner's lifetime, it should really be withheld from other theaters—what then? Without Wagner's personality, the magnetic eye, and the strong hand which draws all, artists and audience, to tiny Bayreuth and holds them here, nobody after him would be in a position to accomplish the same feat.[11] The Bayreuth Festivals will probably die with Wag-

---

[11] Hanslick reckoned without Cosima.

ner, but certainly not his *Parsifal*. The great theaters will give this interesting devout opera without much religious scruple, and audiences in Vienna, Munich, and Berlin will hear and see it, just as do the audiences here, without imagining for an instant that they are in church. People will enjoy the **Ring** and *Parsifal* until, one fine day, they will get tired of being pitched around on a sea of endless melody and led around by stereotyped leitmotives. At that time let us have for the opera a new *reiner Tor*, a naïve composer of natural genius, possibly a kind of Mozart, who will master the "Master" and restore the natural balance between music and drama in the opera.

February 13, 1883

The news of Richard Wagner's sudden death was a painful and shocking surprise. Although it was hardly to be assumed that the seventy-year-old man would further extend the proud series of his works or add to his fame, the disappearance of so extraordinary a personality is, and remains, a loss. Wherever he appeared there was immediate stimulation, excitement, and lively discussion, flowing out from an artistic center in ever-broadening waves to all branches of cultural activity. Wherever the divining rod of his acts or his will pointed, there bubbled forth some hitherto hidden problem. And if it is a hallmark of the path-breaking artist that he provokes questions of principle over and above the immediate aesthetic impression, then Wagner stands at the head of the moving forces of modern art. He shook the opera and all its associated theoretical and practical questions from a comfortable state of repose bordering on stagnation. We hope that the lull now inevitably setting in will not lead back to stagnation again.

When called away, not from spiritual death, but suddenly, from the full exercise of his powers, a man of such comprehensive effectiveness and unexampled success leaves behind him a gap deeply felt by friend and foe. Actually Wagner had no foes in the sense of absolute, one-sided enmity; I have never met a musician so obtuse, or so violently partisan, as to overlook his brilliant endowment and his astonishing art, or underestimate his enormous influence, or to deny the greatness and genius of his works, even granting personal antipathy. Wagner has been fought, but he has never been denied. Those who believe that, with the excogitated and obstinately executed methods of his last style, he has led opera into a treacherous byway are admiringly aware that he broke this path with his own strength and that he created a new genre, a new art. We lift our hats to its boldness and consistency, without, however, giving it our allegiance, and without a moment's infidelity to the "old" art of Mozart, Beethoven, and Weber. The attempt to appraise Wagner's artistic-historical significance in general must be reserved for a later time. Today I wish only to set right the frequently misinterpreted conception of "opposition," and to state, once and for all, that there is no exasperated partisanship against Wagner but only against the Wagnerites. Even the latter may learn moderation— not today, to be sure, but in the near future.

What must console them is the fact of the master's enviably pleasant death. The saying of the Greek poet that the gods summon their favorites young is only half true. Even more fortunate are those who, like Wagner, achieve advanced years and high honors and then depart this life in good health, cheerfully, and without premonition. Yes, Wagner died a happy man. It was recently his privilege to bring his last great work to life in Bayreuth, to rejoice in its actual preparation, and to bask in the full sunlight of such a success as no other artist of any time or nation has enjoyed. I shall always remember him happily as I last saw him, on the balcony of his Festival Theater—which will soon be only a historic monument—rejoicing triumphantly in the all-conquering power of his will. And should one wish to remind us of his mortal weaknesses and passions, we can find no trace of them in our memory. We agree with Grillparzer that death "is like a flash of lightning which transfigures that which it consumes."

BRAHMS' SYMPHONY NO. 3[1]

[1883]

THE still unpublished Third Symphony of Brahms is a feast for the music lover and musician rather than for the critic, who must subsequently describe how it looks and what its beauties are. It is neither one of the rarest nor one of the most inexplicable of misfortunes that the eloquence of the critic declines in inverse proportion to that of the composer. The language of prose is not only poorer than that of music; as far as music is concerned, it is no language at all, since music cannot be translated into it. This may not have meant so much in former and less demanding times. But if one reads today the best of the reviews which appeared immediately following the first performances of the Beethoven symphonies, and imagines himself in the place of the first reader, one must confess that, while he has sensed the proclamation of great and beautiful music, he has been vouchsafed hardly a hint of its individual physiognomy. Only after the Beethoven symphonies had become generally known, and when critics were able to refer to what the reader himself had already heard and experienced, did we gain the substantial instruction of the better Beethoven studies of our own time. The new Brahms symphony has yet to build such a bridge between critic and reader. The former is left with

[1] The world *première* in Vienna on December 2.

Contemporary caricature of Brahms on his way to "The Red Hedge Hog," meeting place of the composer and his cronies.

no other recourse than to compare it with earlier and better known works of the same master.

Hans Richter,[2] in a gracious toast, recently christened the new symphony *"Eroica."* Actually, if one were to call

---

[2] Hans Richter (1843–1916), one of the outstanding conductors of his time. He conducted the *première* of *Der Ring des Nibelungen* in Bayreuth in 1876. From 1893 to 1900 he was Musical Director of the Court Opera in Vienna, and from 1880 to 1890 Musical Director of the Society of Friends of Music. He continued as one of the principal conductors of the Bayreuth Festival until his retirement in 1912.

Brahms' first symphony the *"Appassionata"* and the second the "Pastoral," then the new symphony might well be called the *"Eroica."* The title is, to be sure, not fully applicable, since only the first and last movements strike us as "heroic." In his Symphony in C minor, Brahms plunged with desperate passion into a dark Faustian struggle in the very first dissonant measures. The Finale, with its reminiscences of the last movement of Beethoven's Ninth, does not, for all its ultimate achievements, change the essentially emotional, almost pathological character of the composition. It is the expression of a suffering, abnormally agitated individual. The Symphony No. 2 is a peaceful, often pastoral counterpart. While the thunder of the old Beethoven is still heard receding in the distance, we hear the voices of Mozart and Haydn as if from celestial sanctuary. The Symphony No. 3 is really something new. It repeats neither the unhappy fatalism of the first, nor the cheerful idyl of the second; its foundation is self-confident, rough and ready strength. The "heroic" element in it has nothing to do with anything military, nor does it lead to any tragic dénouement, such as the Funeral March of Beethoven's *"Eroica."* Its musical characteristics recall the healthy soundness of Beethoven's second period, never the eccentricities of his last. And here and there are suggestions of the romantic twilight of Schumann and Mendelssohn.

The first movement belongs among the most significant and masterly compositions Brahms has given us. Wonderful is the way in which, after two resounding chords in the winds, the belligerent theme of the violins plunges down from above and then soars proudly upward again. The whole movement gives the impression of having been created in the flush of an inspired hour. Its second theme, in A-flat, blends incomparably with the movement as a whole. The climax in the development section is of impressive dimensions but, surprisingly, gives way toward the end to a gradually calmer mood, which, in turn, fades away swiftly and beautifully. The two middle movements prepare the listener for no mighty convulsions; they are rather an invitation to peaceful repose. The slow movement does not sing of deathly depression, nor the fast movement of heavenly exhilaration. They are moderate in pace and expression, tender and gracious in sentiment. The slow movement is a very simple song dialogue between the winds and the deeper strings. It would not be out of place in a Brahms serenade. Short, and without organic development or climax, it provides surprises and effects of tone color suggesting the musical conversation of softly sounding, tuned bells. The Scherzo is represented by an Allegretto in C minor, superficially reminiscent of Mendelssohn, which hovers easily in that hybrid, indeterminate mood which Brahms so favors in his middle movements. The piece is simply scored (without trumpets, trombones, and kettledrums) and is rendered particularly effective by the spirited charm of a middle section in A-flat.

For all their fundamental differences, Brahms' first and third symphonies are similar in one important respect: their respective middle movements are rather too small scaled, in content as well as in extent, for the imposing movements which adjoin them. The Finale of the Symphony No. 3 is again an accomplishment of the first order, the equal of the first movement, if not its superior. It rolls upon us with a fast, sultry figure in the deep strings. The theme as such is not impressive, but it immediately experiences the most astonishing development. The eerie sultriness of the opening is discharged in a magnificent storm, exalting and refreshing. The intensity of the music increases continuously. The second theme, in C major, brilliantly and emphatically intoned by the horn, soon makes way for a third, in C minor, even more forcefully introduced. At the peak of all this imposing development, one naturally expects a brilliant, triumphal conclusion. But with Brahms, and with Brahms alone, it is well to be prepared for the unexpected. This Finale moves imperceptibly from the key of F minor to that of D major, the raging winds subside to a mysterious whisper—long sustained chords in the winds are interrupted by the light rustlings of the muted violins and violas in thirds and sixths. The movement draws to a close, strangely, inconclusively, but most beautifully.

Many music lovers may prefer the titanic force of the First, others the untroubled charm of the Second. But the Third strikes me as artistically the most perfect. It is more compactly made, more transparent in detail, more plastic in the main themes. The orchestration is richer in novel and charming combinations. In ingenious modulations it is equal to the best of Brahms' works; and in the free association of contrary rhythms, of which Brahms is so fond and in the handling of which he is such a master, it has the virtue of not seeking effects at the cost of intelligibility.

"TRISTAN AND ISOLDE"[1]

I

WE ARE now familiar with all the stage works of Richard Wagner with the single exception of *Parsifal*, which has been monopolized by Bayreuth. Should the "Consecrational Stage Festival" remain excluded from profane theaters, then *Tristan and Isolde* completes the chain whose ten links Wagner's disciples would have us accept as the ten commandments of modern art. *Tristan and Isolde* is one of the most notable and important of these links. Almost dividing the chain in halves, it first represented definitively the "new style" of Wagnerian music drama. Wagner himself accords it the most important position in his artistic development, and he does not conceal the special enthusiasm he brought to its creation, a circumstance entirely in harmony with his predilection for ardent love stories. In an essay which he wrote in 1878, under the pseudonym of "A Christian Non-Musician," first released—or at least first unmasked—by W. Tappert,[2] love is characterized as the content and basic thought of all the Wagner poems from *The Flying Dutchman* to *Parsifal*. "Throughout *Tristan and Isolde*," according to this essay, "there runs the single, all-powerful, ecstatic

---

[1] First performance in Vienna, October 4, 1883.
[2] Wilhelm Tappert (1830–1907), German editor and writer on musical subjects. In 1887 he published a book called: *Wagner-Lexicon, a Dictionary Containing Coarse, Contemptuous, Spiteful, and Slanderous Expressions Used Against the Master, Richard Wagner, His Works, and His Disciples by His Enemies and Disparagers.*

246

longing of two human beings for an ideal realm of love, released from the sensuality of everyday life, which can be found, however, only in death."

The caution to be exercised with regard to all Wagner's explanations concerning the nature of his works may well dissuade the reader from blindly accepting Tristan as an "ideal Ritter Toggenburg, released from sensuality." [3] The knightly Gottfried von Strassburg,[4] in whose poem the saga of *Tristan and Isolde* has found its most charming adaptation, was far from denying the gay sensuality of his lovers by the superimposition of a sublimating sham holiness. Wagner took the material for his music drama from this favorite epic of our thirteenth century. While the medieval poet, however, did not confine himself to the love story, but rather framed it in a colorful canvas of flowering knighthood, Wagner compressed the material in a long love duet, against which all other persons and occurrences vanish like shadows.

The development of the "plot," dramatically tense and pictorially effective, speaks for Wagner's sense of the theater. We find ourselves aboard the ship which bears the Irish Princess Isolde to a compulsory marriage to King Mark. On the forward deck we see Isolde with her faithful maid, Brangäne; in the background and in the rigging are the busy crew, and to one side, at the helm, the knight Tristan. As we learn from Isolde's narrative, Tristan had killed her fiancé, Morold; and, himself wounded, had been nursed back to health by her. She had first wished to avenge

---

[3] Hero of a poem by Schiller. His lady love enters a convent and the Ritter (Knight) Toggenburg sits in front of her window until he pines away.

[4] Gottfried von Strassburg, medieval German poet, died about 1215. His epic *Tristan and Isolde* was the first artistic and complete rendition of the old saga.

Morold's death and, with drawn sword, had been on the point of doing so; but, charmed by Tristan's glance, she had let the sword drop. She is now incensed by the proud indifference with which he has held himself aloof from her during the journey. She summons him to her, ostensibly to drink to reconciliation before the landing, in reality to die with him. She tells Brangäne to mix a poisonous potion, but the latter, in her anxiety, seizes a phial different from the one designated and mixes the love potion instead. Tristan and Isolde drain the cup. The effect of this libation immediately transforms the defiant enemies into enraptured lovers. As they stand in passionate embrace, the crew herald the landing. The palace of Cornwall appears in the background, and emissaries of the King come aboard to welcome Isolde, who collapses in a faint.

Ignoring for the time being the intolerably boring musical exposition, this first act could hardly have been more effectively constructed as an introduction to the drama. But where is the plot, where the actual drama? We shall certainly not be expected to accept the two subsequent, unspeakably long acts as a drama! Just consider them. In the second act, Tristan and Isolde meet by night in the garden. King Mark surprises them in tender embrace, and one of his henchmen wounds Tristan fatally. In the third act we see Tristan on his sickbed, dying. At the approach of his longed-for "physician," Isolde, he falls lifeless; Isolde dies on his body. King Mark appears, forgives, and blesses the dead lovers. Wagner stretches this meager plot, with insatiable long-windedness, over five hours. That's how long the first performance in Munich [5] lasted. In Vienna, fortunately, liberal use of the conductor's red pencil spared us a good

---

[5] June 10, 1865.

hour. The trouble here, as a sincere admirer of *Tristan and Isolde*, Ludwig Ehlert, put it, is that "not the red pencil but only a sword can really help." This is something for those Wagnerites to think about who are now howling in various journals about the shameless trimming of the *Tristan* score in Vienna. I am rather inclined to regard an uncut performance of this work as a kind of murder committed upon singers and listeners alike.

But even if, as Ehlert suggests, the red pencil should give way to the sword, it could only cut away the rampant excrescences of the music, not the sick core of the drama. This incurable sickness is the complete want of freedom of will on the part of the two principal characters, both governed by a chemical power, the fatal love potion! From a tragedy we demand above all that its characters act of their own free will and that they suffer and succumb accordingly. The origin of their fate must lie within themselves. Romeo and Juliet, Hero and Leander, fall into passionate love at first sight. They follow this passion heedlessly, despite all obstacles, regardless of all obligations, and come to grief. They need no magic potion. The tragic fate of Tristan and Isolde has its origin in a mistake for which neither is to blame. They are helpless victims of a purely superficial pathological process, free of moral responsibility, and thus the very opposite of the tragic heroes of a drama. I am familiar with the arguments brought forward by Wagner's advocates in defense of this love potion. It is only a symbol, only "the poetic representation of real feeling." Such sophistries ignore the real pillars of drama. In the theater we believe only what we see. The love potion, which is prepared and downed with such emphasis, and which exercises its magic effects with such glaring clarity before our eyes, is still a love potion, regardless of how many hundreds of times the poet may have thought it only a suggestion. Reading symbolism into it does not bring us from the dilemma: either the magic potion was superfluous, if Tristan and Isolde loved each other without it, or it is undramatic. Hans Hopfen,[6] in a witty *feuilleton* on the subject, has already demonstrated that the confusion of two different drinks is actually a subject for comedy. I shall enlarge upon his pertinent observation only by reference to Donizetti's *L'Elisir d'Amore*, where the motive is used for dramatic, specifically comic, effect. Wagner has a notable predilection for magic potions, and he overlooks the lamentable part this fairy-tale requisite plays in tragedy nowadays. Just as he took the love potion from the Celtic saga (in *Tristan and Isolde*) so he took from the older German epic (in *Götterdämmerung*) the draught of forgetfulness by which Siegfried is rendered faithless to Brünnhilde.

The poem of *Tristan and Isolde* is decidedly inferior to the libretti of *The Flying Dutchman*, *Tannhäuser*, *Lohengrin*, and *Die Meistersinger*, not only in its want of a dramatically motivated plot, but also in the language itself. Open the book to any page at random and see how long it is possible to take this mad round of bombastic word and sentence dislocation seriously! One particularly brilliant example has for years been the property of the comical periodicals, and has, in this sense, become popular. It is the end of the great love duet:

Liebe—heiligstes Leben—Wonnehehrstes Weben—
Nie Wiedererwachens wahnlos hold bewusster Wunsch! [7]

---

[6] Hans Hopfen (1835–1904), German poet and playwright.
[7] Wondrous rapture—weaving cherish'd visions achieving.
Ne'er daunted by daylight's beam, be our undying dream.
(The translations of this and the following lines from *Tristan and Isolde* are quoted from one of the "authentic" English librettos.)

Other, less famous examples are none the less delightfully characteristic of the poetry of R. Wagner. Thus, Tristan sings before downing the love potion:

> *Tristan's Ehre—höchste Treu'*
> *Tristan's Elend—kühnster Trotz.*
> *Trug des Herzens, Traum der Ahnung:*
> *Ew'ger Trauer einz'ger Trost,*
> *Vergessens güt'ger Trank!*
> *Dich trink' ich sonder Wank.*[8]

Are there really connoisseurs who find this sort of thing poetic, profound—or even German? From time to time, the dialogue is adorned with such archaic turns as the following: *"Befehlen liess dem Eigenholde—Furcht der Herrin ich, Isolde"*;[9] *"Der Wunde, die ihn plagte, getreulich pflag sie da"*;[10] *"Wie ahnte mir, dass es dir Kummer schüf,"*[11] and then there are childish plays on words, introduced with an aspect of profundity, such as: *"Des Schweigens Herrin heisst mich schweigen, fass' ich, was sie verschwieg, verschweig' ich, was sie nicht fasst."*[12]

And yet all these linguistic horrors are as nothing compared to the desperate poetic impotence revealed in the long love duet—in our production, thank God, "shamelessly" cut. The lovers fill whole pages of the libretto with their hysterical metaphors of day and night, night and day.

---

[8] Tristan's honor—highest truth!
Tristan's anguish—brave distress!
Traitor spirit, dawn-illumined:
Endless trouble's only truce!
Oblivion's kindly draught
With rapture thou art quaff'd!

[9] Nay, order him; pray, understand it: I, Isolde, do command it!

[10] The wounds from which he suffered She nursed in skillful wise.

[11] Never dreamt that for thee but sorrow and need had been wrought.

[12] Concealment's mistress makes me silent; I know what she conceals, and I conceal more than she knows.

When and where have two persons in the height of passion spoken to each other in unending comical similes? Tristan and Isolde, on their sylvan bench, philosophize about "day" and "night," "waking" and "dreaming," "living" and "dying," and finally even about the little word "and":

> Doch das Wörtlein und—
> Wär' es zerstört—
> Wie anders als
> Mit Isoldens eignem Leben
> Wär' Tristan der Tod gegeben. . . .[13]

Is that dramatic? And, in the tragic sense, is it dramatic when the deceived husband, catching his wife with her lover, instead of drawing his sword, gives "the faithfulest of friends" a loquacious, tender, edifying lecture?

Where *Tristan and Isolde* ceases to be unintelligible and perverse it immediately becomes commonplace, undistinguishable from any other banal opera libretto. "*Isolde, Geliebte! Tristan, Geliebter! Bist du mein? Hab' ich dich wieder? Darf ich dich fassen? Kann ich mir trauen? Endlich, endlich! An meine Brust!*" [14] And so on. There are not, at least, any word repetitions in *Tristan and Isolde*, such as occur in the earlier operas. Wagner mentions this in his brochure *Music of the Future* as one of its special virtues. This strikes me, however, as one of Wagner's not infrequent delusions. The repetition of one and the same word in ever-changing melodic form is no mere "repetition," and I find it a matter of indifference if the opera composer, assuming him capable of melodic variation,

---

[13] But the sweet word—*and*—
Were it destroy'd,
How else then but with Isolde's last lingering breath
Were Tristan conquer'd by Death?

[14] Isolde! Beloved! Tristan! Beloved one! Art thou mine? Do I behold thee? Do I embrace thee? Can I believe it? At last! At last! Here on my breast!

repeats four or five times on changing melodic sequences the words: *"Wie sich die Herzen wogend erheben,"* [15] or, as Wagner does in Act I, Scene VI of *Tristan and Isolde*, subjects this sentence to three Wagnerian paraphrases: *"Wie alle Sinne wonnig erbeben! Sehnender Minne schwellendes Blühen! Schmachtender Liebe seliges Glühen!"* [16] Which is more monotonous, the repetition of the same few words on varying melodic sequences or the infinite repetition of the same little motive on a sequence of synonyms?

A second delusion goes hand in hand with the first: Wagner's assumption that every word of his "poem" is distinctly heard when sung. This would be conceivable only with an incomparably more discreet and simple orchestration. In such episodes as the first and second allegros of the love duet, the words are lost in the conflagration of the orchestra, and the audience will hardly be able to discern whether the same explanation is repeated four times in the old opera style or given four synonyms in the Wagnerian.

Why do I dwell at such length on the poem of *Tristan and Isolde* instead of considering it in connection with the music? Because, first of all, Wagner himself invited it by publishing the libretto as an independent poem long before he composed the music; secondly, because of the boldness of the Wagner disciples in proclaiming Wagner a great dramatic poet, equal in stature to Goethe and Schiller. The Wagnerites, Wolzogen at their head, consistently speak of him in the same breath with Goethe. Nohl [17] has even gone

---

[15] Sweet in the soul the sunlight is falling . . .

[16] Fill'd is the bosom with rapture enthralling . . . Languishing passion, longing and growing, love ever yearning, loftiest glowing!

[17] Carl Friedrich Ludwig Nohl (1831–1885), German music critic, historian, and biographer (Beethoven and Mozart). His principal contributions to Wagneriana were *Richard Wagner* (1869), *Richard Wagners Bedeutung für die nationale Kunst* and *Das moderne Musikdrama*.

so far as to demonstrate that Schiller and Goethe are decisively surpassed by the dramatist Wagner and, so to speak, antiquated! We have, for the moment, intentionally left to one side the question whether the *Tristan* music will some day be chosen as the music of the future. It is essential, first, to protest emphatically against the assumption that this stammering and stuttering speech, murderous to thought and language alike, this bombastic and excogitated monologue and dialogue, wanting in any kind of natural sensibility, is a poetic work of art designed to be the future poetry of the German people. Artistic taste may for a time suffer such odd sicknesses, but it will never degenerate, in the country of Schiller and Goethe, to the general cultural level of the Wagnerian poetry.

II

Diligent readers of music criticism must, after twenty-five years, be thoroughly fed up with hearing about Richard Wagner's system and appraising each of his operas accordingly. Convinced of the validity of the view that a work of art does not exist in order to prove something, I made every effort during the performance of *Tristan and Isolde* to forget Wagner's theories as completely as he is supposed to have forgotten them during the work of composition. But the experience of the reporter is exactly that of the composer himself: the accursed "system" will not down. *Tristan and Isolde* will always have a certain doctrinaire after-taste in view of Wagner's challenge to apply to it the severest demands arising from his theoretical dicta. Nor should we fail to apply Wagner's plaint about the damage inflicted upon his "single confirmatory work of art" by the death of the tenor Schnorr.[18] It is noteworthy that Wagner's new system was devised and made public prior to the production of this music drama, which followed as a test of the correctness of his reckoning. Wagner was never absolutely free in artistic creation after his emergence as a theoretical writer; in the operas subsequent to *Lohengrin* he had to prove something, above all in *Tristan and Isolde*.

One finds in Wagner the most varied gifts, sometimes mutually complementary, sometimes mutually contradictory. The poet, the musician, and the painter in him are almost without exception interdependent. Those fascinating effects, which, for want of a better term, we call "Wagnerian," arise solely from this rare mixture of creative elements. But between Wagner the composer and Wagner the theoretician the going is not so smooth; they follow lines which, beginning as apparent parallels, inevitably cut across each other in their course. Wagner is far too much an artist, far too much a born genius, to compose consistently according to a premeditated theory; on the other hand, he is too single-mindedly doctrinarian to ignore a theory of his own, thought up and proclaimed as a major revelation. This forces both sides to concessions. And Wagner the theoretician and Wagner the composer actually take such cognizance of one another that the logic of the Wagnerian system comes off with no less damage than the fine beauty of his artistic creation. In *The Flying Dutchman*, *Tannhäuser*, and *Lohengrin* the old and the new flowed fully and directly one into the other. It is only in *Tristan and*

---

[18] Ludwig Schnorr (1836–1865), who created the role of Tristan in Munich and died six weeks later of a chill contracted on that occasion. His wife, Malvina Garrigues (1825–1904), was the first Isolde.

Isolde that we have, according to Wagner's own claim, the perfect realization of his theories.

Actually, *Tristan and Isolde* resembles an opera only in the visible scenery. The chorus, which in *Tannhäuser* and *Lohengrin* is responsible for the most significant effects, is reduced to a few cries of the sailors in the first act. There are no ensembles. The characters do not sing with one another, but rather by turns. Even in the long, long love scene, the voices of the two lovers are united only fleetingly. Musical form, already considerably relaxed in *Tannhäuser* and *Lohengrin*, is totally destroyed, making way for a type of dramatic representation reminiscent of a boundless flood, and governed not by the musical idea but by the word. The essential factor appears to be the orchestra, which weaves the organic musical material from imaginatively spun threads. In no way does song dominate the orchestral accompaniment as the supreme will; it is rather itself the accompanist, following with mere words the "endless melody" of the orchestra. For Wagner, who has declared that pleasure in the familiar terminable melody is "childish," this endless melody—a logical monstrosity—is the panacea of the true music drama. When we charge the songs of Tristan, Wotan, and Parsifal with want of melody, the Wagnerites reply that the opposite is true, that everything in it is melody and only melody. Which is true, too. It's simply another way of saying the same thing. Endless melodizing is no more equivalent to melody than thinking is equivalent to thought, or painting equivalent to a picture.

The same stylistic principle dominates in *Tristan and Isolde* as in the *Ring* and *Die Meistersinger*, only even more consistently. I rate *Die Meistersinger* incomparably higher. There, at least, the golden tree of life sprouts lustily alongside gray theory. The terminable melodies—that is, the real melodies—which stand out so charmingly from the "endless" ones, the full-sounding, multiple-voiced songs, and the infinitely more animated and pleasant character of the story, have actually won for *Die Meistersinger* a popularity to which *Tristan and Isolde* can hardly dare to aspire. Even in the *Ring*, notably in *Die Walküre*, there is a richer stream of musical invention. *Tristan and Isolde* can claim only the advantage of unified, compact form and more human content.

Wagner makes more moderate use of leitmotives in *Tristan and Isolde;* he refrains, at least, from presenting each character with a kind of musical visiting card. The chromatic sigh of the "Love-Potion motive" runs through most of the opera in almost solitary dominance. Only a few less pregnant motives crop up from time to time as reminders of what has gone before. And yet, if *Tristan and Isolde* is reminiscent of its precursor, *Lohengrin*, in the more thrifty application of leitmotives, it has nothing whatsoever in common with Wagner's earlier operas in the form of its musical dialogue. In *Tristan and Isolde* we encounter for the first time the new Wagnerian declamation—allegedly true to speech, actually unnatural which characterizes the utterances of Wotan and Alberich. From this song-speech, destructive of thought and feeling alike, there emerge, from time to time, melodic episodes of delightful, even charming lines, particularly in the love scene. These immediately appealing melodic buds are all too quickly stifled in the quicksands of declamation. And in *Tristan and Isolde* they are less numerous than in any of Wagner's other stage works.

The orchestra plays the most important part, and the

most interesting. As soon as one can forget that the singer is the first and determinant factor in opera and that the accompaniment should be his servant, one follows the incomparably colorful, imaginatively interwoven line of this remarkable orchestra with excitement and often with admiration. We can describe the character of this treatment of the orchestra authentically in Wagner's own words. In his *Reminiscences of Schnorr*, he invites his friend to examine the score, particularly the third act. "You have," says Wagner, "only to examine the score more closely, to follow the musical motives which, from the beginning of the act to Tristan's death, restlessly appear, develop, combine, separate, blend again, grow, abate, finally struggle, embrace, and intertwine; and then you must realize that these motives—which, in order to achieve their significant expression, require not only the most detailed harmonization but also the most independently motivated orchestration—portray an emotional life, alternating between the utmost sensuality and the most firmly resolute longing for death, such as could never previously have been imagined in any purely symphonic movement with similar resources, and which was capable of fulfillment here only through instrumental combinations such as purely instrumental composers would hardly feel called upon to employ." Actually, the orchestral accompaniment against which the dying Tristan shatters his stammering song sounds just about as complicated and breath-taking as this example of Wagnerian prose.

It is from the standpoint of vocal art that Wagner's dramatic style is most open to objection. It would be hard to find music more unvocal, more unsingable, than is to be found in *Tristan and Isolde*. It is almost comical that the same Wagner, in his report on the proposed founding of a music school in Munich, says: "The neglect of song is reacting in Germany, not only on the singers, but even on the instrumentalists and, above all, on the composers." It is too bad that he did not specify the guilty composers by name; I can think of none remotely so guilty as he. The roles of Tristan and Isolde sin not only in their excessive demands upon the voice; because of the unnatural intonation, the dominance of the chromatic and the enharmonic, the restless, inconclusive modulations, they are ultimately difficult to impress upon the memory. They have to be memorized measure by measure, mechanically, like an utterly strange language. Susceptibility of memorization has always been accepted as a sign of the genuine beauty of a poem or a song; music, moreover, is more closely bound than any other art with the fundamental conditions of the memory. Artists who sing *Tristan and Isolde* correctly from memory, even if only strictly according to the written notes, earn my sincere admiration. That they do today what seemed practically impossible twenty years ago is largely Wagner's accomplishment. In having imposed ever heavier tasks upon the singers over a period of thirty years, he has drilled and strengthened their memories—just as one strengthens the muscles through continued gymnastic exercise. It is certainly an accomplishment, but I doubt its value. I can't help but be reminded of the inventions of the Parisian instrument maker, Sax,[19] who, with his new system of pistons, has enabled trombones, horns, and bass tubas to execute the most difficult chromatic passages and trills.

---

[19] Charles Joseph Sax (1791–1865), who, in 1824, invented an "omnitonic" horn, adjustable to any key by means of a piston. He was the father of Adolphe Sax (1814–1894), inventor of the saxophone.

They can do things which would otherwise be impossible. But this technical advance is at the same time an aesthetic danger. Composers are now beginning to write as brilliantly for these formerly simple and dignified instruments as for the flute or the oboe. The instruments enjoy their new technical advancement at the cost of their noble, musical character. That they can now play just about everything is a technical triumph but a musical disaster. It is similar with the gradually extended memorization capacities of our singers, brought about by Wagner's unnatural song writing. They have learned to memorize and to sing the most difficult and unvocal music; the result is that from now on composers will give them only the most difficult and unvocal music to sing and to memorize. Thanks to Wagner, the singers' memories have learned to walk the tightrope, but their voices have broken their necks in the process.

The first act is pleasantly impressive for the pictorial effect of the scenery and the genuinely dramatic conclusion following the tiresome conversation of Isolde and Brangäne. The second act is by far the most significant musically. Right at the beginning, the sound of the hunting horns receding in the distance and the song of Isolde as she awaits her lover show Wagner's talent in its most genuine and brilliant aspects. Even more captivating is the incomparable A-flat episode in the duet, *"O sink' hernieder, Nacht der Liebe"* ("O Night of Rapture, Rest upon Us"). This is enchanting music such as Wagner alone can contrive, a pearl in a long, long duet, but only one. I was struck by the realization that Wagner almost always becomes banal as soon as he tries a jubilant melody (and note that what is involved here is a real melody). The first allegro, with its upward-climbing eighth-note figures and the outcry on the high C, could occur in any opera by Reissiger [20] or Lind-paintner.[21] Hardly nobler is the ever more ardently flaming final allegro, in whose commonplace theme ("unending, eternal") one may find the inevitable, old-fashioned mordent, and whose ultimate ecstasy is thundered out on the four notes G, F-sharp, G, G-sharp.

Just as one was compelled to make cuts of unique dimensions in this duet in order to make it possible for the stage, so also was one forced to similar amputations by the length of Tristan's suffering and death. The "curse," the most strenuous passage of all, was omitted entirely. This was the passage about which Schnorr despaired. Over this third act, so originally and suggestively introduced by the mournful song of the shepherd, there hangs an uncommonly compelling, monotonous sadness. But hardly anyone can bear with its awful length. Here, as in the second-act duet, one asks oneself how a composer of Wagner's eminent understanding of the theater can ignore all sense of proportion. The pathological element in this scene becomes increasingly oppressive and offensive. One waits impatiently for Isolde's *Liebestod*, which achieves its climax and finality on the main theme of the love duet.

Thus the over-all impression of the work, despite its outstanding individual beauties, remains one of oppressive fatigue resulting from too much unhealthy overstimulation —a condition unchanged by the fact that it has been occasioned by a great genius. If one salvages sufficient clarity of thought to analyze *Tristan and Isolde* as a fulfillment of

---

[20] Karl Gottlieb Reissiger (1798–1859), Marschner's successor as director of German Opera at Dresden.

[21] Peter Joseph von Lindpaintner (1791–1856), conductor of the Court Orchestra at Stuttgart and composer of some twenty-one operas, the best known of which was *Der Vampyr*.

Wagner's system, one must confess that even in this consistent attempt to achieve absolutely dramatic music there is much that is illusory. Is it really dramatic when Wagner, at the close of the second act, avoiding any kind of ensemble, fills the stage with deaf and dumb figures who take no more part in the shattering events than the garden benches around them? Or is it dramatic when, after the drinking of the love potion, an interminable, slow orchestral interlude forces the two lovers to stand, motionless, facing each other, so long that even the greatest actors in the world, in such a situation, could not but break down? And, finally, is it dramatic that the mortally ill Tristan spends an hour in the third act singing while he dies and dying while he sings? Even Donizetti's Edgardo and Verdi's Ernani, after fatally stabbing themselves, are content with a few modest measures.

Thus, *"Wahn"* ("Madness") here, too. *"Überall Wahn!"* ("All the world's mad"), as Hans Sachs sorrowfully proclaims.

RUBINSTEIN

———•—•—•———

[1884]

INTEREST is centered at the moment on Anton Rubin-
stein.¹ Exactly six years have passed since he last appeared
in Vienna. And just as he did then, he accomplishes the
miracle of arousing spontaneous enthusiasm in audiences
surfeited with concerts generally and with piano playing
particularly. His four concerts were sold out in a matter of
hours. The last few years have witnessed nothing like it
except in the case of Bülow,² who, since Liszt's retirement,
has shared supremacy with Rubinstein in the pianistic
domain. Rubinstein has an even greater hold on the public,
thanks to the greater immediacy and sensual energy of his
playing.

He gives his concerts alone, without assisting artists
and, unfortunately, without orchestra. In his first concert he
sat for almost three hours and played more than twenty

¹ Rubinstein gave five recitals during this visit to Vienna, on February 14,
20, 23, 24, and 27, offering completely different programs in each. And what
programs! In the fifth, for example, he played a Prelude and Fugue by J. S.
Bach, a Rondo by P. E. Bach, Beethoven's "Appassionata," Schumann's
Kreisleriana, and eleven of his own shorter pieces. As encores he played the
"Waldstein" Sonata, Chopin's Étude in A—flat, and his own *Valse Caprice.* In
the fourth, he played in succession—among many other things—Bach's Chromatic Fantasy and Fugue, Schubert's "Wanderer" Fantasy (opus 15), and
Chopin's Sonata in B-flat minor!

² Hans von Bülow (1830–1894), also a distinguished Wagner disciple,
who served the master with pen and baton (he conducted the *première* of
Tristan and Isolde in Munich) and was Wagner's predecessor as husband of
Cosima Liszt.

pieces, including three sonatas! [3] This may not have been too much for the indefatigable Rubinstein, but it was too much for his listeners. A three-hour opera is endurable because it is a whole, dominated by the greatest multiplicity of content, sound, personality, and scenic device. But twenty piano pieces, one after the other, in a sweltering auditorium —that's too much for even the strongest nerves.

Conspicuous in all of Rubinstein's recital programs is the absence of the name of Brahms. He cannot possibly have simply overlooked the best-known of living composers. It must be that he avoids him intentionally. How strange! For Brahms offers the truly great piano virtuoso the richest treasures of substantial, poetic, unhackneyed music. For us non-virtuosos, Brahms' piano compositions have the single fault of being almost impossibly difficult. And on just that account we like to hear them as often as possible at the hands of masters. It is rather as it was with Schumann, who came into his own as late as he did largely because the virtuosos ignored him. Liszt, with commendable frankness, subsequently censured himself for this neglect, and publicly declared that he regretted, too late, having "thus set a bad example." In this by no means inconsequential respect, namely, his attitude toward Brahms, it is neither to Rubinstein's credit nor to his advantage that he represents the opposite of Bülow.

To hear Rubinstein play is pleasure in the finest sense of the word, a pleasure in which the sensual element plays an important part. His healthy, robust sensuality floods upon the listener with refreshing candor. His virtues are rooted in his unsapped natural strength and elemental freshness.

---

[3] Schumann's Sonata in F-sharp minor and Beethoven's Sonatas in D minor (opus 31, No. 2) and A major (opus 101).

"Rubinstein, the Demon"—so named in a contemporary caricature after his own opera.

So also are the faults into which his rich, but frequently unbridled, headstrong talent easily tempts him. Compared with former years, his playing nowadays is a model of refinement. The melting beauty of his tone, the softness and concentrated strength of his touch, are at the very peak.

Why does he exert such a singular fascination upon his listeners? I believe it is because his virtues arise from a

source rapidly drying up—and not only in Germany—
robust sensuality and love of life. That is an artistic endowment in which one is only too happy to pardon many a
defect, because, among the moderns, it is so rare. Our
composers and virtuosos have little of that naïve, elemental
force which would rather dare than brood and which, in
passion, acts impulsively and without thought of the consequences. They are dominated by the intellect, by education, by refined and more or less profound reflection. They
tend to diffuse bright light with all sorts of blended colors,
to subdue passion, and to indulge in circumlocution. Bülow
may be regarded as their most distinguished representative.
Compared with him, Rubinstein is a naïve, lusty nature.
And that is why we listen to him with untroubled ears and
uninhibited pleasure. He may excite anger now and again,
but with the next movement all is forgiven.

We particularly admired, in his recent concerts, his
sensitivity in the playing of tender pieces. No one can sing
more beautifully than Rubinstein played in his performance
of Beethoven's Sonata in D minor. In Schumann's Sonata in
F-sharp minor the slow movement was ideally beautiful—
an incomparably transfigured image. The Finale, on the
other hand, was overwhelmed in such a manner that even
listeners thoroughly familiar with it were not always able to
keep pace and were often left to guess what he had actually
played. He did Chopin's Barcarolle with charming delicacy,
and then whipped through the C-sharp minor Polonaise,
opus 26, in such a manner that the elegant charm of the
piece, and sometimes even its rhythmic pattern, fell breathless by the wayside. Even Schumann's Fantasy in C major,
which he began wonderfully, was rendered disorderly and
blustery by the exaggeration of the E-flat major middle
section.

That Rubinstein exerts his fascination even in such moments as these is probably because the audience senses that his excesses derive from an irresistible primeval force rather than from mere vanity of virtuosity. Our culture-weary Europe capitulates willingly to this force, rooted in temperament and race, and permits the "divine Rubinstein" many a special prerogative. Yes, he plays like a god, and we do not take it amiss if, from time to time, he changes, like Jupiter, into a bull.

THE
MEININGEN COURT ORCHESTRA[1]

[1884]

AN ITINERANT orchestra, playing not dance music but the greatest works of the symphonic repertoire, is a novelty reserved for our railroad epoch. I even heard people asking one another: "Why a visiting orchestra in Vienna, and from Meiningen, of all places?" Meiningen is, to be sure, a remote little duchy with an enlightened and art-conscious Duke. But it hasn't even an opera. And yet in this very circumstance lies the secret of the Meiningen Orchestra.[2] By permitting his musicians and actors to go on month-long tours, the Duke denies himself much private pleasure, but he provides the most effective stimulus to his artists' industriousness and extends the horizon of their ambition. And since the orchestra of this opera-less court has no duties in the

---

[1] The Meiningen Orchestra gave three concerts in the Musikvereinssaal on November 20 and 25 and December 2, Bülow conducting. Bülow was soloist in the second concert playing Brahms' Piano Concerto in D minor (the orchestra accompanying without conductor) and Brahms was soloist at the third, playing his Concerto in B-flat. The visit also included a concert by Bülow on December 1, the orchestra assisting, in which Bülow played Beethoven's Concerto in G and Liszt's arrangement for piano and orchestra of Schubert's "Wanderer" Fantasy, opus 15.

[2] Most European orchestras, including the Vienna Philharmonic, are essentially opera orchestras. The Vienna Philharmonic, for example, is an independent body whose membership is drawn exclusively from the orchestra of the Vienna State (formerly Court) Opera. Not all members of the opera orchestra are members of the Philharmonic, but all members of the Philharmonic are regularly employed in the State Opera.

theater—Bülow having even done away with the incidental music for stage plays—it is free to dedicate itself to the study of symphonic works and to rehearse them with a frequency and thoroughness which would leave our opera conductors shuddering just to think of it. Add to all this the fact that this unexampled study is directed by a conductor who is heart and soul in the work, who regards it not as a burdensome duty but as a matter of both honor and affection. Only the continuous association of a gifted and enthusiastic conductor with a loyal and dedicated orchestra, daily and hourly at his disposal, can render possible the incomparable ensemble playing which is the speciality of the Meiningen Court Orchestra and which entitles it to appear anywhere in the world—including Vienna—in the full consciousness of its capacities. That is the one factor. The other is Bülow's always interesting choice of programs.

His favorites are Beethoven and Brahms. As far as Beethoven is concerned, this is as fully in order in Vienna as elsewhere; he is, after all, the foundation of all orchestras. With Brahms, on the other hand, what Bülow has done—and continues to do—for the understanding and propagation of his compositions is highly significant. If one had to name the most brilliant of the Meiningen Orchestra's accomplishments, it would be difficult to choose between the performance of Brahms' Variations on a Theme of Haydn and that of Beethoven's Symphony No. 8. Brahms, whose sense of structural design finds its most forceful expression in the variation and its related forms, has given us a masterpiece. The Haydn variations do not reveal themselves to the listener fully at a first acquaintance, but the wonderfully clear, carefully and precisely worked-out performance by the visitors from Meiningen made them about as readily and easily accessible as possible. The performance of Beethoven's Eighth Symphony was a similar accomplishment, rendered even more effective by the audience's familiarity with the work. I have never before heard it so perfectly played. The charmingly and gracefully executed Allegretto excited such an overwhelming storm of applause that Bülow —who had not previously repeated a single piece—was forced to give in to the insistent shouts of "encore!"

There was also an extraordinary reception for Brahms' Piano Concerto No. 2, in B-flat. The composer himself was the pianist, playing with his characteristic rhythmic strength and masculine authority. One sensed that he stood above the work, but this majesty and objectivity sometimes contributed to an impression of carelessness, not to say indifference. Nor was the purely technical execution adequately polished or smooth. It was not, in any case, brilliant. Brahms played as a great musician who had once also been a great virtuoso but now had more important things to do than practice a few hours a day.

Thanks to Bülow, the Meiningen Orchestra has become an analogy for the Meiningen Theater Group which, without individual stars, achieved fame through the excellence of its ensemble. In precision the orchestra is unsurpassed and hardly has an equal. There is probably not another orchestra which could duplicate its feat of playing the accompaniment for Brahms' D minor Concerto—more a great symphony than an accompaniment—with Bülow at the piano but not conducting. An even more astounding feat is that of the whole string orchestra in playing flawlessly Beethoven's formidable Quartet Fugue, opus 133 [3]—a tonal

---

[3] Modern orchestras do it nowadays without prompting such astonishment.

wilderness in which the best string quartets are prone to lose their way. A stunt, to be sure, and thoroughly unenjoyable at that; but the orchestra which can bring it off securely can challenge the mightiest rival. Where the

Hans von Bülow caricatured in the role of Papageno from Mozart's Magic Flute.

Meiningen Orchestra does not measure up to the Vienna Philharmonic is in sensuous beauty of tone, fullness of sound, warmth and temperament of interpretation, and, finally, in brilliance of total effect. One should not forget, of course, that it has only forty-eight men, as compared with the Vienna Philharmonic's ninety. And the fault may well be with the instruments rather than with the players. Bülow's violinists are excellent musicians, but without the compelling force of the Vienna violinists; the double basses and trombones are splendid, the oboes often sharp and shrill, the clarinets and horns good, but not equal to the Viennese. The connoisseur will readily appreciate the effects which Bülow achieves with this comparatively weak orchestra, sometimes by prudent conservation, sometimes by the concentration of all his resources at a given point—as, for example, in the last movement of Beethoven's Symphony in C minor and the Overture to *Der Freischütz*.

Of inventive spirit, and given to experimentation, Bülow has introduced several effective innovations. One of them is the five-stringed bass, which extends down to the low C; the usual four-stringed bass reaches only to E. Another is the Ritter alto viola.[4] Of stronger construction than the common viola, it surpasses it in fullness of tone and reduces the all-too-great distance normally separating violas and violoncellos. And finally, the chromatic kettledrums, which can be retuned by pedals while being played.[5] Another much-discussed innovation—and one which strikes me as of doubtful value—is that of having the orchestra stand while playing. This is actually a reversion to an older custom, possibly attributable in former times to the limited space of the old concert halls and the etiquette of court orchestras. It was probably in Vienna that the fashion of playing while seated first took hold. Dittersdorf, at any rate, writes in his autobiography: "I had long desks and benches made, for I introduced the Viennese custom of playing while seated, and arranged the orchestra in such a way that every

---

[4] Devised by Hermann Ritter (1849–1926), German violinist, teacher, and musicologist. His viola alta was adopted by Wagner for Bayreuth.

[5] The invention of Ernst Pfundt (1806–1871), Mendelssohn's tympanist in the Gewandhaus Orchestra in Leipzig.

player faced the audience." [6] Standing is a kind of insurance against carelessness and ease-taking on the part of the players; sitting conserves their strength. The first is more military, the latter more humane.

Bülow conducts the orchestra as if it were a little bell in his hand. The most admirable discipline has transformed it into an instrument upon which he plays with utter freedom and from which he produces nuances possible only with a discipline to which larger orchestras would not ordinarily submit. Since he can achieve these nuances securely, it is understandable that he applies them at those places where they would seem appropriate to him if he were playing the same piece on the piano. It would be unjust to call these tempo changes "liberties," since conscientious adherence to the score is a primary and inviolable rule with Bülow. It is hard to draw the line. Opinion will vary according to individual taste and the character of specific passages. Metronomic evenness of tempo has, in any case, been disavowed by all modern conductors.

A few things struck me as unmotivated and affected, among them the almost mannered phrasing of the scale fragment which introduces the Finale of Beethoven's Symphony No. 1. And I had reservations about certain rubati in the Overture to *Der Freischütz*. These are interpretive peculiarities common to Bülow's predilection for individual touches; I did not feel them as disruptive intrusions upon the spirit of the compositions. In this respect, however, I should not be inclined to grant the same right to all conductors. In

---

[6] In 1764, when Dittersdorf (Karl Ditters von Dittersdorf, 1739–1799) was Director of Music for the Bishop of Grosswardein (in western Rumania. It was called Nagy Varad during the dual monarchy and is now known as Oradea).

his treatise *On Conducting*, Richard Wagner gave expression to a number of dangerous theories, but when he himself conducted, one readily accepted many liberties—in this very Overture to *Der Freischütz*, for instance. Bülow is entitled to claim the same privileges, since his respect for the great masters is unquestioned and his artistic individuality always interesting. His personal physical mannerisms, however, can hardly be pleasing to anyone. If it were true that the best conductor is he who is least conspicuous, then we should have in Bülow the exact opposite. But Bülow would not be Bülow were he able to stand stock still while conducting. One must accept him as he is, with all his weaknesses and quirks; and indeed we are happy to do so in cordial acknowledgment of his brilliant virtues and accomplishments. Hans von Bülow, the inspired pianist, conductor, and writer, is a real individual, unduplicated in the musical present.

ROSENTHAL

[1884]

IN HIS weak, unprepossessing outward appearance Moriz Rosenthal recalls Tausig. Nor is that the end of the similarity. He also resembles Tausig in the extraordinary brilliance of his playing. Through many years of acquaintance with modern piano virtuosity I have almost forgotten what it is to be astonished, but I found young Rosenthal's achievements indeed astonishing. His technique scorns the most incredible difficulties, his strength and endurance the most inordinate demands. I need recall only two offerings which, in respect to technical difficulties, represent the ultimate in the piano literature: Liszt's *Don Juan Fantaisie* (which he played for the first time with the uncut ending) and Brahms' Variations on a Theme of Paganini, opus 35. In this last piece, Brahms, not content with the obvious tests of dextral strength and velocity, has added latent (particularly rhythmic) difficulties hardly perceptible to the listener but enough to drive the player to despair. Although not comparable to the wonderful Handel Variations as a composition, the Paganini Variations comprise a noteworthy contribution to the piano literature and reveal an interesting and little-known aspect of Brahms' creative talent. The piano virtuoso can as little afford to overlook them as the various Brahms studies (without opus number), his arrangements of Chopin's Étude in F minor in thirds and sixths, Weber's

Rondo in C minor (with the sixteenth-note figure transferred to the left hand), and Bach's Chaconne (for the left
hand alone).

The Paganini Variations (on the last of the twenty-four
Capriccios) suggest a bold campaign of discovery and con-
quest in the field of piano virtuosity, an experiment in the
capacities and possibilities of the instrument. To report that
Rosenthal mastered them faultlessly, and with utter security
and freedom, is to rank him automatically among the first
pianists of the time. Less satisfactory was his performance

of Schumann's Novelette No. 2. The element of virtuosity was intrusive, not only by way of fast tempi, but also by way of certain liberties (slighting of certain notes, separation of melodically related notes and phrases, etc.) which here and there gave a stilted effect to the melodious middle section. I was unfavorably impressed, also, by too frequent recourse to the pedals and by the unlovely violence with which the keys were pounded in fortissimo passages. And yet, these are details characteristic of all the youngsters of the Liszt-Tausig school. Such impetuosity may well subside with the years, as it did with Liszt and Tausig, and make way for more tenderness and warmth. Rosenthal's modest bearing and his quiet and unaffected manner at the piano merit special praise.

LILLI LEHMANN

[1885]

LILLI LEHMANN is unique, if only in regard to a repertoire which ranges from lyric to dramatic parts, from the Queen of the Night to Fidelio, from Zerlina to Donna Anna.[1] After having witnessed her great success as the Queen in *The Huguenots*, a purely coloratura part, it was with almost reproachful admiration that we watched her begin her second engagement as Isolde. Her far from heroic voice is no match for the merciless surf of the Wagnerian orchestra. Such parts demand not only passionate expression and dramatic talent but also uncommon vocal strength. In her own interest, and in that of music lovers generally, I would like to see her safeguarded against such unnatural exertions, to warn her, *nota bene*, against voice-killing roles but not against dramatic parts as such. That so imaginative an

---

[1] It ranged more widely than that—from Offenbach and Suppé to all three Brünnhildes. During her guest engagement at the Vienna Court Opera in the season of 1884–1885 (the engagement discussed in this review), Lilli Lehmann (1848–1929) sang Isolde, Leonore (*Fidelio*), Donna Anna (*Don Giovanni*), Konstanze (*Die Entführung aus dem Serail*), and Norma. In the last opera her sister Marie was the Adalgisa. Since Marie did not like to sing the lower voice in cadenzas, the sisters changed voices, so to speak, every time a cadenza came along. She made her American debut in the following season as Carmen at the Metropolitan, on November 25, 1885, and sang the *Die Walkure* Brünnhilde five days later. It is pertinent to note—at a time when young singers are being charged with impatience—that Lilli Lehmann made her debut as the First Boy in *The Magic Flute* on October 20, 1865, a month before her seventeenth birthday, and pinch-hit as Pamina a few days later.

artist, and one rejoicing in such potentialities as an actress, should feel impelled to break the bounds of purely virtuoso parts and move on to genuinely dramatic assignments is hardly surprising. On the contrary: just as Miss Lehmann's coloratura roles derived their peculiar charm from their rare dramatic inspiration, so do her eminently dramatic roles benefit from the attributes of the former coloratura singer.

The now conventional division of female parts into coloratura and dramatic categories is of comparatively recent origin. Mozart, Beethoven, and even Weber were not aware of this arbitrary division. Their principal soprano parts demanded dramatic energy and, at the same time, a voice more or less well versed in florid singing. Rossini, Bellini, Donizetti, and often even Verdi wrote for artists schooled in virtuosity and yet also capable of dramatic characterization. No one regrets the disappearance of purely bravura parts, but there is every reason to regret the opposite extreme sanctioned by the newest school, according to which genuine technique is not a requisite for dramatic singers. As late as the thirties, the best German representatives of Donna Anna, Agathe, Euryanthe, and Fidelio were singers well versed in coloratura and not above singing such roles as Norma.

An excellent Norma is the rarest thing in Germany today. And what else could one expect? Our coloraturas haven't the voices, and they can't act: our "dramatic" singers have no vocal technique. For this reason alone it was a source of artistic gratification that Lilli Lehmann sang Norma as well as Donna Anna and Fidelio. She reacquainted us with the effects which a voice schooled in virtuosity can achieve when combined with dramatic and

279

passionate expression. Some of the critics made a show of annoyance about the reappearance of an opera which we had not heard for years. I can only say that I am sorry for anyone whom the "dramatic" tendencies of contemporary music have robbed of the capacity to appreciate the simple, beautiful line of these naturally motivated melodies. *Norma* suffers from monotonous stretches, meager accompaniments, and trivial devices. But are there no trivialities in even the best German operas? The difference is only in color. German trivialities are commonly camouflaged as "drama" or "scholarship." Bellini was naïve, even in his trivialities. He was one of the last of the naïve masters. His limited vocabulary was often inadequate for the scope of his emotions, but the emotions were genuine and flowed straight from the heart. With a God-given, if severely restricted, talent he gave to *Norma* and the somewhat weaker *La Sonnambula* the best that was in him. There are excellent things side by side with poor and outmoded stuff. But who since Bellini has written a melody with the sweet long breath of *"Casta diva,"* or a song more expressive in its ultimate simplicity than that of the final duet, *"Qual cor tradisti,"* or a soulful melody so plastically effective as the *"Padre, tu piangi"* in the last finale? One of the best pieces of music Wagner ever wrote, the second finale in *Tannhäuser*, points unmistakably to the final scene of *Norma* as its model in the effective climax, *"Ich fleh' für ihn"* ("I Pray for Him").

In his youth, Wagner had a high opinion of *Norma*. The *Bayreuther Blätter*, in a recent example of imprudent piety, reproduced an old article in which he endorsed the validity of coloratura singing. The editors attempted in a postscript to reconcile these early enthusiasms with his later doctrines

—in vain! The Wagner of the *Ring* regarded every vocal ornament as a crime. The coloratura in *Norma* is no crime; it is rather an obsolete fashion. In all of Germany in Mozart's time, and in at least all of Italy in Bellini's, floridity was considered natural and dramatically permissible in leading soprano parts. It was a generally acknowledged fashion, and it was essential that one know how to wear it in good taste. Sensuous beauty and vocal charm dominated the opera in those days, just as the specifically dramatic dominates now. The ultimate consequences of this "purely dramatic" style—angular declamation, monodic dialogue, endless abuse of deceptive cadence, and the sovereignty of the unbridled orchestra—do all these constitute the irrefutable, sole, and eternal truth? It is a fashion, just as the former preponderance of floridity was a fashion. It will become obsolete sooner or later, and all the more certainly because it is musically unnatural.

Whatever there was of musical unaffectedness in the young Wagner has been destroyed by the Wagnerites. I confess—not without trepidation—that I once found much pleasure in the flowery extravagances of *L'Elisir d'Amore* and *Don Pasquale*, the fine wit of the ornate passages of *Le Domino Noir* [2] or *Fra Diavolo*. I was not then aware of the iniquity of coloratura singing or the perversity of those who enjoy it. The latest issue of the Wagnerite organ, *Parsifal*, has opened my eyes. In a special article on "The Immorality of Coloratura Singing," one Bruno Schrader [3] pronounces this cruel verdict (of immorality) and proposes that the indictment be extended to the representatives and adherents of coloratura singing. Even more significant than the verdict

---

[2] Both by Daniel-François-Esprit Auber (1782–1871).
[3] (1861–1926), German critic, historian, and teacher.

is the justification. Why is coloratura singing immoral? Answer: because of the "damage it has done and continues to do to the popularization and further development of Wagner's works of art." Cimarosa and Mozart, Rossini and Auber are immoral when they offer coloratura singing because they damage Wagner's work. He who enjoys it is equally guilty. Should there exist a monster so immoral as to consider the vocal style of *The Barber of Seville* or *L'Elisir d'Amore* more musical than that of Alberich or Mime, it should obviously be sentenced to starve in the bowels of Siegfried's dragon.

Our vocal virtuosos, according to Schrader, should not be referred to as coloratura singers or even as artists. "Away with that rubbish!" he concludes. "The time for feasting our ears is past. It will not be long before the heavenly strength of Wagner's creations will have purged the temples and thrown the money-changers out."

It is certainly laudable of myself and some of my peace-loving colleagues that we have resolved not to touch upon the question of Wagner without special provocation. Whole libraries have been written about his works, pro and con. It would be best, I think, to observe silence on this exhausted topic for a few years. Only posterity will be in a position to review the subject without bias. But the best of intentions are frustrated by such manifestations as the above. We consider it our journalistic duty to keep the musical world informed of the latest philosophic discoveries of the Wagnerites and of the refined classical language which they employ to popularize them.

Let us return to more pleasant things: to the singing of Lilli Lehmann. Her Norma was characterized in the slow cantilenas by the most beautiful portamento and the securest and finest intonation and swelling of the high notes, in the florid passages by a pure and fluent coloratura. The latter was never a coquettish intrusion; it remained noble, serious, subordinate to the situation. One may conceive of a thunder of passion more imposing, of lightning flashes of jealousy and anger more incendiary—this reservation is applicable to all the climactic moments of Lilli Lehmann's dramatic roles and is probably attributable to vocal limitations rather than to want of temperament, although the latter cannot be entirely denied.

How decisive an actor's or singer's personal appearance may be in determining the final sum of his effectiveness— much more than talent, technique, and schooling—can be observed in Lilli Lehmann in a twofold sense. Nature denied her penetrating strength and sumptuousness of voice, and thus deprived her of the strongest, most immediate means of passionate communication, but it endowed her with a personality predestined not only for the stage but particularly for tragic and noble roles. The tall, slender figure need only appear, lifting the nobly featured head with the darkly arched eyes, and one believes in her at once as Donna Anna, Norma, and Fidelio. There are, moreover, her matchless carriage and her exemplary costumes. Inspired dramatic characteristics develop naturally from the situation; they never appear contrived or imposed from the outside. She does not commit the fault of acting too much or singing too loudly.

In Lilli Lehmann, refined artistic schooling outweighs strong immediacy of feeling. Her creations do not represent the improvisations of a great natural force; they are rather products of a superior mind which finds its way to the core of every interpretive problem and discloses the inner treasure in unblemished perfection.

BRAHMS' SYMPHONY NO. 4

———•◦•◦•———

[1886]

SINCE its first performance in Meiningen,[1] this symphony has enjoyed a series of triumphs. Everyone who had read the enthusiastic reports from Frankfurt, Cologne, and Elberfeld, and even those who had not, expected something great and unique.[2] What symphony of the last thirty or forty years is even remotely comparable with those of Brahms? And yet more symphonies are being composed these days than is generally appreciated. The Leipzig *Signale* lists no fewer than nineteen symphonies performed for the first time last year. It looks as though Brahms' successes had stimulated production, following the long silence which set in after Mendelssohn and Schumann. Not every little talent with a few successful piano pieces and songs to its credit is qualified, however, for such an undertaking. The symphony demands complete mastery; it is the composer's severest test—and his highest calling. Brahms is unique in his resources of genuine symphonic invention; in his sovereign mastery of all the secrets of counterpoint, harmony, and instrumentation; in the logic of development combined with the most beautiful freedom of fantasy.

All these virtues are abundantly present in his Fourth

---

[1] October 25, 1885.

[2] At its first performance in Vienna, in the Musikvereinssaal (Philharmonic Concert) on January 17, Hans Richter conducting.

Symphony; they even seem to have gained in stature—not in melodic invention, perhaps, but certainly in executive craftsmanship. Individual preference may favor one or the other of Brahms' symphonies; my particular favorite is the Third. But I do not want to exclude the possibility that my opinion may change when I have become equally familiar with this latest work. Neither its treasure of ideas nor its chaste beauty is apparent at a first glance; its charms are not democratic. Manly strength, unbending consistency, an earnestness bordering on acerbity—basic characteristics of all Brahms' larger works—constitute the decisive factors. In the new symphony they create their own form and their own language. Independent of any direct model, they nowhere deny their ideal relation to Beethoven, a factor incomparably more obvious with Brahms than with Mendelssohn and Schumann.

The E minor Symphony begins with a simple, somewhat thoughtful idyllic theme, which, after some exposition, finds a vigorous, defiant counterpart. The movement ends strong and stormy. Despite an abundance of ingenious counterpoint, the piece is clear and transparent. The listener does not—and need not—perceive that the theme, with its soft lamentation, is repeated canonlike in the bass.

Deeper and more direct is the effect of the Adagio, the most exquisite movement of the whole work and one of the most beautiful elegies Brahms ever wrote. There is a peculiar sweet and warm atmosphere in it, an enraptured charm which miraculously blossoms into ever-new tone colors, until, at last, it fades away into soft twilight.

The theme of the Scherzo announces itself boldly— Schumann would have called it "forward"—until its brusque humor is tamed by a second, rather commonplace melody. A lively sixteenth-note figure in the violins meanders charmingly through the dialogue of these two themes. Piccolo and triangle are added to the instruments already employed, achieving an effect of lights subtly withheld.

The Finale, although it begins very "energetically" and is ingeniously complex in its nature, seems, on the whole, rather reflective than passionate. Trombones appear, for the first time in the whole symphony, with a series of abrupt chords. They lead directly to the theme [3] which, in eight-measure periods, is continually varied in the form of the old chaconne or passacaglia. This is done with an inexhaustible wealth of structural variation and with an astonishing harmonic and contrapuntal art never conspicuous as such and never an exercise of mere musical erudition. This form is completely novel for a great symphonic finale, and every detail in it is novel too. It is the most ingenious of all, but it is also the least popular, possibly because its size is out of proportion to the melodic material. For the musician, there is not another modern piece so productive as a subject for study. It is like a dark well; the longer we look into it, the more brightly the stars shine back.

---

[3] This statement would appear to be in error, since these chords *are* the theme. The original admits no other translation (*"Sie leiten unmittelbar in das Thema, das, achttaktig,"* etc.), but it may well be rather imprecision or carelessness than faulty analysis.

VERDI'S "OTELLO"

[1887]

Milan, February

I

ALMOST sixty years have passed since Verdi first set foot in Milan. He came as a poor boy from the village of Busseto, where his parents kept a general store. Charitable benefactors had arranged that he should enter the conservatory. The director of this famous institute, Francesco Basily, an obscure scribbler whose name is now known only in the music lexicons, was unable to find the slightest talent in the shy applicant and dismissed him.

Old Verdi may well have reflected upon this when, two months ago, he was honored and celebrated by his jubilant compatriots as no artist has ever been honored before. But it is not of the brilliant *première* of Verdi's *Otello* that I have to report but rather of a later performance, with which the La Scala season just came to a close. It was my purpose to become acquainted with the work, not to participate in a festival. The joyous tribute to Verdi on that fifth of February, 1887, the arrival of visitors from all over Europe, thousands of them, first fluttering with curiosity and later fluttering with pleasure—all this was certainly worth experiencing and will live on in the memories of those who participated. But such an electric atmosphere is not conducive to the exercise of dispassionate judgment. To appraise the new opera objectively, to observe its effect upon a normally disposed public, I judged a twentieth performance better suited than a first.

The *première* commanded the attention of the entire civilized world. Popular anxiety about the fate of a new opera is a remarkable phenomenon, and doubly remarkable when Verdi is involved. It is understandable that all Italy should have held its breath. As artist and man he is the darling of his people. For forty years he has been their greatest composer. *Otello* was thus a matter of national consequence, and the governmental crisis [1] was forgotten, along with the military disasters in Abyssina.[2] But that the leading newspapers of France, England, Germany, and even America should have sent reporters to Milan in the middle of winter to report on its success, even to submit telegraphic bulletins act by act, was a striking sign of the times. Where has anything similar occurred? Granted that travel is twenty times easier and faster—where has there been even a hundredth so much general European interest in a new opera? Weber was the most celebrated German opera composer of his time. Did so much as one single German reporter journey to London to hear his *Oberon?* And when Spohr and Marschner wrote their last operas, did music fans travel even from neighboring cities to Kassel or Hanover to hear them? Even with Rossini's *William Tell* and Meyerbeer's *Le Prophète*, late works of world-renowned composers, we patiently awaited the reports of the Paris newspapers.

"They'll get to us if there's anything to them!" That used to be the attitude about new operas. They were neither so important nor so infrequent! How numerous were the

[1–2] Governmental crisis in Italy in 1887 in connection with the heavy losses suffered by the Italian forces in Dogali in the Abyssinian war.

productive talents in France, Germany, and Italy between the twenties and forties! What a scintillant Milky Way of novelties in comparison with the lonely flickering stars in the operatic heavens of today!

The participation of all Europe in a new tone poem began with Wagner's *Der Ring des Nibelungen*. But one should not forget the fanfare of newspaper articles and brochures which heralded that event years in advance. Nor should one forget that Bayreuth involved not merely an "opera" but an unprecedented "artwork of the future," a revolution, not only of dramatic music, but of the whole nature of the stage. The attractive force emanating from *Otello* cannot be compared with it. It is an Italian opera without special scenic sumptuousness, with neither brilliant processions nor crowd effects. It is a simple lyric tragedy on a familiar subject already set by other composers and involving essentially only three persons. This is where Verdi's real accomplishment enters as the explanation: the trust which he has awakened by his steady advance in objectivity and ability from work to work.

He has interpreted every success as a challenge to do better. His care in preparation has become steadily greater, as has the interval between one opera and another. Five years separate *La Forza del Destino* from *Don Carlos*, and as many separate *Don Carlos* from *Aïda*. The latter was astonishing in the increased intensity and nobility of its dramatic style, in the advance in musical workmanship. Affection for Verdi then gave way to respect, even in "cooler" Germany.

When, fifteen years later, word got around that he had completed a new opera, nobody doubted that it would represent a new step forward. The conviction was general that he could not end his splendid career with an inferior work. There was reason to expect something unique, something significant. And this general expectancy, so different from the usual misgivings about aged composers, explains better than anything else the extraordinary interest in this last, long-matured work of an artist who, to use Boito's fortunate comment, has climbed higher and higher on his own shoulders.

Otello differs markedly from Verdi's older works and drastically from the type of the earlier Italian operas. This is clear right from the start in the plan of the libretto. It is by Boito (the composer of *Mefistofele*) and adheres as closely as possible to the Shakespeare original. Thus the composer's normal impulse to expand musically on his own is completely subordinated to the progress of the drama. Compare this with the libretto of Rossini's *Otello*. In Rossini's first act there is not a trace of Shakespeare. We see Desdemona, still a young girl in the home of her parents, courted by Roderigo, forced by her father to accept him, reconsidering at the last moment, etc. Rossini's librettist was concerned solely with giving the composer and the singers an opportunity to shine independently. Shakespeare's tragedy was treated as though it were an authorless, even worthless subject. Only the last act is true to Shakespeare, and only Desdemona's monologue attempts serious dramatic effects. Rossini paid dearly for this first attempt to permit an opera to end tragically (with the murder of Desdemona). The Italian public of 1816 expressed such displeasure over the gruesome final scene that Rossini had to substitute a happy ending. In the revised version, Desdemona protested her innocence, Otello threw the dagger away, and the two of them, reconciled in a happy embrace, intoned the love duet,

290

"*Cara per quest' anima*" (lifted from Rossini's *Armida*). I myself have seen Rossini's *Otello* with this ending. Today it would be sheerly impossible.

The Italians were not alone among the older opera composers in treating the classics frivolously. It was rather characteristic of the times. This was reflected even in the German theater. When the first German Othello strangled the first Desdemona in Hamburg,[3] so many women fainted that the tragedy had to be given with a happy ending on order of the Senate. And characteristic of our own time is the present respect for the poem. Compare the ridiculous parody of *Romeo and Juliet* in the operas of Bellini or Benda [4] with Gounod's modern version, or the text of Spohr's *Faust* with that set by Gounod! Even Verdi, in his younger days, did not hesitate to reshape classical dramas, among them *Macbeth,* *Die Räuber* (*I Masnadieri*), and *Kabale und Liebe* (*Luise Miller*), according to the prevailing theatrical fashions. One of the nicest examples is to be found in *I Masnadieri*. Amalia, clothed in deep mourning, appears at the grave of old Count Moor and expresses her grief in a plaintive adagio. How was the composer then to crown the aria with the indispensable bravura allegro? Very simply. Just as she sings the last measures of the adagio, a servant rushes to the churchyard and hands her a letter. She opens it: "Ah, from my Carlo!"—and breaks into the most spirited of allegros. That Verdi and his librettist have not permitted themselves similar liberties with *Otello* was to be taken for granted. They have followed Shakespeare even more faithfully than Gounod did in *Romeo and Juliet* or Ambroise Thomas in *Hamlet*.

---

[3] On October 26, 1776.

[4] Georg Benda (1722–1795), Bohemian composer, credited with originating the idea of music drama with spoken words.

The choice of *Othello* as the subject of an opera does not strike me as an especially happy one—or, to put it as objectively as possible, I find it uncongenial. Of all tragic passions, jealousy is the least ideal, the least musical. It is, as Vischer [5] once said in a Shakespeare reading, a dirty, sticky passion. Ugliness is justified in music only when introduced by way of contrast or as a recurrent element. In treating such a subject as *Othello* it must inevitably achieve an embarrassing dominance. Music which must describe how a cold, evil spirit infects a narrow-minded husband with the poison of calumny, first drop by drop and then in whole doses—such music has to fulfill a difficult and certainly not the most beautiful of missions. Iago, who is much in the foreground in the Verdi opera, is a subtle monster, hardly more capable of musical representation than Franz Moor (*I Masnadieri*). We hate him. And, indeed, we hate Otello hardly less. The strangling of the sleeping Desdemona is the most gruesome of all tragic endings. Shakespeare's dramatic genius and his extraordinary psychological insight enabled him, by many subtle devices, to motivate the character and brighten the grim proceedings with gaily colored scenes and witty speeches. A musical setting has to forego much of this. And Verdi has always been drawn exclusively to the pathetic and the tragic; like Bellini, the Italian Spohr, he has no humor, hardly even a vein of natural gaiety.

A casual remark by Verdi that *Othello* would make a good opera subject prompted his young friend Boito to write the libretto—a nice demonstration of unselfish devotion. Verdi began the composition four years ago, in his seventieth year. Boito has shown fine literary sensibility as well as a

---

[5] Friedrich Theodor Vischer (1807–1887), German aestheticist and writer.

deep knowledge of both music and the stage. He has been able to embody many passages from Shakespeare word for word without recourse to literary violence. It is unfortunate that he found himself compelled to leave out the entire first act and begin with the second. He can hardly have failed to notice what fine material there is in Shakespeare's exposition: the threatening crowd in front of Brabantio's palace, waking the old man in the middle of the night with the cry, "Up! Your daughter is being abducted!" And the meeting of the senate to consider the charge against the Moor, Othello's narrative and the incomparably beautiful vindication of Desdemona—all these offer attractive opportunities to the composer. According to Boito, he and Verdi racked their brains to find a way of retaining this first act without making the opera too long. The Italians will not stand for five-act operas (in which we share their taste); and for this particular drama of jealousy it seemed to the authors that the prelude in Venice could well be passed up. Aside from this abridgment, Boito has departed from Shakespeare only in the omission of Brabantio and Bianca and in some modest lyrical trimmings. Otherwise the drama is mirrored in the opera almost scene for scene. Verdi submerged himself in the original with similar reverence and devotion and modulated his once so resonant voice to blend with the poem.

II

Have you ever examined an old ivy plant attached to a tree or to a wall? You will find that its first, lowest leaves change their form near the middle of the trunk; the jagged outlines become rounder and disappear entirely in the thin leaves at the top. It is the same plant, but with a threefold re-forming of the leaves. With this picture I should like to answer the familiar question, whether Verdi, in his *Otello*, has become an entirely different composer. He has remained the same, the old undamaged trunk, although in the long course of his growth the leaves have gradually changed from their original form. The sharp, challenging rhythms and melodies of his first period (*Nabucco*, *I Lombardi*, *Ernani*) are more rounded in his second (*Rigoletto*, *Il Trovatore*, *La Traviata*). In *Aïda* and *Otello*, they achieve noble simplicity. He who has steadily followed Verdi's development will perceive in *Otello* a further growth of the same trunk; there has been no grafting, least of all with anything from Bayreuth.

That the music of *Otello* is "Wagnerian" is the same fable which was circulated about *Aïda* and which was given credence in some quarters. There is not a scene, not a measure, for which Verdi owes any obligation to the composer of *Tristan and Isolde*. There are neither leitmotives nor endless melody; song is dominant throughout—the voice! The orchestra, even in its liveliest moments, serves the voice as supporting accompaniment. That decides the question whether a composition is "Wagnerian." Only *Tristan and Isolde*, *Die Meistersinger*, the *Ring*, and *Parsifal* are Wagnerian in the sense applicable today. In these music dramas the method of composition, the style, is Wagner's exclusive invention. Whoever else employs it learned it from Wagner.

Otello, as I have said, betrays not the slightest trace of this method. If, however, one chooses to call Wagnerian every sharper emphasis on the dramatic, every device of characterization or illustration in the orchestral accompaniment, every relaxation of the old restrictions of form, then *Fidelio*, *Der Freischütz*, and *Euryanthe*, not to speak of the operas of Marschner, Meyerbeer, and Gounod, are Wagnerian. The instinctive, consistent progress from the purely

294

musical to the characteristically dramatic can be attributed, in Italian operas as well as in German, to the spirit of the times. Wagner comprehended this spirit consciously and with extraordinary talent and success in *The Flying Dutchman*, *Tannhäuser*, and *Lohengrin*. He didn't create it; he followed it. This intensified dramatic emphasis which in *Tannhäuser* merely compresses the musical outline but doesn't do away with it, is like a charge of electricity in our whole atmosphere. It is peculiarly Wagnerian only in the manner of its expression in Wagner's last operas.

People who think in terms of slogans professed to scent the "music of the future" in Verdi's operas thirty years ago, when Wagner's name was hardly known beyond the borders of Germany. Even so serious a critic as Fétis [6] saw in *Simon Boccanegra* an attempt at the "music of the future of contemporary Germany." Even more common was the assertion, in connection with *Don Carlos* and *Aïda*, that under Wagner's influence Verdi had "gone dramatic." And yet it was plain to all that Verdi was endowed by nature not only with a great fund of melodic invention but also with a dramatic talent forceful to the point of crudity, which distinguished him immediately from Rossini, Bellini, and Donizetti. At the same time he has always remained honest. Only twice, to his disadvantage, has he acquiesced in a denial of his own individuality and nationality: in *I Vespri Siciliani* and *Don Carlos*, five-act tragedies written in French for the Grand Opéra in Paris and redolent of a bad—because badly assimilated—foreign influence. Finally we encounter in *Aïda*

---

[6] François Joseph Fétis (1784–1871), Belgian musicologist, critic, and historian, author of *Biographie Universelle des Musiciens* (1837–44), *Histoire Générale de la Musique* (1869–76), and many other theoretical and historical studies.

and the Requiem a Verdi remarkably advanced and clarified, but in no way Wagnerian.

I was perfectly clear in my own mind about the Wagnerian aspects of *Otello* after looking through the score. I was anxious, nevertheless, to add tangible, factual criteria to these rather abstract ones. My visit to Milan offered me ample opportunity to do so. Three estimable musicians who have had intimate contact with Verdi over a period of years, the composer Boito, the critic Filippo Filippi,[7] and the publisher Giulio Ricordi, told me that Verdi knows none of Wagner's later operas. He had heard only *Lohengrin* in Italy. *Tannhäuser* he first heard in Vienna in 1875, and possibly *The Flying Dutchman*. Of the impression made upon him by these works, he said only that they interested him. It had always seemed to me highly improbable that so meager and late an acquaintanceship with Wagnerian music could have exercised any influence on Verdi's style. It is unthinkable in view of a remark made by the far younger and rather pro-Wagnerian Boito in regard to Verdi's taste. Boito described it as the sheerest nonsense for young composers to follow in Wagner's footsteps. "Wagnerism," he said, "is the sickness of our time. It is a scourge."

Otello, in its stern dramatic character, represents a further clarification and simplification of the style dominant in *Aïda*. The material itself determines certain essential differences. While *Aïda* offers a spectacle rich in variety and pomp, with dances, festival processions, and massed crowds, *Otello* is concentrated upon a very simple situation, animated more by the emotional experiences of the three principals

---

[7] (1830–1887), leading Italian Wagnerite, author of *Richard Wagner, eine musikalische Reise in das Reich der Zukunft* (1876), and editor of *Gazzetta Musicale*, of Milan.

than by surprising developments. It offers no orchestral noise, and it is elaborated by fewer odd tonal combinations than *Aïda*. There are moments of inspired harmonization and modulation, but there are also many rude progressions. The predilection for chromatic chord sequences, for the shift from major to minor in the same key, is more prominent than before. The chorus, as necessitated by the subject, is relegated to the background, playing only a modest and decorative role in the first and second acts and none at all in the last; only in the finale of the third act does it come fully to the fore. Dramatic truth and consistency are dominant. The scenes progress from one to another without sharply definitive finales. The duets and trios, departing from the old forms in which ensemble singing prevailed, are rather in dialogue form, the voices joining in ensemble only at the very end. Song remains the decisive element, but it follows closely the course of thought, feeling, and word. Independent, self-sufficient, symmetrically constructed melodies appear less frequently than does that cross between recitative and cantilena which now dominates modern opera. Repetition of words is to be noted only in the choruses and the large ensembles. Not the slightest tribute is paid by way of ornamentation or brilliant passages to vocal virtuosity, and all the effective climaxes involving high chest tones are called for by the situation. Neither unvocal line nor excessive strain is imposed upon the voices. Correct declamation, never as close to the Italian heart as to the French, has been carefully respected, and the variety of effect reproduced with as much scruple as talent.

If the right choice of color for every mood and the emphatic notation of every turn of speech were the single objective of opera, then we could unhesitatingly declare

Otello to be an improvement over *Aïda*, and Verdi's finest work. This understanding devotion to the poem does not, however, release the opera composer from other obligations. He must, above all else, be a musician, and on this basis we expect music not only in accord with the text but also attractive to us simply as music—individual, original, and self-sufficient. Not only should it provide the animating coloration for the poet's sketch; it should itself provide musical picture, sketch, and color. In a word, we demand of the opera composer beauty and novelty of musical ideas, particularly melodic ideas. And from this point of view *Otello* strikes me as less adequate than *Aïda*, *La Traviata*, or *Un Ballo in Maschera*.

Does the inspirational strength of a composer really grow in accordance with the growth of his self-denial, his aesthetic repose, his technical skill? He who finds Goethe's *Wanderjahre* superior to his *Werther* may well prefer *Otello* to Verdi's earlier operas. It is a noble and ultimately respectable work, and of special biographical interest as a monument to the artist's clarification and to the comprehensive strength of a popular favorite at the end of a splendid career. In this, Verdi has achieved what Sophocles described as the most enviable of human objectives: "to grow wise in old age." But wherein lies the wisdom of old age in art? Mostly in negative virtues: in denial, avoidance, and self-limitation. For opera, the most sensuous of musical creations, the wisdom of old age is seldom so rewarding as the genius of youth. Verdi's *Otello*, more unified, more solid, purer than his earlier operas, does not breathe their natural freshness and power. The master set himself a noble objective, but much of worth has been sacrificed in its attainment: naïveté and youth. And youth in music is melody. In

298

his earlier operas the young Verdi did not always know quite what to do with his melodies—but he had them.

We prefer to see nations, as well as individual artists, effective through those virtues which are their natural endowment; thus, the Italians through fresh and fulsome melody. Even in Verdi's operas feeling has always come to the surface in the form of melody. Who is not acquainted with the many Verdian melodies which express real feeling with compelling forcefulness, unlike the *buffo* music in Rossini's tragedies which exercises a certain sensual charm quite independent of its relation, or want of relation, to the dramatic situation? They stand out in Verdi's earlier operas like beautiful flowers, always more or less surrounded by weeds. There are no weeds in *Otello*, but there are also few roses. Nor do I overlook the individual striking melodies any more than I underestimate the dignity of the opera as a whole. Desdemona, in several scenes, has heartfelt music, indescribably touching moments of pathos. There we hear the familiar, warm, deeply vibrant voice of Verdi—it is his voice, but it tells us nothing new.

The love duet of Otello and Desdemona closes with an expressive phrase which, as it is recalled in the death scene as a melancholy memory, has a double significance; it reminds us of other Verdian melodies. We can hardly compare this now famous and certainly irreproachable duet with the final duet between Amneris and the convicted Rhadames, with the death scene of Rhadames and Aïda, or with the Andante of the love duet in *Un Ballo in Maschera*. Even the mood, the foreboding sadness, which dominates the fourth act, has its analogies in Verdi's earlier operas, specifically the remarkable Prelude and Leonora's monologue in *La Forza del Destino*, the last act of *La Traviata*, Leonora's sustained airs in *Il Trovatore*, the concluding part of Aïda's first-act aria, etc. How much more direct and immediate is the flow of musical invention in these earlier examples! How these bittersweet melodies pursue us, even without thought for their connection to the opera! From the *Otello* music we can pick no melodic buds of such enduring fragrance; the fragrance remains behind in the theater.

I can share the universal admiration for the fourth act only in respect to the masterly mixing of colors, not in respect to the musical sketching. Desdemona's mortal fear is mirrored with shocking realism in the dismal sounds of the orchestra and the repeated interruptions in her song, but the whole vague, elusive scene leaves me musically unsatisfied. Verdi's Desdemona—really *"pallida morte futura,"* like Vergil's Dido—touches us more deeply with her farewell song than the more composed Desdemona of Rossini; but as a piece of music, Verdi's "Song of the Willow" is definitely inferior to Rossini's. Verdi finds tones for Otello's pangs of jealousy which recall Shakespeare's wonderfully effective: "Oh! it comes o'er my memory as doth the raven o'er the infected house." With the final appearance of Otello, bent on murder, the penchant for graphic representation borders on the bizarre: a long ritornello on mere muted basses moves gruesomely up and down in unison, punctuated by three dull blows on the big drum—"like three shovelfuls of earth on a grave," observed Boito. The use of the drum for horror effects is Verdi's own idea. He first tried it out in the wonderful duet between Rigoletto and Sparafucile. There is no dearth of such characteristic devices in *Otello*. Indeed, one listens to the whole opera with rapt attention; it is only that in the course of the evening one sometimes has to wait rather long for a musical piece effective as such.

The libretto, to be sure, does not offer many occasions for musical pieces of absolute form, occasions where the progress of the drama does not require episodic treatment, but still there are some: Iago's drinking song, with chorus; the song of the Cyprians gathered around the festival fire; and the homage to Desdemona, with mandolin accompaniment. In these pieces I missed exactly that which I would have expected to find in these single lighter points of repose in the tragic story: Verdian temperament and healthy, ruddy-cheeked melody. It is almost the end of the second act when Iago's pretty andante, *"Era la notte,"* offers us our first novel, catching theme, strongly reminiscent, by the way, of Amelia's appearance at the gypsy's hut in *Un Ballo in Maschera*. The great ensemble at the end of the third act, with Desdemona's touching song soaring high above the chorus, is an effectively constructed, well-rounded piece, associated with the good old-fashioned tradition. Beautiful in sound, and extremely expressive, it will have an effect everywhere, and did so in Milan, despite the lamentable inadequacy of the prima donna.

It would be premature to go further into the details of *Otello* as long as the opera is unknown in Germany and the reader has not the possibility of comparing notes. Besides, a single hearing of such a comprehensive novelty—moreover, in foreign and therefore disconcerting surroundings—hardly offers security for a detailed judgment. As far as prophecy goes, *Otello* can expect in German theaters a success equal to that of the more recent Milan performance, if not to that of the first. It will appeal to German audiences because of its artistic sincerity, its distinguished manner of expression, and its dramatic execution. Our close acquaintance with the Shakespeare original can only serve the under-

301

standing of the opera and its ultimate success. German opera houses are said to be preparing for its production, and well they may. Even if certain expectations prompted by hyper-enthusiastic reviews remain unfulfilled, it is a work which hardly another composer alive today could match.

BRUCKNER'S EIGHTH SYMPHONY

[1892]

THE Philharmonic Orchestra devoted its entire concert to a new symphony by Bruckner.[1] It is the eighth in the series and similar to its predecessors in form and mood. I found this newest one, as I have found the other Bruckner symphonies, interesting in detail but strange as a whole and even repugnant. The nature of the work consists—to put it briefly—in applying Wagner's dramatic style to the symphony.

Not only does Bruckner fall continually into Wagnerian devices, effects, and reminiscences; he seems even to have accepted certain Wagnerian pieces as models for symphonic construction, as, for example, the Prelude to *Tristan and Isolde*. Bruckner begins with a short chromatic motive, repeats it over and over again, higher and higher in the scale and on into infinity, augments it, diminishes it, offers it in contrary motion, and so on, until the listener is simply crushed under the sheer weight and monotony of this in-

---

[1] At a Philharmonic Concert on December 18, 1892, Hans Richter conducting. Bruckner, an Upper Austrian, settled in Vienna in 1868, where he acted for a quarter century as Court Organist, teacher of counterpoint at the Conservatory of the Society of Friends of Music, and Professor of Musical Theory at the University of Vienna. He was consistently and bitterly opposed by both Hanslick and Brahms, and the story is told that once when Emperor Franz Josef asked Bruckner what he could do for him, the composer asked him to do something about Hanslick. Bruckner's music is still enormously popular in Vienna.

terminable lamentation. Alongside these upward surging lamentations we have the subsiding lamentation (after the model of the *Tannhäuser* Overture). Wagnerian orchestral effects are met on every hand, such as the tremolos of the violins *divisi* in the highest position, harp arpeggios over muffled chords in the trombones, and, added to all that, the newest achievements of the Siegfried tubas.[2]

Also characteristic of Bruckner's newest symphony is the immediate juxtaposition of dry schoolroom counterpoint with unbounded exaltation. Thus, tossed about between intoxication and desolation, we arrive at no definite impression and enjoy no artistic pleasure. Everything flows, without clarity and without order, willy-nilly into dismal long-windedness. In each of the four movements, and most frequently in the first and third, there are interesting passages and flashes of genius—if only all the rest were not there! It is not out of the question that the future belongs to this muddled hangover style—which is no reason to regard the future with envy. For the time being, however, one would prefer that symphonic and chamber music remain undefiled by a style only relatively justified as an illustrative device for certain dramatic situations.

Even before the performance we had heard such provocative reports of the extraordinary profundity of the new symphony that I took care to prepare myself through study of the score and attendance at the dress rehearsal. I must confess, however, that the mysteries of this all-embracing composition were disclosed to me only through the helpful offices of an explanatory program handed to me prior to the

---

[2] Also referred to at that time as "Wagner tubas." The reference is presumably to the tenor tuba (in B-flat) and the bass tuba (in F), something between horn and tuba, with characteristics of each.

Caricature by Otto Boehler of Hanslick cordially doffing his hat to Bruckner—presumably before the accompanying critique was written.

concert. The author of this dissertation is anonymous, but we easily discerned the fine hand of Schalk.[3] From him we learned that the irksome humming theme of the first movement represents the figure of the Aeschylean Prometheus. An especially tiresome part of this movement is charmingly

---

[3] Josef Schalk (1857–1911), pianist and composer, pupil of Bruckner, teacher of piano at the Vienna Conservatory, and writer. He was the older brother of Franz Schalk, the conductor.

305

described as "most awful loneliness and quiet." Right next to Prometheus stands *Der deutsche Michl*.[4] Had a critic uttered this blasphemy, he would probably have been stoned by the Bruckner disciples. But it was the composer himself who gave the Scherzo the name of *Der deutsche Michl*, as is plain to be seen in black and white in the program. With this authentic pronouncement before him, however, the commentator (Schalk) doesn't hesitate to find in the *Michl*-Scherzo "the deeds and sufferings of Prometheus reduced in parody to the smallest scale."

What follows is even more exalted. In the Adagio we behold nothing less than "the all-loving Father of Mankind in all His infinite mercy!" Since this Adagio lasts exactly twenty-eight minutes, or about as long as an entire Beethoven symphony, we cannot complain of being denied ample time for the contemplation of the rare vision. At long last, the Finale—which, with its baroque themes, its confused structure and inhuman din, strikes us only as a model of tastelessness—represents, according to the program, "Heroism in the Service of the Divine!" The blaring trumpet figures are "heralds of the Gospel truth and the conception of God." The childish, hymnal character of this program characterizes our Bruckner community, which consists of Wagnerites and some added starters for whom Wagner is already too simple and intelligible. One sees how Wagnerism educates, not only musically but also in literature.

And the reception of the new symphony? A storm ovation, waving of handkerchiefs from the standees, innumerable recalls, laurel wreaths, etc.! For Bruckner, the concert was certainly a huge success. Whether Hans Richter

---

[4] The term is used to represent a kind of sturdy, oafish peasant.

performed a similar favor for his subscribers by devoting an entire concert to the Bruckner symphony is doubtful. The program seems to have been chosen only for the sake of a noisy minority. The test is easy: just give the symphony in a special concert outside the subscription series. This would be helpful to all concerned, save probably the Philharmonic Orchestra.

RICHARD STRAUSS'S "DON JUAN"

$$[\,1892\,]$$

WE HAVE had, at last, an opportunity to hear *Don Juan*.[1] Not Mozart's—no, quite the contrary. The name of the composer is Richard Strauss. Described in general terms as a "tone poem," the work is closest in content and form to the symphonic poems of Liszt. The score is prefaced by a lengthy extract from Lenau's [2] *Don Juan*. "The charmed circle, the infinitely distant . . . Of many kinds of beautiful, stimulating femininity . . . I should like to traverse in a storm of pleasure," and so on.

That Strauss consciously cultivates the imitation of painting and poetry is demonstrated in his other symphonic poems. He has not, as yet, gone as far as a new English composer (Wadham Nicholl) [3] who called his orchestral composition, *Hamlet*, a "psychic sketch"! But the tendency is the same: to use purely instrumental music merely as a means of describing certain things; in short, not to make music, but to write poetry and to paint. Hector Berlioz is the common father of this ever-multiplying younger generation of tone poets. With Liszt and Wagner he makes up the

---

[1] At a Philharmonic Concert on January 10, Hans Richter conducting.

[2] Nicolaus Franz Niembsch von Strehlenau (1802–1850). The poem dates from 1844.

[3] Horace Wadham Nicholl (1848–1922), English composer and organist. He was organist of St. Paul's Cathedral, Pittsburgh, Pennsylvania, and later at St. Mark's Church, New York.

triumvirate to which one may attribute essentially all that these youngsters can, and will, do. In the one-sided study of these three orchestral geniuses, the younger generation has developed a virtuosity in the creation of sound effects beyond which it is hardly possible to go. Color is everything, musical thought nothing. What I said about Nicodé's *Das Meer* [4] goes double for Richard Strauss: "Virtuosity in orchestration has become a vampire sapping the creative power of our composers."

These outwardly brilliant compositions are nothing if not successful. I have seen Wagner disciples talking about the Strauss *Don Juan* with such enthusiasm that it seemed as though shivers of delight were running up and down their spines. Others have found the thing repulsive, and this sensation seems to me more likely to be the right one. This is no "tone painting" but rather a tumult of brilliant daubs, a faltering tonal orgy, half bacchanale, half witches' sabbath.

He who desires no more from an orchestral piece than that it transport him to the dissolute ecstasy of a Don Juan, panting for everything feminine, may well find pleasure in this music, for with its exquisite skillfulness it achieves the desired objective insofar as it is musically attainable. The composer may thus be compared with a routined chemist who well understands how to mix all the elements of musical-sensual stimulation to produce a stupefying "pleasure gas." For my part I prefer, with all due homage to such chemical skill, not to be its victim; nor can I be, for such musical narcotics simply leave me cold. It's a pity that there is no "free stage" for emancipated naturalism in

---

[4] Jean-Louis Nicodé (1853–1919), German conductor and composer. *Das Meer* (1888), his opus 31, was a Symphony for Men's Chorus, Soloist, Orchestra, and Organ.

instrumental music. That would be the fitting place for "tone paintings" à la Richard Strauss.

We could almost wish that many more such tone paintings might be composed, simply to provide the *ne plus ultra* of false licentiousness and precipitate a reaction, a return to healthy, musical music. The tragedy is that most of our younger composers think in a foreign language (philosophy, poetry, painting) and then translate the thought into the mother tongue (music). People like Richard Strauss, moreover, translate badly, unintelligibly, tastelessly, with exaggeration. We are not so sanguine as to expect the reaction against this emancipated naturalism in instrumental music to come immediately—but come it must.[5]

---

[5] And come it did.

RICHARD STRAUSS'S
"TOD UND VERKLÄRUNG"
("DEATH AND TRANSFIGURATION")

[1893]

THE composer of *Don Juan* has again proved himself a brilliant virtuoso of the orchestra, lacking only musical ideas.[1] He places various brightly colored slides in his magic lantern, whose alternately melting sweetness and flaming fervor occupy our senses. What we are supposed to make of it, whether death and the devil or death and transfiguration, is taken care of by a descriptive program.

This time, too, we have a previously published poem to see to it that we don't go wrong; the music follows it step by step as though it were a ballet libretto. "In the dingy little room, feebly lighted by the stump of a candle, the sick man lies on his cot." Long sustained minor triads above the quiet sobbing of the violins. "He sinks exhausted into a deep slumber." Soft harp arpeggios and a little figure for the flute, then a broad melody for the violins. After this introduction, the most successful episode of the whole composition, a furiously surging C-minor Allegro, tells us that death will no longer let its victim slumber and that a "horrible struggle" is about to begin between them. Later, as delirium sets in, the music rises in intensity and abandon

---

[1] At a Philharmonic Concert on January 15, Hans Richter conducting.

311

until it becomes a glaring tumult. The kettle drums are belabored with wooden drumsticks, the trombones "must be played enormously *marcato*, with bells raised to the public!" A dreadful battle of dissonances, in which the wood-winds come screaming down in chromatic thirds, while the whole brass section thunders and the fiddles rage. Who can object when the composer tells us that he must describe the very death struggle, the groaning and moaning, the fevered resistance of the departing brother? We can only wonder: must this really be?

After the pictures of a cheerless life, filled with struggle, have passed before the eyes of the dying man, the death knell sounds. For forty measures we hear dismal beating of the tom-tom, then a long session of two harps arpeggiating against one another above mysterious mutterings in the strings; finally, a pianissimo dying away. The poor young fellow has been released from his suffering, charmingly described in the program as *"Welt-Erlösung, Welt-Verklärung."*

Tod und Verklärung belongs, with *Don Juan*, among the products of refined overcultivation in our music. All the happenings in the poem are, as we have said, illustrated with brilliant virtuosity, sometimes even with really new color combinations. This explains the sensual-pathological effect which so merciless a representation has upon the listener. The realism lacks only the final step: the dimly lighted sickroom with the dying man upon a real stage, his death struggle, his visions, his death—all in pantomime—plus Strauss's music in the orchestra. That would be no more than consistent and may, in time, actually be tried. That which I said in general about *Don Juan* goes for *Tod und Verklärung*. The basic characteristic of Strauss as a sympho-

Richard Strauss as conductor.

nist is that he composes with poetic rather than with musical elements and, through his emancipation from musical logic, takes a position rather adjacent to music than squarely in it. *Tod und Verklärung* also strengthens our previously expressed opinion that, in view of the quick and rapturous acceptance of this composer, the unhealthy tendency will not soon be overcome, although it will eventually provoke a healthy reaction.

In his latest short story, Paul Heyse [2] addresses to a

---

[2] Paul Heyse (1830–1914), German poet.

young *plein-air* painter the following pertinent words, which may well be applied to the case under discussion: "I observe in the new radical tendency to slight the beautiful in favor of the sheerly dramatic no more than a growing pain in our time. A wise aesthetic pathology would no more attempt to suppress such phenomena than would rational physical hygiene attempt to obstruct the cleansing processes of the human body, even when they break out conspicuously upon the skin. It is probable that our schoolbook aesthetics would have become downright dry without this violent reaction. I have seen so many 'tendencies' which professed to be the only true ones run into the sand and make room for even 'truer' ones, that I am no longer unduly disturbed when everything which claims some spiritual value or attempts to offer pleasure through charm and nobility of form is decried as 'old hat.' "

Tod und Verklärung received stormy applause from one portion of the public and hisses from others. Everyone, however, must have felt the first chords of the Schumann Piano Concerto [3] as a heavenly balm.

---

[3] Played by Ilona Eibenschütz.

" H A N S E L A N D G R E T E L "

[1894]

Hansel and Gretel triumphed just as completely in Vienna [1] as it had triumphed previously in the major musical centers of Germany. Such a great success in the most varied places and under the most varied circumstances—a success such as no other German opera has enjoyed since Nessler's [2] *Trompeter von Säckingen*—is inconceivable without particular merit. Humperdinck cleverly discerned the complete novelty and surprise of presenting a simple children's tale on the operatic stage. The effect consisted, initially, of the contrast between the plot and our whole current opera repertoire. The first counter to the long dominance of an already tiresome orientation in art has a nearly irresistible force. Under Mascagni's leadership, the tragic one-act operas were triumphant as a reaction to operas four hours long. And to these brutal miniatures, already becoming tiresome, the strongest possible contrast is—the children's fairy tale. On the one side we have criminals, suicides, betrayed lovers and couples; on the other, a little brother and sister whose only pain is hunger and whose greatest pleasure is a candy bar— no passion, no love story, no intrigue. It is another world —and a better one.

---

[1] At the Court Opera, December 18, 1894.
[2] Viktor Nessler (1841–1890). The opera was given at the Metropolitan in 1887, three years after the *première* at Wiesbaden.

Apart from this contrast of plot, however, there is another inner and more precarious contrast—between the plot and its musical treatment. It is a false contrast, a conflict of style. Humperdinck could not have been unaware that the simple fairy tale offered him not only a novel, promising theme but also a strong obstacle. Simplicity was the attraction but also the hazard. He who knows *Hansel and Gretel* in Grimm's Fairy Tales can imagine only a children's theater for its dramatization, a theater not only playing for children but also played by children. It is said that Mrs. Adelheid Wette, nee Humperdinck,[3] the author of *Hansel and Gretel*, never thought of it as an opera. She wanted to dramatize the familiar fairy tale for her children—thus, an unassuming children's performance in the drawing room, perhaps with operetta music à la Grétry [4] or Isouard.[5] But this was not enough for Humperdinck. With his little children he wanted to get hold of the big children, and not at home but in the opera house. He would not have gone far with simple childish music and naïvely plain settings. Our opera public would have become bored after the first two scenes and demanded more seasoned stuff. Thus: a children's fairy tale with brilliant adornments, a large orchestra, and the most modern music, preferably Wagnerian.

No sooner said than done. The composer set to work and solved his task ably and successfully. He has attained his goal—whether with acceptable artistic means or not is disputable. The naïveté of the fairy tale resists, in my

---

[3] The composer's sister.

[4] André Ernest Modeste Grétry (1741–1813), Belgian composer, prolific writer for the opera and the *opéra comique*, sometimes called "The Molière of music."

[5] Niccolò Isouard (1775–1818), French opera composer, contemporary and rival of Boïeldieu.

opinion, the contrived Wagnerian style; there is an inner conflict between the subject and the manner of its presentation about which none can be in doubt, not even the composer, who asked for the contradiction and even needed it for his success. The general public, which loses itself in the plot and the few nursery rhymes, easily overlooks this false contrast; but the aesthetically acute are made uncomfortable when an overartificial, pompous orchestra illustrates the scolding of the mother, or when music directly descended from the *Ring* accompanies the children while they pick strawberries. Courageously welding together these contrasts, Humperdinck, as cleverly as Wagner in his day, has understood and satisfied the spirit of the time. The public desires new themes and yet adheres to Wagnerism. Humperdinck satisfied both requirements.

He divides his opera into three acts. The Overture introduces the majority of the leitmotives, collectively, juxtaposed, diminished, and augmented. All these motives have, of course, been christened by the Wagnerians: "Evensong" motive, "Sandman" motive, "Children's Dance" motive, etc. The Overture, by this contrived, polyphonic construction and the restless tumult of the middle voices, makes a pretentious and yet uncertain impression. One would never guess a children's tale from it. It also reveals a method, or mannerism, of the composer which is more a mechanical continuance than free musical creation: the boundless use of sequences in which every motive is repeated (often half a dozen times) in the next higher degree.

The first act begins prettily: During their parents' absence, Hansel and Gretel try to pass the time and forget their hunger. Gretel sings the familiar nursery rhymes, *"Suse, liebe Suse, was raschelt im Stroh?"* ("Suzy, Sister

Suzy") and *"Brüderchen, komm tanz mit mir"* ("Brother, Come and Dance with Me")—all very pleasant. But between times, they talk to each other in the awkward declamation of *Die Meistersinger*, while the orchestra goes in for the same nervous splitting of motives and the same contrapuntal precocity. This is the case throughout the whole opera wherever there is conversation or dialogue. The mother enters, scolding, and sends the children out into the woods to collect strawberries. The broommaker comes home and is alarmed to find them gone; he rushes to the haunted forest to look for them. An interlude, entitled "Ride of the Witches," illustrates in shrill orchestral colors the broommaker's gruesome narrative; a weak "Ride of the Valkyries"—on brooms.

With the rise of the curtain, we see the children in the woods. Again Gretel starts with a pretty nursery rhyme: *"Ein Männlein steht im Walde"* ("A Dwarf Stands in the Forest"). The children happily eat their strawberries, but then, at nightfall, they become frightened. The sandman sings them to sleep after they have prayed their evensong. This is all well done musically, and is full of atmosphere. We noticed, for instance, the effective treatment of the echo and the cuckoo calls. In this idyl in the woods, Humperdinck shows himself a real poet. But the ace of trumps is yet to come: A shining light penetrates the mist and illuminates a staircase leading down from heaven, on which fourteen angels descend to surround and protect the sleeping children. A whole army of angels appears behind them, rising up to the roof of heaven, Archangel Michael with sword and armor among them. It is a magnificent scene with truly picturesque effects. The accompanying music does not reach the same level as in the preceding scene in the woods.

With its flourishing brass, into which, after the recipe of the *Tannhäuser* Overture, shrill, jagged violin figures intrude, it displays too crude a pomposity.

The third act is too long in proportion to its content. Despite effective episodes, such as the awakening of the children, it falls short of the first two. The scenes with the witch follow the fairy tale: Gretel pushes her into the burning oven, and the children sing and dance with joy. The parents retrieve them. Thus ends the fairy tale. But Humperdinck has added another ending which we relate only with hesitation, since it is utter nonsense. In front of the witch's house we see a long row of life-sized marshmallow statues representing "children turned to marshmallow" by the witch and now redeemed by Hansel and Gretel. With a Wagner apostle, there is no way of escaping a "redemption." With Wagner it was a fixed idea, from *The Flying Dutchman* to *Parsifal*. This gingerbread redemption sounds like a parody on redemption. Why does the witch catch children? In order to turn them into gingerbread? No, in order to fry and eat them. This we hear continually from the stage and see it prepared before our eyes. That the witch does not eat the children but turns them into marshmallow statues and puts them as a fence round her house gives the lie to all the foregoing and overthrows the whole fairy tale. And this nonsense, which disfigures the whole work, was only committed for a superficial and unbeautiful theatrical effect. The audience, enjoying itself from beginning to end, did not, of course, object to this contradiction. It broke into applause the like of which has rarely been heard in the opera house.

It cannot be said that the success was unmerited. Humperdinck is not only a gifted and able musician, he is also a man of spirit and cultivation, an artist with poetic and picturesque fantasy. But as far as his creative musical power is concerned, I cannot, on the basis of this opera—I know nothing else—consider it very strong. He is no musical inventor in the true sense, no *Originalgenie*, as they used to say. Wholly his is only the fortunate idea of bringing a well-known children's tale upon the stage as an opera. There are two musical inventors in *Hansel and Gretel*: first, those unknown, unsung mothers and nurses with whom the nursery rhymes originated and, second, Richard Wagner. Humperdinck's personality is completely submerged in Wagner, a fact which can be explained biographically. Having the closest personal ties with Wagner the father and Wagner the son, he hovers at present like the Holy Ghost above the German *Musikdrama*. He not only composes after Wagner's method; his score swarms with reminiscences from the *Ring* and *Die Meistersinger*. They are so easily recognizable and so numerous that it is unnecessary to enumerate them. The restless modulation and predominant enharmony; the polyphonic texture of the accompaniment, which often completely veils the leading thoughts; the declamation, stumbling around in the most distant intervals, with five-six chords or diminished sevenths at the end of a cadence; the unsteadily shifting instrumentation and the refined orchestral effects—this is Richard Wagner to the core.

Humperdinck has chosen the nursery rhymes, which appear either in an original or slightly altered form, with great skill; they constitute the irresistible charm of the whole work. What he offers from his own means as an inventor of melodies is insignificant and cheaply sentimental. None of Humperdinck's own melodies struck me as beautiful or genuine. I was more impressed by his dramatic and graphic gifts. I do not underestimate his merits and am pleased at the general success a young German composer has achieved with his first work. But this does not prevent my speaking up against those exaggerations in which most of the musical journals are indulging. "Not since Mozart," we read in one periodical, "has dramatic art seen so enlightened a humorist as Humperdinck!" "Ingenious composition," "epoch-making masterpiece" are the most current terms for the score. And then there is young Siegfried Wagner's statement that *Hansel and Gretel* is the most important opera since *Parsifal*. In other words, the best in full twelve years? An irritating pronouncement, and the worst of it is—that it is true.

TCHAIKOVSKY'S
"SYMPHONIE PATHÉTIQUE"

————— •—•—•— —————

[1895]

TCHAIKOVSKY'S *Symphonie Pathétique* achieved a lively success in the last Philharmonic Concert.[1] Although this may be attributed in large part to the magnificent performance, the success of the composition was profound enough to pave the way in Vienna for other compositions of this prolific composer. We know very little of his work, and our acquaintance was not well initiated. The only larger orchestral works of Tchaikovsky heretofore presented in Vienna —*Romeo and Juliet* and the Violin Concerto—both fell flat. Only the *Song without Words* in F major, played so delightfully by Rubinstein—a trifle, but charming—and the graceful string quartet in D major have enjoyed any sort of success.

The new symphony surprised us, first of all, by its peculiar form. In the first movement, an introductory Adagio leads to a nervous, passionate Allegro. This gives way to a dreamy Andante in D major which, following a short interlude, dominates to the end. Thus it happens that in this first fast movement a slow tempo prevails. Another peculiarity is the Scherzo, in five-four time. This disagreeable rhythm, actually a continual wavering between simple

---

[1] At a Philharmonic Concert on March 3, Hans Richter conducting.

and compound time, is used rarely and only episodically (as in Delibes' *Le Roi l'a dit* and in the third act of *Tristan and Isolde*). Consistently retained through a long symphonic movement, it is disturbing to listeners and players alike. The ear is always substituting more comfortable measures, dividing five-four into two and three parts, or into three and two—an intolerably worrisome procedure. It is, moreover, superfluous, since the piece could be adapted to six-eight time without damage.

The two following movements turn the usual musical order upside down again. The third has the character of a finale: rousing, heroic, calling ultimately upon the full means of the orchestra. And the fourth movement, the Finale, an *Adagio lamentoso!* We are not so pedantic as to take offense. Although the usual sequence of the four movements of the symphony has its psychological reasons and is historically acknowledged, it is no iron barrier excluding exceptions or changes for all time. The criterion will always be whether or not the chosen order lacks psychological motivation or inner relationship. There is obviously a hidden poetical program at the bottom of this symphony; the first movement, with its rhapsodic shifting between adagio and allegro, between major and minor, points to a passionate tragedy of the heart. Most listeners would probably wish for a program to save them guessing; I consider it, rather, proof of the composer's musical temperament that he lets his music speak for itself and prefers to leave us guessing rather than force a laid-out course upon himself and us.

The *Symphonie Pathétique* has a special place among the compositions of Tchaikovsky in that there is not a trace of national Russian color. What lamentably trivial Cossack cheer we had to suffer in the Finale of his Serenade, opus 48, in his Violin Concerto, in his D major Quartet, or in the third movement of his Suite, opus 54! There is nothing of this kind in the symphony, whose character is downright West European and reveals a nobler mind and a more heart-felt interest. The first and the last movements particularly, which I consider by far the best, contain episodes of touching emotion and pure beauty. In the second movement, there is nothing extraordinary except the loathsome five-four time; the third, brilliant and animated in the larger first part, loses, toward the end, all sense of what the normal ear can tolerate in the way of noise and length. Liszt and Rubinstein have not been without influence on it. At any rate, we thank Hans Richter for having made us acquainted with this origi-nal and intelligent composition which, despite unbeautiful, purely operatic characteristics and a merciless length, has made a strong impression.

JOHANN STRAUSS

———•◦•———

[1899]

WHEN we buried Johann Strauss, Senior, fifty years ago, I remarked in an obituary that Vienna had lost its most talented composer. This was annoying to musicians and laymen alike. They refused to admit that a correct but characterless piece of concert or church music could reveal less talent, less in the way of natural resources, than a melodious, original waltz.

In this sense, I can only repeat the same plaint today, at the grave of the younger Johann Strauss.[1] Vienna has lost its most original musical talent. The sources of his melodic invention were as fine as they were inexhaustible; his rhythm pulsated with animated variety; his harmonies and his forms were pure and upright. He named one of his waltzes "*Liebeslieder.*" The designation was applicable to all of them: little love stories of bashful courtship, impulsive infatuation, radiant happiness, and here and there a breath of easily consolable melancholy. Who could enumerate even the most charming of Strauss's numerous dance pieces! It's too bad that each ball season, like Kronos, pitilessly devours its own children in order to make room for others. Thus it is that we are as little familiar with Strauss's earliest and best waltzes as though they dated from the time of Maria The-

---

[1] He died on June 3, 1899.

resa. They are not obsolescent; they have merely been crowded aside and neglected.

One waltz among the hundreds deserves to be named specifically: "The Blue Danube." As I once wrote many years ago, one has only to sound the first three notes of the D major triad and all cheeks instantly glow with enthusiasm. "The Blue Danube" not only enjoys unexampled popularity; it has also achieved a unique significance: that of a symbol for everything that is beautiful and pleasant and gay in Vienna. It is a kind of patriotic folk song without words. In addition to Haydn's national anthem, which celebrates the Emperor and the ruling house, we possess in "The Blue Danube" another national anthem, one which celebrates the country and its people. Wherever Austrians are gathered together abroad, this wordless "Marseillaise" of peace is their national song and their symbol of recognition. Whenever Vienna or Austria is toasted at a banquet, the orchestra strikes up "The Blue Danube." Its melody has the effect of a motto.

Johann Strauss modernized, extended, and enriched the Viennese waltz created by his father. He made a school, and it has become almost compulsory. What is heard today in the way of waltzes is mostly rewritten Strauss. However hard they may try, our operetta composers cannot write two measures in waltz time without involuntarily copying him.

After having spent his melodic store on dance music for twenty years, Strauss became dissatisfied with so narrow a form. He decided to have a go at the theater, and in 1871 he wrote his first operetta, *Indigo*.[2] The transition to dramatic composition was not easy. The strict waltz and polka

---

[2] Now known as *A Thousand and One Nights*.

rhythms had become too much a part of him. *Indigo* was not wanting in melodies, but it was plain that they were not born of the text. Strauss himself confessed to me that I had been right in my supposition that his librettist had had to supply words—for better or worse—to music already written. He outgrew this dilettante method in his later operettas, if not without strenuous effort. He remained, nevertheless, more a pure musical inventor than a creative dramatic composer.

A tragedy for *Indigo* was the incredibly stupid, commonplace book. This tragedy was not the only one of its kind in Strauss's career as composer for the theater. Many of his fifteen operettas were victims of bad librettos and vanished quickly, despite many musical beauties. His librettists ignored the specific nature of his talent, the fact that it required lighthearted, animated materials, that it breathed most freely in its native air. They loaded him, instead, with exotic adventures set in Italy, Spain, and France. His masterpiece, *Die Fledermaus*, certainly owed its enduring and extraordinary success to its charming music, but the latter would have been unthinkable without the gay plot and the Viennese setting. Wherever, as in *Die Fledermaus*, his material was replete with good humor and fun and provided the pretext for the free flow of dance rhythm, Strauss gave of his best and most genuine. In sentimental or even tragic scenes his pulse stopped, and he tended to become forced, uninteresting, and banal.

This is demonstrated in many parts of *The Gypsy Baron*, next to *Die Fledermaus* his most popular operetta. The libretto offers some new characters and a number of likely situations. The music is excellent, as long as it does not lapse into sentimentality or tragic passion, as in the second

*Johann Strauss, who, according to
custom, played the violin as he conducted in uniform.*

finale. Of his earlier operettas, *Das Spitzentuch der Königin*
and *Der lustige Krieg* seem to me to have disappeared too
quickly from the repertoire. The same goes, among the later
ones, for *Der Waldmeister*. The text of the latter, for all the
meagerness of the plot, is cheerful and harmless. The music
is attractive, if not up to earlier standards. What stands out
even in Strauss's less inventive operettas is the genuine
musical feeling, the natural flow of song, and, finally, the
wonderful orchestration. At the *première* of *Der Waldmeister*,
Brahms remarked to me that the Strauss orchestra reminded him of Mozart.

Toward the end of his career, Strauss was seized by the natural but nevertheless infelicitous ambition to write a large work for the Vienna Court Opera. He took a mighty leap and composed the three-act *Ritter Pazmann*. But every genius has his limitations. Strauss's genius was for the smaller forms, for dance rhythms and good humor; he was weak in large ensembles, dramatic characterization, and the expression of passionate feeling. His nature reacted noticeably against the dull, conventional plot, which brought a lot of serious people together in sentimental situations often bordering on the tragic. He had to deny himself, to make himself over, and this could lead to no good end. With a real comic opera in the older form, such as *Czar und Zimmermann*, he could have established himself in the Court Opera, too. But the long-drawn-out verses, uninterrupted by recitatives or spoken dialogue, forced him into a continuous arioso from which it was seldom possible to derive a rounded musical piece. One admired the skill with which he worked his way into this hitherto strange genre and style. But it was not our Strauss!

We have lost not merely a brilliant talent, a herald of Vienna's musical fame, but also a thoroughly lovable, forthright, and well-disposed man. It is impossible to speak and think of oneself more modestly than Strauss did. His elastic figure, unbent by the years, with the full head of hair and the blazing eyes, will be sadly missed in Vienna. He was a last symbol of cheerful, pleasant times casting a fading light upon our uncheerful, disrupted present.

THE WAGNERITES

———•◦•———

[From the Autobiography]

MY REVIEWS of *Der Ring des Nibelungen* and *Parsifal* have been bitterly attacked. A calm, reasoned opposition has not been my lot; rather scorn and angry words. The Wagnerites have nicknamed me "Beckmesser," thereby demonstrating that they comprehend neither their master nor his most readily understandable character. Beckmesser, the town clerk in *Die Meistersinger*, is the prototype of the pedant absorbed in trifles and superficialities, the narrow-minded quibbler and stickler who chalks up every false note, every deviation from the "rules," as a sacrilege and thinks that with the summing up of individual errors he has ruined the singer. I have never attacked Wagner over trifles, never tracked down individual irregularities in his works—my reviews over a period of forty years are proof that I have never gone in for that kind of pedantry.

Far be it from me to approach a significant personality with the measuring rod of formal correctness, with orthographic and grammatical faultfinding. To Wagner's music dramas I have applied only larger points of view, only the fundamental requirements of the art of music. What I have held against him is his uncompromising subordination of music to the word; his unnatural and exaggerated manner of expression; his destruction of the singer and the art of song, by unvocal writing and orchestral din; his repression of

melodic song in favor of declamatory recitation; his paralyz-
ing monotony and immoderate length; and, finally, the
unnatural stiltedness of a poesy contrary to every finer feeling for language. When I have discussed details, it has
usually been to praise rather than to find fault. Such
criticism is anything but Beckmesserish. It is rather the
Wagnerites who resemble Beckmesser—for it is possible
to be Beckmesserish in adoration. They permit themselves
no rest until they have sought out the most insignificant
note, the most commonplace phrase, the most innocent
sixteenth rest, and glorified it as a work of matchless genius.
This Beckmesserism in the Wagner literature is still on the
increase. Now that the larger aspects of Wagner's art have
been appraised, the critical pasture land is bare, and the
admiring Beckmessers have no other recourse than to get
down to the work of moles and ants. The results fill volumes.

Edmund von Hagen [1] wrote a whole octavo volume on
the poem (!) of the first scene (!) of *Das Rheingold*. The same
author wrote "the significance of the morning summons to
awake in *Parsifal*" on sixty-two octavo sheets and apolo-
gized in the foreword for the brevity of his dissertation,
attributing it to "the result of an over-rich spiritual content"! Is that not Beckmesserism? And is it not Beckmesserism of the worst kind when Hans von Wolzogen, in his
Leitfäden, explains ninety different leitmotives of the
Nibelungs and, in his *Poetische Laut-Symbolik*, elucidates the
psychological effect of every single consonant and allitera-
tion Wagner ever used? Wolzogen explains, for example,
that in the first scene of *Das Rheingold* "Alberich's exciting
call to the nixies carries the hard, incisive N-sound ap-

---

[1] 1815–1907

propriate to his character as the negative force in the drama and in sharp contrast to the soft W of the water sprites. Then, when he begins to climb after the Rhine Maidens, the sounds of Gl and Schl, together with the light, slippery F, illustrate his sliding and slipping on the rocks. Woglinde calls a *Prosit* to his snorting and sneezing with the appropriate combination Pr (Fr), etc." So it goes through the whole opera.

From another of the doting Beckmessers, Moritz Wirth,[2] we have a brouchure on King Mark, in which it is proven that this unhappy husband is the central figure of *Tristan and Isolde*. The various Beckmessers have argued about the age of King Mark in polemical essays; one says he is fifty, another says seventy. There are books and dissertations on the "character of Eva," on "the relationship of Erich to the Flying Dutchman and to Senta," a whole collection of arguments about Brangäne's love potion, etc. One would have thought that this flood of useless and tiresome babble would have begun to subside from the high water mark of the year 1876. But the contrary has been the case. The interpretive and canonizing Beckmessers simply won't die off. New Wagner detectives turn up every minute, each having just sniffed out some hitherto hidden profundity.

What I call the Beckmesserism of adoration may be experienced in Vienna in plastic and tangible form. There exists here a Richard Wagner Museum, to which a rabid

---

[2] Friedrich Moritz Wirth (1849–1917), German musical essayist. The catalogue of his other effusions on Wagner gives an even better idea of what Hanslick was talking about: *Bismarck, Wagner, Rodbertus; Drohender Untergang Bayreuths; Wagner-Museum und Zukunft des Wagnertums; Fahrt nach Nibelheim; Entdeckung des Rheingoldes aus seinen wahren Dekorationen; Mutter Brünnhilde; Der Ring des Nibelungen, das Weltgedicht des Kapitalismus; Der Ring des Nibelungen als Wotandrama*, and *Parsifal in neuem Lichte*.

Wagnerite,[3] eager for sacrifice, contributed his life's savings and twenty years' work. Two gigantic volumes in lexicon form contain the (still incomplete) catalogue of the treasures of this museum. Among them are entered "one of Richard Wagner's steel pens," "Richard Wagner's visiting card," "a ticket of admission to the platform of the railroad station for the arrival of Richard Wagner," "pictures of all the hotels in which Richard Wagner has stopped," etc.

I sincerely believe that a ten-year moratorium on books about Wagner would be of the utmost advantage for his art. Does anyone really think that an honestly strong and effective music drama requires all this philosophic rubbish by way of commentary? When a real example of musicology appears, something to rescue us from this insupportable flood and set us up on a peaceful, fruitful island—such a work, for example, as Spitta's [4] sixteen essays *Zur Musik*— it is promptly set upon as "very dull" by the *Leipzig Musikalisches Wochenblatt* "because the name of R. Wagner is not mentioned more than three or four times in the whole book!" There can be no doubt that this sort of thing has hurt the cause of the master more than the derogatory criticisms of cultivated men. It has even become too much for "the master," despite his not inconsiderable susceptibility to incense.

Not a few intelligent persons have seen fit to desert the Wagner camp. I shall pass over Nietzsche, whose remarkable book, *Der Fall Wagner*,[5] has, of course, been denounced

---

[3] Nikolaus Oesterlin (1842–1898). His museum, founded in Vienna, was moved to Eisenach after his death.

[4] Julius August Philipp Spitta (1841–1894), eminent German musical historian and Bach's first authoritative biographer.

[5] *Der Fall Wagner* (*The Wagner Case*) was written in 1888, and Nietzsche's "incipient insanity" was medically confirmed about a year later. ᵃ

as a sign of incipient insanity, despite the fact that it is clearer, more reasonable, and more convincing than his earlier hymns of praise. Bülow, too, who did more for Wagner than anyone else, wrote to me in January, 1891, that he "rejoiced in his late—but not too late—cleansing process" and considered himself cured of his former "*Nibelungen* mania." In the same letter, Bülow winds up certain observations on Gluck's *Armide* with the words: "The sorceresses are extinct, and so far as having Klingsor hang Kundry for us as a ghost of Armide, I quite agree with you."

It is only natural that the exalted hero worship of the Wagnerites and their challenging attitude should not have been without effect on the object of their attacks. I and some others who share my views would probably have written more dispassionately about Wagner had not our pulses been agitated by the immoderate, often ludicrous excesses of our adversaries. The consciousness of being in the minority embitters the most honest soul and sharpens the vocabulary. I readily confess that in my case this may have happened from time to time. But I must protest the statement of Max Nordau in his book, *Degeneration* (this most thorough annihilation of the whole business of Wagnerism), that "Hanslick held out a long time before he finally struck his colors in the face of the overpowering fanaticism of the hysterical Wagnerites." I do not know upon what Nordau bases this utterly false declaration. My most recent discussions of Wagnerian composition and Wagnerian literature are evidence to the contrary. After I had spoken my mind on Wagner for full two-score years, my task was finished. There is hardly anything new to be said on the subject. I would be as wanting in taste as the Wagnerites themselves were I to make every single production of *Tristan* or the

Ring the occasion for a reopening of the question. Graphomania, or pen fever, is, as Nordau correctly observes, a characteristic symptom of the ills of Wagner and the Wagnerites. As for myself, I suffer neither from graphomania nor cowardice. I know that I represent a small minority, and I know that I shall not live to see a reversal of taste in this regard. Younger critics may. I shall not dare prophesy how long Wagner's music will command public enthusiasm, but I do not doubt that in fifty years the writings of the Wagnerites will be looked upon in amazement as the relics of an intellectual plague.

INDEX

About the Editor and Translator

VIENNA'S GOLDEN YEARS OF MUSIC *was edited and translated in Vienna itself, where Henry Pleasants III was stationed as a civilian member of the American Military Government. He has since been transferred to the State Department, and is at present assigned to Berlin.*

For twelve years before the war, Mr. Pleasants was music critic for the Philadelphia Evening Bulletin, *and since his metamorphosis from critic to public servant he has continued writing musical reports on the European scene for the New York* Times *and* Herald-Tribune. *Most of his musical education was gained at the Curtis Institute of Music, where he was a baritone, and he continues his deep interest in the art, which is shared by his concert-pianist wife, the former Virginia Duffey.*